FENCING

the modern international style

Also available from SKA Swordplay Books:

István Lukovich, *Electric Foil Fencing: advanced competitive training*
Laszló Szabó, *Fencing and the master*
Imre Vass, *Epée Fencing: the complete system*

the modern international style

by István Lukovich

SKA Swordplay Books

Staten Island, New York

Original title: Vivás. Sport, Budapest 1975
Translated by István Butykay
Translation revised by John Harvie
Professional checking by Béla Bay,
Róbert Duronelly and Jenö Kamuti
Figures by Attila Bénö
Cover photo by Gábor Kreisz
Design by János Lengyel

ANALYTICAL TABLE OF CONTENTS

Getting the most from this book

This book warrants a new edition because it remains still the most complete and thorough presentation of fencing in English. Not a word of the original text has been omitted or altered. However, several new appendices make it an even more complete and valuable resource for fencers around the world: a history of fencing, discussions of safety and the priority rules, and a collection of fencing resources -- an expanded booklist, a page of Internet resources, and the addresses of fencing suppliers and national organizations around the world.

István Lukovich has trained fencers from their first beginners' calisthenics to world championships and Olympic gold. In this book, he teaches the leading style in the world today – the modern international school. It is an eclectic system, but still deeply classical at heart. It blends two ancient rivals, the French and Italian schools, stirs in original elements, and adapts the result to the demands of modern fencing. (See Appendix A: The history and development of fencing.)

The task Lukovich sets himself is to make the beginners who learn his method into skilful and enthusiastic practitioners – fencers who do well, understand what they are doing, have fun in the process, and do it all within the essential spirit of the sport.

Fencing: the modern international style is a guide to all the fencing actions, and the reasons behind them, as the international school teaches and understands them. The text itself is thorough as well as concise. The illustrations are invaluable. They contain essential information about positions and actions, as well as nuances that words can't always convey. The result is not a leisurely essay for an armchair athlete, but a practical handbook for an active participant. It is a book to be worked through -- a book for fencers and coaches to read, reread, and study.

When he wrote this book, Lukovich thought that most of his readers would be coaches in training. A great teacher is imparting his life's work to another generation. But everyone can read it with profit. Beginners will find themselves "going to school" in a system designed specifically for the demands of today's Olympic sport. Every basic move is not only described, but also taught and explained from the ground up, with clear illustrations. On the other hand, advanced competitors as well as coaches at every level will find new insights into familiar actions and concepts.

For competitors and coaches

If you are an advanced fencer or a coach, this book is aimed at you. You know something about fencing – perhaps a lot – and you need to fill in your knowledge and get a fuller and more systematic view of what you're doing.

If you fence, you'll naturally go straight to the repertory of actions and the tactical advice for each weapon. Don't forget to review the basics, though – otherwise, you may find yourself suddenly floundering because you were taught a slightly different position, or learned a slightly different vocabulary from the ones used here.

If you are a coach, or thinking of becoming one, you owe it to yourself to read the first chapter. It's the clearest description imaginable of why fencing is *not* a massively popular sport, why coaching it is so demanding (and sometimes discouraging!), and ultimately, why some people find it one of the most rewarding possible activities. (If you're a beginner sneaking a look at this page, you might want to read that chapter to be sure that a sport like fencing — which demands so much physically, emotionally, and intellectually — is for you!)

As a coach, you will notice that the book is helpfully arranged, both according to the order of a normal fencing *practice* and a normal fencing *curriculum*. Whether you want to know what to do for warm-ups tomorrow, or how to plan a half-year fencing course — whether your concerns are practical or theoretic — this book will be of assistance, both immediately and in the long term.

In short, coaches, competitors, and knowledgeable lovers of the sport should find this book conveniently arranged and immediately useful.

For beginners

Beginning fencers can use this book whether they are taking a course, joining a club, taking private lessons, or just trying to understand the sport better.

Look at the pictures first, beginning especially with Chapters IV and V, which deal with footwork and foil fencing. The pictures are an integral part of the teaching. Especially if you are not already a member of a strong club with many advanced fencers, the pictures will do more than almost anything else to give you a feeling for the sport.

Assume the positions shown in the book. Practice in front of a mirror until you begin to be comfortable. Don't make any fast or violent moves yet, just try to assume and hold the positions.

Practice the moves at home with something in your hand. A broomstick might seem tempting, but it won't give you the feel of a fencing weapon. Choose something small enough to control with your fingers (so you don't have to grip it with your whole hand like a club or a hammer and lose the precision that a fencer needs). A pencil isn't big enough, but a half-inch (12-mm) dowel will do well. Any length that projects beyond your hand will work; a standard three-foot dowel will approximate the length, though not the balance, of a real weapon. For maximum convenience, you might want to flatten a top and bottom along the last six inches or so, to approximate a handle.

Read the text. Start at the same place I suggest you start looking — the material on footwork (Chapter IV). Skip the sections on stretching and warming up for the time being. Most readers these days know the importance of a preliminary stretch and warm-up – it's super-important! — before any strenuous activity. But you won't be doing anything strenuous yet. Learn the footwork in Chapter IV slowly and carefully. Don't try it for speed yet. Build slowly. Aim for smoothness, relaxation, and technical accuracy at this stage. Come back to Chapter IV often, even after you've gone on.

It may seem illogical to learn the footwork before you learn to use the weapon. The fact is that weapon work and footwork require different kinds of coordination, so that it can be hard to learn them simultaneously. Footwork is simpler than handwork in the sense that it involves larger muscle groups that are easier to coordinate. Also, by starting with footwork, you can begin to build the strength and speed to deliver your attack to the target when it's necessary.

Then go on to the foil chapter (Chapter V). Foil is the weapon most commonly adopted by beginners – even beginners who are going to wind up fencing sabre and epee. Lukovich therefore placed a great deal of fundamental material in this chapter. When working through it, try first to get the general idea, then recheck the paragraphs that deal with common faults that may need correction.

As you are working through this material, go back and start doing the stretches, warm-ups, and exercises presented in Chapter III (Task-oriented and Inductive Exercises). Lukovich placed them earlier in the book because they belong to the early part of a practice session. Now that you know something about what you're doing, you can use them. If you belong to a club or team, you are probably doing some version of these exercises already. In that case, you might want to add just a few exercises designed for your own specific needs – whether it's to become more flexible, strengthen a particular muscle group, or improve coordination.

Now go *forward* in the book and learn about sabre and epee. Sabre and epee are not just different weapons. They are rightly called different disciplines. Each offers a different perspective on the sport. In each of them, you aim for a different target, fence at a different distance, and employ different techniques. In addition, epee does away with the scoring convention used in foil and sabre. Each change of perspective can help you see why the weapon of your choice "makes" you fence in a certain way.

By the time you have worked your way through the book in this way, I hope that you have acquired some equipment and found a place to fence. (Appendix E offers listings of suppliers around the world, fencing federations, and Internet sites.)

In a club, and working with good instruction, you will be able to turn the principles in this book into a sound practice.

Good luck and good fencing!

Stephan Khinoy
Staten Island, New York, 1997

The publisher gratefully acknowledges the generous sponsorship of Blade Fencing Equipment, Inc., for its generous sponsorship, as well as invaluable advice, in producing this book.

Author's Foreword

This book discusses the general theoretical questions related to fencing, the methodology of training, and the problems that arise in teaching. It contains material on all three weapons used in fencing, on the teaching of the sport, and the activities of the coach.

Chapters are built upon each other and identical problems are considered in one paragraph in order to avoid unnecessary repetitions and possible overlapping. For this reason, and to promote a more complete understanding, it is necessary to study each and every section on each weapon, as well as the chapters on the other weapons and the other technical aspects.

István Lukovich

I. THE SPORT OF FENCING AND THE VOCATION OF THE COACH

Fencing can be defined as a sport practised in pairs and employing a weapon (foil, sabre or épée). The objective is to hit the opponent with a thrust in foil and épée, or with a cut or thrust in sabre, in a manner and on a target area specified by the rules of fencing. Sabre and foil are conventional weapons; that is, their use is controlled by agreed-upon rules. Épée, however, has retained within its sport framework much of the duelling nature of its origin.

Fencing can also be defined as a mental and physical effort. It mobilizes the individual's motor system, intellectual powers and emotional energies. All three are involved simultaneously, each one complementing the others and intensifying or multiplying their influence. An earlier description of fencing appropriately expresses the above idea as follows: "The necessity to hit the opponent while trying to avoid being hit makes the art of fencing extremely complicated and difficult because the eyes that see and watch coupled with the mind that considers and decides must join with accuracy and speed the work of the executive arm."

While fencing a bout, the competitor relies on a number of special qualities and abilities in addition to basic physical abilities. Many of these are of a psychological nature or background.

Technique, which remains one of the essential requirements for success in fencing, is the pathway leading to the specific internal world of fencing and provides the means of expressing the special qualities and abilities needed. It brings to life the concepts and skills of the fencer which, along with the tactics that are the soul of fencing, inspire and infuse the sport with colour and variety. Technique, therefore, should not be regarded as important only in a formal or aesthetic sense.

Fencing requires more than an average ability to concentrate on an objective. The fact that actions, movement and competition are restricted in the early stage of fencing tests the young fencer's will-power and patience and his aptitude for persevering in the repeated performance of technical exercises over extended periods of time.

Despite the many efforts made to develop a complex method of instruction which includes every important element of the sport, a major problem inherent in fencing is that tactical training inevitably follows in the wake of technical instruction. A great deal of hard work is needed, therefore, to acquire the broad range of experience that enables a fencer to become an accomplished competitor.

In its early days, fencing was looked upon as the domain of high society, an aristocrat among sports. Although its days of "splendid isolation" have long since passed, fencing is still not a mass participation sport which enjoys widespread support. The reasons for this include the fact that:

- fencing cannot be measured objectively and, as such, does not allow direct comparisons in terms of results. The skill and knowledge of a fencer can be evaluated only individually or in comparison with fellow fencers or the great competitors of the past,
- actual combat (bout fencing) comes only after prolonged practice and preparation. Considerable time elapses before a fencer is truly ready to fence his first bout,
- fencing allows much less space and opportunity for movement than most other sports. During the initial stages of instruction, the specific spatial and corresponding time limits within which elements are practised restrict the beginner's desire to move and restrain his freedom of movement,
- at the level of the beginner, fencing demands a remarkable degree of concentration rather than offering pleasure and recreation,
- the real pleasure of fencing can be experienced only at a highly advanced level. In this respect, fencing differs from other sports which offer this experience from the very beginning,
- fencing recruits from a much narrower interest group than the more popular and amusing sports which attract large numbers,
- the fencer has to learn and relearn his sport on three separate occasions — when being introduced to the technical elements, when using these elements in bout fencing and when applying the acquired experiences of technical training and bout fencing to competitive fencing. Such a prospect often has a discouraging effect at an early stage of the process on even the most talented young person,
- in order to enjoy fencing, a person requires a certain degree of inside knowledge and understanding. Only the initiated can recognize and fully appreciate the tactics and strategy underlying the actual movements exhibited. The uninitiated generally fail to see the most essential elements because they can only identify with fencing through external and formal factors. They cannot draw any true experience from their observation, or can do so only to a very limited extent,
- fencing can never be a simple amusement or a useful pastime. Nor can it be just a form of physical exercise for dilettantes. The long and thorough preliminary training required rules out any possibility of "pure entertainment".

Fencing demands the sweat of both student and coach. To choose fencing as a sport either as competitor or as coach is to take on a demanding and difficult task.

Few sports afford the coach the opportunity to experience directly and concretely the day-to-day development of the student. The fencing coach, however, personally takes part in training sessions as a matter of course. He imparts his knowledge to each student directly through his own physical and spiritual labour.

It follows from the nature of fencing that a competitive career can be a fairly long one. Add to this the fact that a coach's strength and availability are less than infinite and it becomes evident that, even in the ideal case, the fencing coach cannot expect to train more than three or four talented generations of students to the level of competitive fencing.

Ambitious coaches, therefore, cannot be indifferent to the qualities of prospective students. Many adopt a strictly practical approach to the selection process if they are in a position to do so. Setting different tests to determine which students are potentially gifted, they choose from the material available and are ready to train only those selected on the basis of the test results.

Other coaches, however, are opposed to such preliminary selection procedures. They argue that fencing with its inherent difficulties and stumbling-blocks, and not tests, should constitute the actual selection process. If the nature, specificity and complex character of fencing is considered, the latter approach is subject to fewer errors in judgement and therefore is sounder. Simple tests are not sufficient to reveal whether or not a person has any aptitude for so complex a sport as fencing. The history of fencing provides numerous instances where people identified through test results and measures of ability and aptitude as having identical potential did not all reach the same level or become great fencers.

Tests measuring a single ability are usually inadequate because they deny potential fencers the opportunity to use other abilities to counter-balance any given weaknesses; yet this is exactly what happens in the competitive situation. To attach an absolutely determining role to tests is to make a grave mistake. It is interesting to note that a number of the great competitors of the past would have been judged unsuited to fencing had they been subjected to some of the tests used today. Relying on tests excludes from fencing late maturers whose talents become evident and evolve only after they have acquired knowledge in all aspects of the sport. This group may include hard-working young people with great strength of will who, through prolonged practice and training, flourish as great competitors but who, at the outset of their careers, fail to reveal any of the qualities for which they ultimately become admired and envied.

Previously the recommended age at which youngsters should take up fencing was 12 or 13. Today, however, even coaches who consider children of 10 or 11 as not yet physically and mentally ready for the sport do start to work with this age-group. They do so for objective reasons.

The age limit for entry into all sport has dropped, and fencing is no exception. Nevertheless, it remains a sport that can be practised successfully over a long time, a point mentioned earlier. Two major factors contribute to the fencer's longer-than-average active sports life. First, expertise can be acquired only through fencing many bouts against a wide variety of opponents.

Second, the special fencing abilities developed normally last longer than basic physical abilities. The competitive career of a truly successful fencer, therefore, begins at the point at which careers usually end in other sports. In most sports, performance declines in proportion to the decline of physical abilities. In fencing, it is at this stage when attributes enabling a competitor to enjoy prolonged success often become fully developed. Qualities such as sang-froid, poise, quick thinking and precise observation, balance in defence, sense of distance, the ability to recognize the opponent's intention, foresight and anticipation, facility in the execution of complex movements, timing and reflexes, and so on emerge after several years of fencing. This expertise improves given a longer, not shorter, training period.

Success in fencing is not achieved through one specific ability or quality. It results from a number of elements and conditions which are organically related, which presuppose or perhaps substitute one another, and which assume different forms under changing circumstances. The particular opponent and the situation of the moment arising from a permutation of highly variable physical, mental and emotional factors combine to determine a given result. Each result is unique and not open to comparison. Because of this, a bout, although described in terms of fencing actions, cannot be reproduced or recur exactly as it happened.

II. THE PROCESS OF INSTRUCTION AND PRACTICE

II.1. Warming up

There can be no doubt as to the importance of warming up despite the seeming lack of attention, mainly in the physical aspects, given to this activity by some outstanding competitors who have been training regularly for years. The reasons for this stem partly from the specific character of fencing and partly from the individual's personality and need for warming up.

The following factors justify intensive warming up for beginners being trained in groups:
- inexperience,
- muscles not adequately prepared,
- movements practised are complementary in nature to fencing and require greater intensity of effort and exaggerated range of performance.

The coach should personally direct the group warm-up of beginners. The exercises to be performed, their duration and intensity are a principal and mandatory part of the training session.

In the case of beginners, a sharp distinction exists between general and specific warming up. For more advanced fencers, the division is less pronounced and, for competitors, it practically ceases to exist. The general warm-up of a competitor is effected in part or in full by his working on specific fencing exercises. This gradual removal in the distinction between the two parts results in:
- a shorter warm-up period,
- a change in the nature of warming up which focuses primarily on psychological and mental aspects, with the physical aspects taking on a secondary importance.

An economical and concentrated warm-up which varies in terms of both duration and nature:
- is an instinctive defence against prolonged loading,
- accepts the fact that a fencer must warm up several times over the course of a competition,
- recognizes that warming up the highly important phychological elements (mobilizing the mental abilities, focusing attention, arousing fighting spirit, activating tactical thinking) is more essential than a physical limbering up,
- allows a greater or lesser part of the physical warm-up to be transferred to preliminary bouts, depending on the fencer's level of expertise and the strength of the competition in question.

Because neither general nor specific gymnastic exercises are sufficient to answer the needs of psychological warming up, fencers are advised to warm up in part or in whole through actual fencing. Bout fencing as a method of warming up has become a widely adopted phenomenon.

Certain fencers need more physical warming up than others. They include:

- those who tend to be lethargic at the start of competition,
- those who suffer from excessive pre-competition nervousness,
- those whose musculature is quite pronounced,
- those who tend to stiffen up between rounds of a competition.

Some hits scored at the end of a warm-up bout are designed to calm the competitor and to confirm his imagined or actual state of readiness. Partners chosen for warm-up bouts are selected according to individual needs and interests.

Warming up with a fencing lesson is not a generally adopted method. Its use at competitions of major importance can be traced mainly to psychological reasons.

The warm-up is determined by a number of internal and external factors including:

- the fencer's familiarity with the competition venue,
- the temperature in the hall,
- whether the competitor is prone to injury or is lucky enough to be relatively resistant to injury,
- the level of competition,
- the competitor's level of fitness and physical condition,
- the competitor's need for a warm-up and the habits to which he is accustomed,
- the nervous system of the fencer.

Warming up exerts an influence in two different directions. On the one hand, it mobilizes in the most efficient manner and to the extent required the energies needed to give a maximum performance; on the other hand, it reduces, and in some instances completely eliminates, factors which have a detrimental influence on performance.

II.2. The major areas and stages in the preparation of a fencer

In the course of his preparation and as his skill and expertise develop, the fencer should experience a variety of training methods with ample differentiation in form.

The collective or group training of beginners has become universal even though such a form is alien to the nature of the sport. It was established as a result of the increased interest in fencing and the consequent need to create economic methods to train large numbers of people.

Eventually collective training gives way to paired work, a form which is representative of the actual character of the sport. At this stage, the coach or another fencer acts either as a partner or as an assistant.

Different methods of training coupled with tactically or technically oriented work supplement each other. More effective work results from the judicious combination of the various elements of fencing and different training methods, sometimes even when they are diametrically opposed.

II.3. Collective activities as a necessary method of training

It is rare for a fencing coach to train beginners individually. Normally he starts coaching young fencers in groups.

"When individual training could no longer meet increasing demands, attempts were made to develop new methods of teaching beginners which would at the same time allow the identification of young talent and give basic training. Group training, tried and proven valuable in the practical instruction of fencing masters, was handy and readily adopted, although not adequate in every respect for the teaching of children." So wrote László Szabó on this question in his book, *Fencing and the Master*.

i. A critique of the traditional method
As fencing developed and coaches pushed the use of the individual lesson to the utmost, the many advantages inherent in group training remained overlooked. Indeed, as time passed, group training made little if any progress; rather, it became rigid, almost military, in its character. The virtually exclusive reliance on exercises performed uniformly and simultaneously on command expressed this trait. Also, the explanations given were too brief, too *pro forma* and too academic. The material taught was overtly theoretical and was drilled in a mechanical style and pace that stifled individual rhythms and characteristics. All this combined to make group training monotonous, tedious, uninteresting and unimaginative.

The application of this method left the beginner an outsider even after much training. The material and the method of instruction kept him from gaining insight into the essential structure of the game. It was too superficial, focusing learning, primarily, or even solely, on the technical side.

This conventional method of collective training proceeded in a linear fashion selecting only particular elements from the whole. Each action and variation was taught in isolation, with the result that the beginner had to face a new problem after each step in the process. Developing some correlation of action over time through this method was impossible and, in some cases, it even masked the objective or logic of the material. The constant use of commands also accustomed the student to unrealistic stimuli. This conservative method failed to inform and communicate. It could neither stir the beginner's enthusiasm nor arouse his interest.

Fortunately, this common, formalistic and, to a certain extent, art-for-art's-sake approach with its primarily and overwhelmingly technocratic and redundant nature has become obsolete. Group training methods have proven able not only to teach beginners the basic elements of technique but also to make them aware of the subtler elements of fencing. Although progress was slow and group training remained virtually unchanged for years, attempts to restructure the method have adjusted it by broadening the basic content and variations to conform to the actual character of fencing. So developed, it assists the coach both directly and indirectly in bringing out each student's individual talents. By the same token, the coach's search for exercises which imitate the actual bout atmosphere has led to the creation of numerous instructional variations.

Rather than describe individual variations, the following examination looks at general principles and attempts to summarize certain points and approaches with a view to establishing a common denominator for current and future coaching methods.

The need to rationalize collective training methods arises from today's modern age and life-style. Group training should not only be a form of instruction but also act as an ambassador and propagator of fencing and represent its standard of excellence. The coach's ability to promote, to influence and to convince are not unimportant since fencing must compete with other sports, each with its own particular appeal.

The principal objective of group training must be to enable the beginner to test not only his natural aptitude but also all the physical and mental abilities required in fencing. In other words, the beginner should from the very outset come to understand fencing not just on the physical level but also on the intellectual plane, recognizing and assessing the need for the self-development of emotional, psychological and physical abilities through independent activity.

The new approach to collective training:
- tries to make the beginner aware of what fencing is all about in the shortest possible time,
- encourages the beginner to use his own mind from the very first moment,
- maintains the parallel development of the physical and mental elements in all aspects of fencing,
- offers a rich, varied and colourful programme in both the preparatory and the actual fencing material to be learned,
- does not attempt to introduce an element through the physical without establishing the relevant and appropriate emotional and intellectual background,
- offers the beginner the opportunity to develop his personal characteristics of rhythm, cadence and dynamics.

In order to achieve the afore-mentioned objectives,
- unnecessary formality and formal phases are eliminated in regard to the process of training and when giving technical instruction,
- individual movements and positions are linked by a common characteristic,
- the hands and feet are prepared at the same time,
- beginners are trained not only in groups but also in pairs and individually,

- technical standards are approached gradually and indirectly,
- beginners are given the opportunity to assess and test their own abilities,
- a richer variety of training methods is adopted,
- a greater number of preparatory and specific exercises is employed.

To realize all the objectives listed above requires that the traditional framework for group training be replaced by a broader and more contemporary repertory of methods. The same applies to general and specific exercises. Also, the art-for-art's-sake approach to teaching and subject matter must give way to a more realistic, more varied and more diverse training method which arouses, engages and intensifies interest.

ii. The organization and content of group training for beginners

Today's methods of group training for beginners involve many more diverse and complex tasks than were included in its traditional form. The following problems must be overcome within the framework of group training:

- physical and mental preparation for fencing,
- the teaching of fundamental technique and its systematic application,
- the development of specific fencing abilities to the highest level possible under the conditions of group training.

With very young fencers, even certain aspects of general physical training are taught within the collective format.

Group training viewed as a necessary evil, and approached with such an attitude, has little value in fencing training. The most that can be hoped for from a method in which the coach confines himself to barking out commands without explanation and with a minimum of demonstration and which offers only the mechanical practice of positions and footwork is a basic technical level. Much more is required of the collective fencing lesson if development is to proceed at a quicker pace.

The nature of group training does allow for broader approaches beyond mere command and drill, methods which should be discarded. Ultimately, commands should be used only to get the group started or to change the pace of group actions. A command can provide the reference for action but never the atmosphere.

Programmes for collective training should be planned and conducted to arouse maximum interest. A well-organized and lively session which includes a variety of interesting fencing exercises can approximate the same physical, psychological and intellectual effects as those experienced in the average individual lesson. Such a session naturally places a heavier load both physically and mentally on the coach.

Group training is suited to both the initial and the intermediate stages of instruction. Whenever interesting new material is to be introduced, it is a good idea for the coach to hold a joint session which includes more advanced students who can help in the discussion and demonstration of the material.

It is possible, even necessary, to design group training sessions for fencers who have been working on their own for several years. These should be held at the start of the competitive season.

The ideal number of students in a group ranges between 15 and 20. Students with similar qualities, of approximately the same height (most difficult to arrange) and at comparable levels of technical development should be grouped together whenever possible since this facilitates training. If differences are too great, healthy rivalry is hampered and progress retarded.

One coach is usually in charge of the training of one group. If two coaches work together (an ideal situation which allows for more effective work), one must be in full charge of the session, while the other assists him in the work. For example, the second coach may participate in demonstrating the exercises to be practised and in correcting the students' errors.

Students can practise collectively, in pairs or individually within the framework of group training. These three methodological variations should be applied in a manner related to and determined by the students' progress.

The coach who limits group work to the practice of one or two basic elements fails to take advantage of the realistic fencing atmosphere which this form of training may take on through his organizational and leadership efforts.

Eventually, paired exercises should predominate in group sessions and a number of particular variations should be included to maintain interest levels. Collective practice can precede, assist or supplement paired exercises.

The most frequently used formations in group training include the single line, the double line, the chessboard array and two lines facing each other.

The exercises practised during a training session may be executed either on command or at the students' own pace. With the former, movements are performed in unison by the group members; with the latter, the students do not have to execute movements at the same time nor in a uniform manner.

If the programme involves inductive or task-oriented exercises, commands should not be used. Such exercises accomplish their objectives more satisfactorily when done at the students' own rhythms.

Having performed the basic exercises, the students should then practise in two lines facing each other. This formation gives them a feeling for spatial relationships, distance and the different images presented by right and left-handed opponents.

Some coaches prefer to keep the same pairs together, while others change the pairings from time to time. Practice with the same partner builds familiarity between the two, a valuable asset when working in pairs. Changing partners, however, helps to develop the student's ability to adjust to opponents with different styles.

Equipment such as mirrors, targets and dummies which aid in the acquisition of technique should be exploited during group sessions.

II.4. Preparation to accustom the beginner to actual fencing

This area of teaching has not been as fully explored as others. No final method has been absolutely established, but a number of variations do exist. At this time, they remain experimental.

The following points attempt to set out the concepts which must be considered by the coach, regardless of his theoretical biases, during the period of preparation designed to accustom students to actual fencing.

(a) Fencing can be defined as a combat between two opponents which requires a combination of physical and mental effort. It is not simply a show of strength but equally a demanding test of the intellect.

(b) Tactics are the heart and soul of combat. During the fight, the fencer thinks like a chess player. Tactics are as important as technique and, at some points, even more important.

(c) The fencer's movements are compact and precisely defined, thus demanding a well-tuned sense of motion. Exaggerated or distorted movements may be anticipated easily and are, as a consequence, bound to fail in actual combat.

(d) In addition to correct and accurate technical execution, appropriate timing of movements plays an important role in determining a fencer's success or lack of it. Actions done in haste are as disastrous as those executed hesitatingly or too late.

(e) In most instances, hand actions and footwork are performed independently. The timing of hand and feet are often different, varying in terms of speed, rhythm and range of motion. In certain cases, however, harmony between hand and feet needs to exist.

(f) The number of variations possible in fencing actions is almost limitless. This is due not only to the many formal movements which exist but also to the changes of rhythm between hand and feet from action to action and even within a single action.

(g) Movements within varying dynamics play a decisive role in fencing. Alternating fast and slow movements, interspersed with long or short pauses, should be adopted. These pauses are an integral part of the rhythm of an action.

(h) Attention must never waver. The fencer needs to have the kind of attention that combines intensity and concentration with elasticity, that can simultaneously recognize a number of factors without any significant loss of efficiency, that can be divided easily and quickly, and that is transferable, adjustable and mobile.

(i) The capacity to recognize the situation of the moment during a bout and select the appropriate reaction is essential to the fencer. He must be able to distinguish movements designed to mislead him from those which constitute a real threat.

The tasks to be fulfilled in the preparation of the beginner are as follows:

- the presentation of the sport of fencing in a way which underlines its characteristic features,
- the clarification of the nature and essence of fencing's specific abilities and needs through simple exercises,
- the preliminary elaboration of the necessary physical and intellectual conditions with the aid of task-oriented and inductive exercises.

There was a time when beginners were taught conservatively. Preparation for actual fencing was ignored and technical elements were introduced immediately. Today, the indirect method is more readily applied.

Training methods which include play and game situations are spreading throughout the fencing world. It is unlikely that the stature and seriousness of fencing will be harmed if freer and more flexible training methods are selected for preparation, especially since today's students are beginning their apprenticeship at a younger age than ever before.

If the movements learned in the preparatory stage take root in the mind of the future competitor, then he is actually engaged in a fighting situation despite his lack of technical knowledge. This condition can be exploited by tapping abilities used under actual bout conditions. Such an approach reduces the time needed to teach young fencers because they discover a great many things from and about the various tricks and secrets of deception.

Once it has been demonstrated that the combat atmosphere can be recreated and that the physical and mental efforts needed for fencing can be evoked even without possession of technical skills, exercises must be designed which faithfully represent the characteristics of fencing and, at the same time, remain preparatory blocks suited to building a fencer. The following points should be considered by the coach in developing such material.

(a) The hand and feet should not always move in unison as is usually the case. Their timing and range of motion should vary; that is, movements are not necessarily symmetrical.

(b) Co-ordination that differs from the instinctive, natural or habitual should be incorporated.

(c) Complex and diverse actions that pose a challenge to the students should be present.

(d) Both major and minor muscle groups should be involved in the execution and refinement of individual movements.

(e) Execution under varying conditions and circumstances should be possible.

(f) The possible intrusion of extraneous factors which could distract attention should exist.

(g) The freedom to choose and to try alternate actions should be allowed.

(h) Both physical and mental abilities should be mobilized.

(i) The components of fencing should be developed comprehensively.

(j) Situations in which the unexpected must be overcome should arise.

(k) The patience to wait for the decisive moment to act should be cultivated.

(l) Preparatory and misleading actions and feints should be used in conjunction with actual movements.

Using his ingenuity and imagination, the coach can invent many tasks, games and gymnastic exercises which precede fencing training proper and which still relate to the general and specific requirements of the sport.

Such exercises induce in the beginner, either simultaneously or alternately, the use of body and mind, physical abilities and psychological qualities, and general and specific fencing elements. Through these exercises, the learner gradually acquires proficiency in movements which lead up to actual fencing; that is, his skill level improves and broadens in scope. He learns how to evaluate his own abilities, how to use them to advantage; in other words, he has his first flirtations with tactics.

The appropriate use of preparatory exercises can create conditions which, at a later stage, facilitate the student's ability to analyse and unravel the complex of actions, abilities and problems he inevitably must face. This applies even to tactics.

The task of the coach is to guide beginners through the work described above. Once the students have gained an insight into the realm of fencing and have made the necessary adjustments to the new conditions, the coach may proceed to the teaching of actual fencing movements.

Prior to starting technical instruction, the coach must discuss the essence of fencing with his students. He reveals its specific internal reality and the logic which governs it. He explains the importance of each component, its influence on and relationship to the others, and the ways in which required abilities and characteristics can be applied.

This broad overview can be practised with the aid of well-known paired exercises performed in a playful atmosphere. These exercises and games, introduced in advance of technical training, offer the future fencer an opportunity to discover himself as a fencer and to assess his abilities. They awaken his imagination and intensify his interest in fencing, consolidating and deepening his commitment to his chosen sport.

If the student is to internalize fencing in all its complexity, he must possess an elastic, adaptable and flexible neuromuscular system and an accompanying practical intelligence. The ability to assimilate the many elements of fencing is proportionate to the existence of the above attributes. These qualities are determined only in part at birth by heredity. Much depends on the method adopted by the coach to effect preparation and instruction.

Beginners should first be familiarized with the atmosphere of fencing and the field of play. To many, one-to-one combat is based upon unusual and unknown concepts. Young fencers should be made aware of them as soon as possible.

The tasks best suited to familiarizing beginners with technical fundamentals are those which are based on simple or well-known solutions, which place the students in situations resembling actual fencing conditions, and which rely on a given dominant ability. The coach's ingenuity, imagination and ability to inspire his students to practise are also revealed in the structure of the set tasks.

Any playful task or exercise which incorporates any element similar to actual fencing serves the above objectives. It is paradoxical that the simplest and most insignificant exercises are often the ones most likely to illustrate and demonstrate vividly but briefly the most abstract concepts of fencing, such as those encompassing the theme of tempo and, at a later stage, connected abilities in relative speed.

The inclusion of such exercises and games in a training session should be varied in a way that reveals to the students the essential concepts and nature of the abilities to be learned. They should also create the specific milieu and atmosphere of combat; that is, they contain the germs of actual fencing which include technical norms as well.

Basic gymnastic exercises, or more relaxed games with or without the gymnastics, can make up the preparatory material.

After a while a broader variety of basic gymnastics should be used. Complex and diverse tasks which are more and more related to actual fencing should increasingly be set. Once the students understand the basic structure of the exercises, their execution should be intensified. The degree of difficulty can be increased by adding to the complexity and diversity of the exercise.

Ways to make the exercises more difficult include condensing them, combining them and performing them in an asymmetrical fashion. They should be performed with changes in pace and rhythm, with variations in dynamics, and with possible alternatives left to the choice of the students. In structuring the exercises, the coach should strive for complexity, the simultaneous engagement of several abilities, increased involvement of intellectual qualities and the introduction of fundamental tactical forms in order to match the multiple objectives of fencing.

Variety arouses, maintains and intensifies interest. It twigs the imagination and thereby involves the fencer's mind in his training. Later, the student will find certain solutions and variations for himself. Once he has reached this stage, he participates actively and creatively in his own training.

Variations of schoolyard games and physical education activities adapted to fencing training play a major role in the preparation for actual fencing. With few restrictions and high emotional changes, these adapted games allow students to experiment with acquired technical elements under changing conditions and circumstances and amid numerous distractions. Also, they can bring to light important hidden qualities of the student and can intensify the spirit of combat as well. Individual approaches and unique solutions to problems are fostered through these adapted games. Finally, they help to alleviate nervous tension and fatigue caused by the boring and repetitive practice of technical elements.

II.5. The nature and variations of individual training

The crossing of two blades in the fencing lesson is the ultimate form of paired exercise. The coach acts as the student's partner, opponent, teacher and adviser all at the same time.

In the lesson the student gets to practise with a partner well-versed in all technical aspects. The coach, doubling as the opponent, can offer maximum or minimum resistance and can specifically limit the choice of action.

Contact with and control of the blade are the main advantages inherent in the fencing lesson, benefit not ensured by any other form of practice or training. Because of this, the coach must not ignore the correction of errors even in cases where the lesson is designed to assume the characteristics of an actual bout.

All fencing lessons have things in common, but they also differ one from another depending on the style of the coach. Each coach adds his own personal touch to the universal fundamental actions of the fencing master.

The most noticeable differences appear in terms of the atmosphere of the lesson which has its own particular emotional and dynamic character. This issues from the personality and background of the coach and his relationship with the student.

Whether they want to or not, coaches mould students in their own images. The greatest of them leave an unmistakable imprint on a generation of fencers, but without stifling or restricting the expression of the student's individual characteristics.

Coach and student join in a creative partnership, each complementing the other and leading the other to new horizons.

The primary objective of the fencing lesson is to teach technique, maintain it and refine it. For this reason, the classical technical lesson should play a leading role in the training of a fencer.

The addition of tactical elements through a wide range of exercises which resemble bout fencing can be introduced in the technical lesson to make a more colourful and varied experience.

The structure of the lesson depends greatly on the fencer's personality, his skill level, his needs and his immediate frame of mind. There is no universal recipe which suits everyone. Theoretical schemes do exist, but the structure, manner and extent of their actual application varies widely.

A fencing lesson lacking in enthusiasm or dedication is tiring and unproductive. Distinguishing between routine lessons of the same length at a regular hour and repetitive lessons based on the same action helps the coach to avoid the above problem.

For the lesson to have any benefit, the student must come to it in optimum physical and emotional condition. He must also bring a high level of self-motivation, imagination and a desire to do creative work. Likewise, it behoves the coach to prepare himself properly so that he arrives relaxed and fit when coming to give the lesson.

It is virtually impossible for the coach to keep a written daily record for each student. He should, therefore, commit to memory the key material and structural elements of previous lessons. This requires no extra energy on the part of an experienced coach. Such an outline of the lesson just completed serves as the framework and core for the development of the next.

The number of students with which a coach works has a decisive influence on his efforts. Complete and thorough work of substantial content can be performed only if the number of students allows the coach sufficient time to prepare.

Fencing lessons abound with abridged technical jargon which must be learned by everyone. This specialized terminology allows a more efficient use of the available time and adds a personal character to the lesson. Even among coaches who speak the same language, differences in usage and expression distinguish one from another. This special communication adds to the intimacy of the lesson.

The primary means to the end in fencing, the individual lesson establishes a bond between coach and competitor which does not exist in other sports even when coach and athlete are friends. A lesson involving a coach and student who know each other well will be good even if one of the partners is off form or tired.

II.6. The division and objectives of the fencing lesson

In principle, a fencing lesson is composed of three distinct parts: the introduction, the main body and the conclusion. Though they are separate, there are no sharp lines of distinction between them in practice. They are intertwined in such a way that they appear to be a single unit even to those versed in fencing. Only the people involved in the lesson can sense one part from the others.

i. The introduction

The introduction of the lesson is more than just a simple warm-up. Warming up, in the narrow sense, is left to the student. In the introduction, the coach extends and refines the warm-up to attune the fencer's nervous system to the lesson proper.

The fencing lesson differs psychologically from all other types of training, such as free fencing, footwork and target work. Tuning the nervous system, therefore, is essential to this form of practice which has special requirements to be satisfied.

The student may arrive for his lesson fresh from fencing a bout or not having been active at all. This requires that an emotional transition period be provided. Those who come directly from fencing must be relaxed and calmed; those who have been inactive prior to the lesson must be energized and "pumped up".

The lesson introduction should establish contact with the student and reveal to the coach what the student is capable of doing at that time. It should direct the emotional and physical state of the student and revitalize him. It should promote relaxed movements, set the correct distance and co-ordinate the actions of hand and feet.

The time devoted to the introduction is quite short. In this brief spell the coach must attune himself to the student. This demands a concentrated and condensed effort on the part of the coach. In most instances he seeks to harmonize the student's physical and emotional states simultaneously through the same actions. This is done by exerting a psychological influence, inspiring, adjusting the effects of the student's warm-up and calling on physical and nervous reserves. At the same time the coach assesses what the student's condition will allow in terms of the lesson material and regulates the co-ordination of hand and feet.

Often physical co-ordination can be established before psychological balance. For a tired student, one who is slow to relax or one who is frustrated, efforts to establish emotional harmony can continue beyond the lesson introduction.

It goes without saying that every student is different. The coach, therefore, should experiment with each one to find out what approach works best. The principle of using differentiated training methods should be applied as early as the lesson introduction.

Outstanding coaches establish contact with the student through their personal charisma and powers of suggestion. This almost negates the need for the introduction, except in the case of an inexperienced student. Coaches of this calibre exert the necessary influence, usually created with the introduction, through the way they take up a position, how they hold their weapon or the tone of their voice. Under such conditions, a fencing lesson can begin without any introduction at all.

ii. The main body of the lesson
During the introduction the coach outlines for himself the material which will constitute the main body of the lesson. New material should be presented early, while the student is still physically and mentally fresh.

A predominant motif should permeate the entire lesson, thus forming a logical unit. The related elements which follow like episodes make the principal material to be learned more appealing and varied. They can also introduce, supplement or conclude the material.

The new material recurs as a motif or refrain throughout subsequent lessons until it has become part of the routine material to be practised.

Within each lesson offensive, defensive and counter-offensive actions should be blended together as they might occur in actual fencing, keeping in mind general fencing theory and the particular concepts of the weapon being used. If the new material to be introduced is of an offensive nature, the coach should include elements chosen from the arsenal of defensive and counter-offensive actions or, if defensive or counter-offensive material is being taught, they should be balanced by practising some offensive movements.

The coach often has to improvise in the course of a fencing lesson. This may result either from a problem with the element or subject being presented, or from instinctive reactions of or comments by the student.

Pauses in the fencing lesson provide moments of complete or relative relaxation.

The coach can make use of these breaks, which may vary in length, to analyse, summarize or emphasize differences and variations in the actions just practised. The time can be used to discuss personal problems, to explain tactics, to provide demonstrations, and so on.

The pauses inserted between various elements of the lesson aid and abet the perfection of technical execution. Adjusting the length of breaks can create a more favourable starting state in the student. This helps to eliminate errors which stem from too quick a start and those which inevitably occur in movements "produced on the assembly line". It also prevents other inhibiting factors and unnecessary muscle use in the execution of movements and reduces the effects of emotional distractions and useless experimentation which diminish attention.

iii. The conclusion

In general, the lesson conclusion condenses or summarizes the newly acquired subject matter in combination with emotional or psychological follow-up drills, thus readying the student for bout fencing.

In practice it is rarely possible to provide a gradual and complete physical and emotional decrescendo except, perhaps, in the last lesson of the training session if time is available because the students usually carry on training either on their own or in pairs after their lessons.

The lesson normally concludes with a short, suggestive and energetic episode which condenses and mobilizes the fencer's energies for the bout fencing to follow. This is particularly true in the case of a slow-paced technical lesson. A series of lunges combined with simple actions and done with increasing intensity and speed from a medium distance are useful to this end.

A lesson which continues when the student has been emotionally drained or physically worn out is virtually useless. It is important to end the lesson at just the right moment in order to preserve the student's motivation in subsequent training.

Obviously errors can and should be corrected in all three parts of the fencing lesson. The theory of how to make corrections changes from part to part. Most of the coach's efforts directed to correcting errors occur within the main body of the lesson.

A number of factors and circumstances determine the length, content and style of the fencing lesson. They include the number of students trained by the coach, their skill levels, their mental and physical states at the time, the competition schedule, and so on.

II.7. Types of fencing lessons

There are several types of fencing lessons. Some of the basic ones are lessons which are designed to:

- attain and maintain competition form,
- drill mechanics and technique,
- treat a particular subject,
- reform and correct movements,
- teach movement variations and tactics.

There are also silent lessons, lessons for warming up with the blade and lessons for developing other special skills and abilities.

A fencing lesson can focus on one subject area or deal with a variety of subjects. It can be instructional or motivational. It can create a stable environment or a constantly changing one for the student.

Any clear distinction between lesson types can be seen only when the nature, content and objectives are extremely different. Many synonymous terms may refer to transitional and similar types.

Rarely does a coach give a purely typical lesson, except in the case of a beginner or a more advanced fencer who is returning after a long absence due to illness or injury. The great majority of lessons are a blend of types with differing natures and objectives, each figuring more of less in the overall composition of the total lesson. This provides advantages in complex preparation as compared to a series of lessons, each dealing with a separate and independent theme.

In practice lessons of different profiles are mixed together. The difference from one lesson to the next is sensed rather than clearly defined on the basis of an obvious specific formula. This is particularly true in the case of analogous lessons.

The most readily discernible difference exists between the lesson built on mechanics (the technical lesson) and the one built on varied and alternative movements (the tactical lesson).

i. The technical lesson

"The mechanical lesson is undoubtedly the most important if not the only method of drilling the technical elements of movements and actions. This type of lesson plays a role in the development of so many abilities and the acquisition of so many skills that no training or instruction can be successful without this fundamental form," these words were written by László Szabó in *Fencing and the Master*.

The pure variation of the technical lesson is used only with beginners. In it, the student practises actions in a stationary on-guard position without changing the distance, tempo or rhythm.

Beginners internalize technique in the course of a technical lesson, concentrating their attention on the quality of execution. This is coupled with the most essential physical elements, such as quick and energetic starts, rapid execution and, of course, tempo.

In the case of competitors, the technical lesson is used to maintain, renew and correct technique or to re-establish movement precision after a competition.

Often during a technical lesson, the student loses his concentration and falls

28

into the constant rhythm of movements in the lesson. This can cause practice to become all too monotonous.

This shortcoming of the technical lesson can be overcome if material is presented skilfully in a "serial dosage". Breaks of appropriate length between successfully accomplished segments can avoid or neutralize any potential loss of attention.

If the lesson is longer than usual, inserting pauses does not suffice to break the monotony. Segments of a different nature and character should be included to intensify and extend the student's attention. This has a relaxing effect when concentration fades. Only students with a high threshold for repetitive work can withstand the monotony of a long technical lesson.

It is impossible to ignore, or to completely eliminate from training, the technical lesson. Nor would it be wise to underrate the technical lesson since it serves as the foundation of learning. Everyone, without exception, begins his training in fencing with this type of lesson and it recurs from time to time at later stages of development when necessary, such as when a competitor loses confidence, suffers a physical injury or psychological breakdown, loses his precision, or when the coach must correct a recurring error which could become an ingrained fault if left uncorrected.

There have been, are and always will be great talents who, though trained only with technical lessons throughout their competitive careers, develop into superior fencers. Others never reach such heights, even when nurtured with lessons that assume bout characteristics.

ii. The tactical lesson
The tactical lesson is built upon the possibility of alternative action, in other words, on the inclusion of bout characteristics. This type of lesson is designed to stimulate fencing actions under varying conditions and circumstances, but that does not mean the primary criterion of the tactical lesson is to keep the student constantly on the move. The coach tries to recreate bout conditions in every aspect through a theoretically logical sequence of actions. In this way, the tactical lesson shapes the fencer's technical profile, style, competitive personality and overall approach to conducting a bout.

The coach may choose to concentrate on a single action or on several movements of opposite nature and characteristics in the tactical lesson. In the former, "the vegetables that garnish the meat" must be varied; that is, the starting position, the setting and the finishing touch can be altered. Also, preparatory and transitional movements and those designed to camouflage and reconnoitre should change. If the latter option is chosen, then the setting and other surrounding elements of the lesson usually remain constant. Other ancillary movements also maintain a uniform appearence.

Generally, the tactical lesson begins with a bit of a technical lesson.

iii. Other considerations

The coach should give lessons with his non-dominant hand to accomplish certain psychological objectives. Such lessons help students to overcome fear or apprehension when faced with this unfamiliar situation by building the fencer's self-confidence and sense of security, if considered necessary, a few of these lessons given a week or two before a major competition should suffice.

Lessons used as warm-ups also have primarily psychological purposes. In a pre-competition work-out, the coach must adapt the lesson to the student. It is the student who must be served in the choice of speed, rhythm, intensity and form. The inclusion of key actions also helps to enhance the psychological influence of the warm-up lesson. The task at this point is to assist the fencer in achieving a successful experience and to build his self-confidence in order to have a calming influence. Errors should be corrected only in an indirect manner.

II.8. The coach's use of the blade and its role in the lesson

The success of a fencing lesson depends largely on the way in which the coach handles his weapon; that is, the manual skill of the coach.

The preconditions necessary for the execution of a fencing action are created by the coach's presentation of his blade in reciprocal or complementary positions and movements. In some cases, these blade actions should be accompanied by actual footwork or its approximation as required.

The cardinal requirement needed to create conditions with the blade is that such presentations approach reality as much as possible when simulating a given situation. No matter how close lesson conditions approximate reality, they can never be completely identical because:

- although more than mere assistance, a lesson is never a real bout,
- the coach starts his attacks from a closer distance than an opponent in a competitive situation,
- the coach's presentation of the blade does more than create conditions.

In reference to the last point mentioned above, the coach uses his blade to create conditions by making reciprocal movements which assist the correct technical execution of the student's actions. These movements not only create and ensure the possibility of an action but also offer stimuli and assistance at the same time; that is, the coach may facilitate or hinder the student's execution through his method of presenting the blade. In a lesson that assumes bout conditions, the moment at which the final thrust or cut is to be executed and the appropriate manner of execution should be clearly indicated.

Proper blade presentation is a combination of natural ability and practice. Based on the amateur's instinctive sense of the blade, it is more refined, expressive and evocative in its ability to offer assistance. All the coach can add through his blade to the creation of conditions is invaluable to the assistance he provides the student during the lesson.

Rarely is the blade assistance offered by the coach of a merely physical quality. Even with beginners, he inevitably includes psychological associations connected with emotional reactions and consequences, initial intentions and ideas, and logical processes. Usually, these are hidden within the actual physical presentation. On occasion, however, artificially imposed verbal cues relating to the manner of execution fulfil the emotional or psychological role.

A correctly presented blade demonstrates to, motivates and inspires the student. It makes him execute actions and think.

The coach's blade presentation can create an ideal, realistic, exaggerated or unique situation. It should be suited to the student and present to him a particular type of fencing or the style of a certain opponent so as to achieve very special objectives.

The varied characteristics listed above can be applied to all technical elements of an action: size, range, limits, speed, direction, frequency and rhythm. All elements do not have to be presented in any given way at the same time.

One indication that the coach and student have accommodated to each other is the degree to which the student is familiar with the universal signals given with the blade and the particular accents of the coach's presentation. There can be a harmonious lesson only if the student is in possession of such knowledge.

Each coach has his own unique style of blade presentation. As time goes by, each adds something of his personality to the general technique of the fencing master. Such individual traits take much practice to develop before becoming integrated into his general patterns of presentation. Even the most mechanical of coaches who invests little of his being into the universal technique of the master eventually develops his own specific and characteristic presentation of the blade.

In practice the coach employs other complementary movements to enhance blade presentation. Usually, they come about instinctively. Those which might provoke harmful, misleading or incorrect actions on the part of the student, or which might lead to occupational injuries, should be avoided.

II.9. The role and forms of paired exercises

Technique acquired through fencing lessons is not sufficient in and of itself. Other possible forms of training must be fully utilized in order to develop an automatized technique which suits the particular characteristics of the student.

The fencing lesson and bout fencing are two of the possible methods of preparation. They lie at opposite ends of the spectrum. The fencing lesson represents the "purest" form, while bout fencing (or free fencing) is the most versatile and realistic. Paired practice acts as the bridge between these two extremes.

Paired exercises recreate the characteristics of a bout in a realistic manner.

In the course of paired exercises, the coach may play many different roles.

(a) With beginners, he should try to match students of similar abilities as partners. If he wants to achieve a very specific objective, he may wish to pair a more talented fencer with a weaker one.

(b) He should describe and demonstrate, or have students demonstrate, the exercises to be practised. Fencers should play both roles in the exercise, even in the course of demonstration.

On occasions when the coach does not have the opportunity to include certain actions in the fencing lesson, he can match experienced fencers together to practise such movements, such as fencing at close quarters, special ripostes to the back of a ducking opponent or to the shoulder of an opponent attempting a sidewards esquive, and so on.

i. Attack/defence exercises at the wall

One fencer (the defender) stands with his back to the wall to prevent his retreating. The other fencer (the attacker) tries to hit the defender with a predetermined action from a given distance. The defender tries to parry the attack and riposte in a set manner. The defender does not have to react to every action of the attacker.

The primary objective in this type of exercise are the development of the attacker's ability to execute simple or first intention actions precisely and quickly and to initiate these actions without giving away his intention, and the development of the defender's ability to execute a secure riposte after taking a parry, even at the last possible moment.

At first, only the simplest actions should be practised. The material used in attack/defence exercises can expand gradually to include compound attacks, a wide range of parries and counter-attacks.

ii. Conventional practice in pairs

Once the desired level of proficiency in attack/defence exercises has been attained, the students may advance to conventional practice in pairs. The conventional practice in pairs is actually free fencing in which certain limits in the choice of actions are set. In this form both fencers have the opportunity to attack and defend as the situation calls for.

The coach should gradually broaden the range of actions employed in conventional exercises, always keeping in mind the students' skill levels.

iii. Systematic bout fencing

The systematic bout is one step removed from actual bout fencing. The fencers are given a certain set of actions to integrate into the bout and must execute them systematically without tipping their hands to the opponent.

Although such a bout has a competitive character, with hits being recorded, the fencer's main aim is to execute the specified actions as often as possible.

The basic elements best developed in the systematic bout include sensing tempo, changing speed and rhythm, and using preparatory movements and others designed to disguise the fencer's intentions and distract the opponent.

The students should try to apply their list of actions against a wide variety of opponents. This teaches them how to present the same movement in many ways.

II.10. Controlling the student's movements and correcting errors

Although one of the purposes in any systematically organized training is the prevention of technical faults, it is impossible in the course of learning to avoid errors completely. No process can expect to teach unknown material to a beginner without some errors.

Even if the coach considers every possibility in the organization of training, he still has to contend with a number of errors of varying severity. These must be reduced, or totally eliminated if possible, step by step in the course of practice situations where the student's actions can be controlled.

The beginner should be taught to execute movements as closely resembling the theoretical ideal as possible. With advanced fencers, the coach may make certain allowances for individual style and interpretation. The factors which influence and mould a competitor's characteristic technique should be modified only if such modification is not at the expense of results; otherwise they should be accepted as they are.

Initially any deviation from the ideal should be considered as an error. Later, however, this approach must change since individual differences must be judged by different standards and in different manners. Many personal idiosyncrasies should not be categorized as errors or important aberrations from the absolute. It is natural for individual tendencies to appear after a time. Anatomical structure as well as personality traits present specific obstacles at certain stages and work against the maintenance of pure classical technique. More often than not, these obstacles prove to be impossible to overcome.

Often it is difficult to decide, even after appropriate consideration, what should be treated as an error to be corrected and what should no longer be dealt with. In the latter case, the deviation remains in the student's technique in a limited way, becoming a factor which shapes and moulds his individual style.

It is extremely important in fencing that the student learn a technique which is as error-free as possible. Not to do so poses major difficulties at later stages because it is very difficult to eliminate ingrained bad habits and replace them with correct movements. Because fencing includes many movement elements which are unfamiliar to the beginner, the coach must treat technical errors strictly and not ignore them under any circumstances.

The coach needs a number of qualities and abilities in order to correct errors. These include:

- ambition,
- unlimited patience,
- the ability to find and to analyse the causes of errors,
- a thorough knowledge of corrective procedures and the imagination to find and develop new methods when necessary,
- the ability to choose the right procedure for a particular problem,
- the skill to implement the required method.

The student, too, must possess certain things, among which are:
- will-power and intense concentration,
- a willingness to correct errors,
- a tolerance for the tedious work required,
- self-control and self-reliance to work on correcting errors.

In short, the coach and the student must be equal partners in the process in terms of determination and effort.

The order of activity in the correction of errors is:
(1) comparing the actual movement to the model one as explained and demonstrated,
(2) stating the errors and their order of significance,
(3) exploring the underlying causes of the most significant errors,
(4) selecting the most suitable corrective measures (usually through practical trial-and-error),
(5) informing the student in a positive way about the errors and the methods of correction.

Corrections are positive when the coach, rather than just making a statement of fact, gives instructions on how to perform the movement properly or the way to correct the fault. For example, instead of saying something like "Your knee is not in line", the coach gives the student the instruction "Turn your knee outwards". The use of such imperatives does not confirm the actual error committed, but rather engages the student in an indirect way in the correction necessary.

This positive approach to correcting errors is designed to strengthen the stimuli and reflexes necessary for correct technical execution. Incorrect and unnecessary movements are not reinforced and, as a result, weaken and eventually disappear.

Errors in initial positions and major movements must be corrected from the very start. Success in eliminating them normally leads to the decrease of any ancillary faults.

Secondary errors that are unrelated to the primary one being corrected obviously have to be treated separately.

The errors of beginners should be corrected in a period without movement. Corrections should be made continually, introduced gradually in the course of the movement, and made in proportion to the intensity of the action.

Complete sentences, used to indicate corrections to be made, are inevitable at the early stages of training but become shorter formulations of thoughts as time passes. For a coach and student who are very familiar with each other, one word can suffice to call attention to a recurring fault or some element to be corrected; that is, the coach may only say "knee" for the message to be communicated to the student. Continuous corrections made during the course of the training session must be brief in order to make the best use of the available time, to maintain the continuity of training and to conserve the coach's energy.

Methods of error correction can take several forms, including:

- verbal,
- manual; that is, with the blade and unarmed hand working together or separately.

A student who needs more explanation than average in order to understand a movement normally needs more of the verbal type of correction. Visually or motor-oriented students tend to respond better to the manual form.

For a more complex method of correction, the coach can experiment with a combination of the two types mentioned above, using them together in the interest of achieving success.

There are advantages and disadvantages to each of the methods of error correction which must be considered when choosing between them.

The verbal correction of errors:

- lets the coach to define the importance and emphasis of technical reformation, and demonstrates from a number of different points of view,
- allows the coach to instil the speed and rhythm of a movement in the student, to accentuate the key elements and to verbally accompany elements to make them more obvious,
- helps to heighten the student's awareness of more refined elements and methods of execution.

Manual error correction:

- usually refers to errors in blade movements,
- indicates without delay what correction the student must make,
- underlines and characterizes the nature of the error,
- is more expressive and representative than the briefest verbal communication,
- stimulates and inspires more than the verbal method,
- does not depend on the coach's ability to express himself in words,
- saves the coach's voice,
- makes corrections only through positive elements,
- can be integrated in the blade assistance used to create learning situations.

Since verbal corrections by nature often lead to negative communications by the coach, he should pay particular attention early on in his career to developing a positive manner of expressing his messages. The inevitable monotony inherent in extended verbal corrections must be avoided when possible by changing the working tone of voice and emphasis of the delivery. To counterbalance the tedium of error correction, the different methods should be used alternately or combined and associated in any appropriate manner.

Error corrections should be firm, compelling and move the student to act accordingly. They should characterize and illustrate symbolically and precisely the point or nature of the correction, and also provide a concrete basis on which the student may make the necessary adjustment.

A coach making corrections with weapon in hand should not abuse his position through a brutal, intimidating or supercilious use of the blade.

The verbal correction of errors is effective even with a new student. Correction with the blade, however, is practical only when coach and student have established a *rapport* since the student must recognize and adjust accordingly to the signals and messages coming from the coach's blade.

The underlying causes of errors can be of a physical or a psychological nature. Errors can stem from:

- insufficient understanding or misinterpretation of the action,
- false or distorted images of the movements,
- rigid fixation on a single element which inhibits any other viewpoint,
- lack of confidence,
- insufficient muscular or other physical abilities needed to execute movements,
- inadequate intellectual or psychological qualities needed for problem-solving,
- poor kinesthetic sensitivity.

The coach, especially one with less experience, should view the student's movements from several different angles and distances on a number of occasions before making a concrete reference to any error. This is more easily done in group training than in the individual lesson. Instead of standing in one place, the coach should move among the group members as is necessary and to the extent possible in order to get a more complete image of the students' movements.

In the case of the individual lesson, the coach should leave his position in front of the student only if there is no other way to find the source of the error. Errors not visibly discernible can be discovered and evaluated through other mediating elements such as excessive firmness in the blade, decreased fencing distance, and so on.

Some errors may be detected when the coach is supervising other activities outside the lesson. He should make time, therefore, to observe those activities when he is not giving lessons.

The most important processes in error correction are:

- repeated explanation or verbal instruction,
- repeated demonstration,
- the giving of direct and indirect assistance,
- the creation of situations which lead to correct technical execution,
- independent practice in front of a mirror which allows the student to control his actions visually,
- the isolation of incorrectly executed elements from the others,
- the adjustment of situational factors such as starting position, preparatory or introductory or concluding movements,

- the disguising of the faulty movement within familiar elements,
- the execution of the movement from a different position directed to the opposite side,
- the elimination of inhibiting preparations and the reduction of the time of preparations,
- the return to practice under standard conditions,
- continuous, rhythmic and uninterrupted work,
- the brief or extended suspension of practice of the faulty movement,
- the interruption of the movement at the point where the error occurs,
- the comparison of the faulty execution with the correct execution in an emphatic manner which makes the student sense the difference.

Opposing strategies can be employed to gain the desired effect. The coach can:

- focus the student's attention in order to intensify his concentration, or distract the student to reduce his excessive attention on one point,
- increase or decrease the intensity of a movement,
- change the speed and frequency of action,
- exaggerate or refine elements of execution (the former mostly in the case of hand movements, the latter for foot movements),
- make situations more difficult or easier,
- increase or decrease the length of pauses between movements.

II.11. A discussion on the abilities required for fencing

A debate has been under way in fencing for many years concerning what are the necessary abilities, their order of importance, the possibility of their development and the best methods to use to develop them. In order to support their position each side has argued with and referred to evidence gained through particular cases of application yet to be verified scientifically.

Rather than come down on one side or the other, the following discussion confines itself to making a few fundamental statements. They are necessary, not to carry on the debate, but to serve the interests of fencing.

Starting from the natural basis of fencing, rather than referring to statements concerning the general theory of training, is likely to reduce the possibility of logical errors and misinterpretation.

Fencing can be described as an extreme branch of physical training which possesses a specific character. The conditions necessary for success and the demands on the fencer are far from being recent in origin. They go back a long way and have changed through time mostly in terms of style and proportions of the weapon.

Considering that fencing is:

- a sport requiring more than a single ability (the fencer needs many at his disposal giving him a broad range of possibilities from which to choose, unlike athletes in many other sports),

● not only an individual sport but also the sport of individuals,

everyone can establish his own ranking of the abilities needed and their importance.

If the above viewpoint is compared with the generally held concept, it then becomes evident that categorical statements about the abilities needed for fencing are as useful as similar statements concerning styles and tactics or preparation and training.

A fencer can succeed through the use of a wide range of abilities. No listing can rank with absolute certainty those abilities which are the most important and unchallengeable. No single ability can solve every problem just as no single condition or element can settle old scores. Only in theory can one ability or another be said to be the absolute one.

No absolute scale or measurement exists because no final or uppermost limit can be defined. Each fencer can be judged as better or worse than another depending on the particular ability being compared. Since no concrete method of measurement can apply, all judgments must be based subjectively on appearances.

A student who shows striking potential in the early stages of training often develops into a talented and successful fencer. The later-maturing individual, on the other hand, whose hidden abilities surface gradually, can not only equal the quick-rising fencer but may even surpass him to a considerable degree.

A fencer must mobilize physical and intellectual energies in a given situation which is very specific. The motivations and other factors which lie behind the eventual scoring of a hit are decided by the situation at hand, the choice of the action to be used and the difference in the abilities of the two combatants.

A competitor has not only to take advantage of his own strength and skills, but also to exploit the weaknesses and mistakes of his opponent. For this reason, it is unnecessary for the competitor to bring to the fore all his abilities on every occasion.

From time to time the fencer must use one or another of his specific abilities to the maximum. It is more often the case, however, that a bout is won or lost not by virtue of the fencer's strongest point, but by the role played by less significant abilities.

The same factors and components do not always contribute to the success of even the highest calibre competitor. In some instances, a single ability, or rather its advantageous application, is sufficient to score a hit. On other occasions, however, success comes only through the proper combination of several qualities and abilities.

One of the advantages of fencing as a sport is that a person's lack of, or weakness in, a certain specific ability does not have to be fatal. Weaknesses can be compensated for, substituted with, or balanced by the use of other abilities. When they are combined, the effects of the separate components are multiplied and intensified. Thus, this allows the fencer to overcome any particular shortcomings.

That a fencer lacks talent in the most obvious or spectacular of abilities does not at all spell disaster. Using practical intelligence and skill, the competitor can make up for certain weaknesses quite adequately.

Abilities have both a physical and a psychological side. Each physical ability has a corresponding psychological or emotional one. Reaction time is paired with speed of movement, indomitable spirit with muscular endurance, willpower with physical strength, and so on.

Many assumptions which have no scientific basis in fact are made about abilities in general and specific abilities in particular. To clarify problems connected with abilities is no simple task even in sports less complicated than fencing. Settling the question cannot be done by simply referring to some authority or by reducing it to "common knowledge". Only when special abilities can be analysed in terms of their composition, and thus classified, can any significant step forward be taken.

General physical abilities can be developed outside fencing. Specific fencing abilities, however, can be developed to the required levels only in tandem with technique, keeping in mind that abilities and skills are closely related. Specific abilities cannot be separated from technical activity; that is, the manipulation of the weapon. Fencing brings these abilities to the surface and develops them to their highest level. Only active fencing effectively develops these abilities necessary to the sport.

There are many who think that the development of abilities through fencing is inefficient and ineffective. They frequently try, therefore, to improve the fencer's skill, strength and speed by borrowing movements from other sports. Such an approach can be useful with beginners, but is not always applicable in the case of experienced competitors since the abilities brought out are cruder in form than those required in fencing. They must be refined, differentiated and made to resemble fencing abilities more closely. Such borrowed movements can frequently disturb the internal co-ordination so essential to fencing.

It has become fashionable in most sports, fencing included, to find seemingly complementary sports to use for further development of abilities. They should not, however, be practised at the expense of the athlete's actual sport. As yet a model variation which is not quite fencing but not a general activity, and which would develop abilities closely allied to fencing, has not yet been found.

So many properties are necessary for fencing that only a theoretical model of such a parallel activity can possess them all. This model is often approached by fencers in different ways and to different extents as they train.

II.12. Technical development and the development of fencing abilities

Intensive physical and emotional preparation for fencing should be followed by the explanation and subsequent instruction of the necessary technical fundamentals. The student who has been given the time and opportunity to mature is better prepared to solve technical problems. The maturation process acquaints him with the most essential requirements and the ways to put them into practice. Through it, he experiences first hand the influences exerted on him by motivations, essential abilities and qualities, and learns how to put those influences into action.

Play-oriented methods and optional free forms of training used in the preparatory stages should continue to be used at the stage of technical development. In adopting these methods, consideration must be given to the introduction of new material which approaches certain technical norms to replace the old preparatory material. This is particularly important in the teaching of fencing positions and footwork, and can save time if properly organized. The coach who is able to develop smooth transitions between the situations and movements already known to the student and those which are new and unfamiliar should have fewer difficulties in putting technical norms into practice than the coach who resorts to more conservative training methods. Such transitions establish relationships between the two levels in the course of instruction, drawing parallels between the somewhat difficult but important initial fencing actions and their technical variations in a concrete way that facilitates learning. These parallels relate artificially created movements to naturally taken positions and actions, point out and build upon movements found in everyday activities which have something in common with fencing movements, and establish the new material in a simple and logical manner.

Artificial positions and footwork may be employed as task-oriented or inductive exercises for the sake of expediency, but they have little else to offer. Fundamental gymnastic forms create more opportunities from which the coach can deduce the positions and movements already known to the student and, from this, which fencing actions are most essential to develop.

In order to shorten the time taken to reach the desired goal, technique must be established in a rational way. Nothing should be taught that would overtax the student or be a waste of time for beginners. In bout fencing attention and energies must at all times be focussed only on the essentials.

More rapid progress can be aided by limiting "academic" practice, relaxing the rigid enforcement of precision in positions and their treatment as basic elements of order.

Training methods should not automatically follow formal standards; nor should they necessarily conserve and respect traditions. An art-for-art's-sake approach or overly spectacular methods ought to be avoided. Even in the initial stages of training, methods should be chosen which give life to the cold, and sometimes boring, technical material.

The on-guard position, steps forward and backward, the lunge and recovery must be taught in as simple a manner as possible. A natural path should be followed, with the overriding objectives being optimum use of time and the inhibition of errors. These viewpoints should influence the methods chosen from the outset of training.

In contrast to the conservative approach, the coach should teach the on-guard position, not the initial position, as the first fencing position.

Taking up the on-guard position from a straddled stance, with the feet parallel and almost two foot lengths apart, reduces the likelihood of the student making a mistake. Keeping the trunk erect, the student bends both legs as the first step. This immediately locates the rear knee in the correct position, where it remains throughout the taking up of the on-guard position. Following the sequence described below, the rear knee never caves inward, a fault commonly seen when using the traditional approach. The leading foot is rotated 90° to the outside, turning on the heel with the toes raised. The student then faces along the line of the leading foot which is directed toward an imaginary opponent. With this, the on-guard position has been taken up.

When learning steps forward and backward, the student should first execute short steps done virtually on the spot. Stride length should increase gradually without allowing the centre of gravity to rise or the position of the body to shift. Steps should be completed without delay, and care should be taken to lift the rear foot energetically and to maintain the distance between the feet.

Beginners with stiff or muscular shoulders should be allowed to hold their free arm loosely, behind and parallel to the trunk. This runs contrary to conservative thinking. It does, however, inhibit the raising of the shoulder and the stiffening of the muscles of the shoulder girdle.

The positioning of the arm which holds the weapon should be done by lowering it from a loosely bent high position rather than by lifting it from a low position as suggested by the traditional method. This is done in the interest of maintaining a relaxed arm position which in turn keeps the shoulder from tensing.

In teaching the lunge the coach should begin with the final position of the action. From a straddle position with the feet parallel and over three foot lengths apart, and with the trunk held erect, the leading leg should be bent and the leading foot rotated 90°, turning on the heel with the toes raised. Proceeding in this manner ensures the placement of the rear foot firmly on the floor. The student also senses the flexing of the ankle and the straightening and positioning of the rear knee in the appropriate manner.

The return to guard should be taught first from the final position of the lunge, in which the feet are widely separated. In the return movement, the pulling action of the rear knee must be particularly emphasized. Once the student has acquired the above movement, he can be taught to execute the lunge from the on-guard position. At first, the action should resemble a long step forward rather than a proper lunge. This not only facilitates learning and gradual progress, but also prevents the usual faults from occurring. The lunge should be likened to a forward step in which only the leading foot advances, while the rear foot remains stationary as the rear knee extends to allow the leading foot to move forward.

The coach can make his job easier if the methods he uses allow the student to experience some success in their initial attempts. The above methods not only demonstrate correct form but also instil the necessary internal sensing of the various components of the movement.

When teaching particularly complex movements, the coach should refer in his introduction to the rhythm pattern. This can be taught beforehand even if it is done at some expense to form.

Rhythm is the corner-stone in both the teaching and the learning of movements. It is often more significant than form. Correct rhythm in the execution of an action is the key to rapid learning. It helps to avoid excessive intensity, the development of harmful ancillary movements, overly large movements, the signalling of the intention to move, and so on.

Once the student masters the characteristic rhythm of a movement, he must learn to change the rhythm. To accomplish this, the coach must on occasion break the regularity of routine execution. The student's neuromuscular system can then be developed to adjust in accordance with the situation.

A competitor able to alternate between fast and slow movements, to insert short or long pauses in his actions, to catch the opponent off guard by starting an action following an unexpected break in continuity, or to change rhythms of the components of a movement in an irregular fashion, has a great advantage over his opponents, especially those whose execution is very mechanical.

General rhythm patterns outline only the initial and basic forms of technical movements. To teach differences and variations in rhythm constitutes yet another chore for the coach. Differences in rhythm, even of the slightest magnitude, can have a decisive effect at high competitive levels. Just as they are difficult for the coach to teach, so are they equally difficult for the student to identify and learn.

Only a fencer of high technical skill and with a well-developed sense of rhythm can change his rhythm patterns during the course of a bout.

Care and patience are required in the teaching of technique. Increasing the student's repertory of actions at a forced pace can never bear good fruit. The fencer does not have time to develop the muscles needed nor to establish the subtle co-ordination and refined sensory differentiation required, thus, the movement cannot properly mature.

The coach must never sacrifice technical development for early results of dubious value. Much patience is demanded in waiting for the student's technique to mature to the point where he is ready for bout fencing in the competitive sense.

The coach must never waver in his insistence that the student acquire the fundamentals. No exceptions can be made in respect to these essential requirements. Without confining the student to the pillory of classic technique, the coach must lead him ever closer to universal technical norms.

It is natural, however, that technique grows into style with the passage of time. To eliminate the individual characteristics of style will most certainly kill the fencer's personality.

To have any success, the coach must formulate the logical sequence in which to transmit technical material. This sequence also has to correspond to the nature of fencing, general pedagogical principles, tactical concepts and the fencer's particularly unique qualities.

Relaxed, fluid movement has an extremely important role to play in fencing. The more complex and faster the movement, the more compact the execution must be and, therefore, the more difficult and more important the need for relaxed muscles becomes.

The quality of a movement determines not only its character but also to a large extent its effectiveness. If a movement is too rigid or inflexible, its path is extended and speed acquired through technique lost. Any unnecessary tightening of the muscles prior to execution results in slower physical speed. Movements which are too bound up or mechanical also constitute an obstacle to accurate execution. They inhibit the fencer's ability to sense the subtle differences and changes in rhythm, and to take advantage of the tempo. They also lead to premature fatigue.

Muscle spasm not only paralyses the fencer physically but also emotionally.

All this can be avoided if the coach teaches the student how to attain and maintain optimal muscle condition before and during a bout. A readiness to act quickly and stability can coexist only when the fencer's muscles execute movements in a relaxed and harmonious manner.

Learning the proper muscle control is one of the most difficult and intricate tasks facing the fencer. Maintaining the muscles in a ready state must become virtually instinctive. Competitors who become accustomed to keeping their muscles constantly relaxed are rarely subject to tension developing, even at critical moments in the heat of the action.

Good technique, correct execution of fencing movements and the co-ordination of hand and feet result in the most economical expense of energy.

To help the student learn how to execute actions with relaxed muscles, the coach can try using several teaching techniques, including the use of distraction, the breakdown of movements into components or, oppositely, the insistence on a continuous and evenly paced execution. If these fail to achieve the desired effect, the coach should have the student imitate the action in a way which focuses attention on the correct sensing of speed and rhythm. He can also give the student more time for warming up, for settling his attention, for preliminary and preparatory movements, and for actual execution of actions; in other words, he changes the speed of the work, the load and intensity of training, the length of pauses, and so on.

It is a good idea for the coach to work separately with those students who have the stiffest muscles. He should devise for them specific objectives to be reached and appropriate task-oriented or inductive exercises which they can perform on their own, even at home.

Once the student finally senses the feel accompanying relaxed muscle states, increased speed of actions becomes possible. By isolating the antagonistic muscle groups or reducing their involvement the student can transmit strength in the sequence and proportions necessary to facilitate speed.

Only gradually should the coach embark on a process to increase speed, change speed and rhythm, and vary strength of execution.

To promote speed, the coach should polish technical execution to perfection. This contributes to reducing the time of execution by co-ordinating hand and foot movements and eliminating advance indications of any impending movement. Since movements are based on the principle of finding the shortest distance between two points, the fencer should not betray his intent by superfluous pre-parations. Lateral deviations kept to a minimum, and properly co-ordinated hand and feet, result in extra speed. Anyone can acquire these by drilling the initiation and execution of actions in a varied manner.

The genetically determined speed of execution of the nervous system cannot be altered. Speed as one of the elements of fencing, however, can be developed in both fast and slow-moving fencers.

Initially, the student learns to start an action from a stationary position. Train-ing him to start an action in tempo on a given cue should be introduced as a second step.

Tempo can result from both physical and psychological factors. Physical tempo is predicated on movement. Movement is not, however, a criterion of psychological tempo. Even a fencer who stands motionless can be caught and hit in a psycho-logical tempo. Rarely are tempos purely physical or psychological in nature.

Psychological tempo requires much understanding, anticipation, foresight and intuition. Physical tempo taken from the hand or foot can be taught; psycho-logical tempo cannot. It can only be trained under the actual conditions of bout fencing.

In order to teach tempo, several fundamental conditions must exist. These include properly directed attention, technical maturity and the necessary speed of execution. A student whose attention wanders, whose movements are large and sweeping and who operates at a slow speed cannot possibly take advantage of the fleeting occurrences for tempo actions.

The coach teaches tempo by inducing the student's movements through visual and tactical stimuli. In the early stages of training, highly visible and exaggerated cues are used by the coach to induce tempo actions. Gradually, the time given for the execution of an action should be reduced. At advanced stages, even a mo-mentary signal should not be given so as to approach actual bout conditions and thus teach the student to sense and take action in tempo under realistic competitive circumstances.

It is not enough for the fencer to start an action in tempo; he must finish it in tempo as well. The hit has to arrive before the opponent regains his ability to act. Thus, a close relationship must exist between tempo, speed and technique.

Situations in fencing, in terms of both space and time, are brief in duration and constantly changing in a way unlike many other sports. Under these condi-tions, success is only possible through subtle technique. Less polished, sweeping movements do not comply with these restraints of space and time.

Taking actual conditions into consideration, the coach should tolerate only necessary technical deviations since movements done in too broad a fashion result not only in the revelation of the fencer's intent but also in the reduction of speed. The principle of finding the shortest distance between two points must guide all efforts because only an action executed within effective spatial limits can take advantage of the split-second timing involved in tempo.

The development of skill and the training of fast, economical movements including compound movements and their variations, as well as the taking of action in tempo, should be a recurring theme in the fencer's practice sessions for years.

Technical development should be combined as early as possible with the development of abilities. Keeping distance, changing the distance undetected by the opponent and developing the total range of analytic actions are elements which should be introduced in training as soon as possible.

For advanced fencers development of abilities must complement technical practice. A comprehensive lesson requires maximum attention, intense concentration and great effort from both coach and student. The biggest advantage in a lesson, however, is that it simultaneously involves both physical and intellectual abilities. It combines and associates the most important of them to enhance their effects or to minimize their deficiencies, and teaches technique and tactics.

The training of beginners initially is done in groups. Paired practice, which is more representative of fencing, must be introduced as soon as possible. Today, paired practice plays a more important role from the very outset than it did before. Several elements should be taught earlier than is traditionally the case. These include keeping distance, breaking distance without detection, taking the tempo from the opponent's hand or feet and preparing actions to fill time or distract the opponent. The fact that a fencer learns certain things early has a decisive influence on his competitive career.

Group training only provides the outlines for technique. It is the individual lesson which strengthens technical execution and tailors it to the particular student. To this end, the lesson has to incorporate actual fencing actions and movements in combination with the spatial and temporal elements found in fencing.

II.13. The basis of fencing strategy

It is beyond doubt that technique and tactics are intertwined and influence each other in any combat sport, fencing included.

A wide technical repertory can lead to extremely rich and varied tactics which are difficult for the opponent to unmask. Poor and superficial technique produces primitive ideas and solutions.

It is obvious that only tactical ideas supported by repeated technical drilling can be translated into practical realities. The more developed the technique at the fencer's disposal, the less likely his tactics are to break down.

Only a fencer who is more than familiar with all possible offensive and defensive actions can develop real tactical ideas. It is of no avail if the fencer has good ideas but cannot put them into practice.

Most coaches focus on technique, partly due to the fact that fencing is not worth doing and has little chance of success with only a limited technical repertory. On the other hand, it is more difficult to teach technique in fencing than it is in some other sports, such as basketball or other team sports.

Since most coaches do not believe that tactics can be taught, only a few include tactical training in their lessons. There are even fewer who incorporate tactics within the framework of group training.

Previously technique and tactics were acquired separately. The student learned technique from the coach and then picked up tactical skills on his own through bout fencing, self-education and experience. This sequence was virtually dictated by the quest for absolute technical perfection. It was possible only through the infinite patience of the student. It was not unknown for beginners to be trained only in footwork for up to two years.

Today a different philosophy prevails. People are less patient. They want results as quickly as possible. This trait and the relationship between tactics and technique must be considered when amalgamating tactical and technical training, which is now the prevailing approach. No longer can the fencer rely solely on the conclusions he may draw from personal experiences of success and failure; he needs to be trained in tactics.

The coach's principal task is to bring the student up to competitive standards both in terms of mechanics and strategy at the same time without technical flaws or loss of time. Before, much time was lost through idling in training.

To achieve the above objective, an intense synthesis of technique and tactics is required. Because technical training invariably precedes tactical instruction, the two principal components of fencing cannot be taught totally in parallel. The possibilities in comprehensive instruction, however, should not be abandoned.

It is possible to train a fencer in tactics even if he lacks a concrete technical foundation. The teaching of tactical ways of thinking, therefore, can start prior to actual fencing training.

Schoolyard games adapted to fencing are useful in giving students a taste for tactics. Depending on the coach's objectives, such games can be modified and made simpler or more complicated. The advantage of these games is that they are familiar to the students and thus save time because the necessary techniques are already known. Despite the limited means at their disposal, the students not only think but also act tactically. The experience gained assists them later in their fencing to find solutions to typical fencing problems by drawing conclusions in a similar manner as done in the games and transferring learned ideas to actual fencing.

By nature, fencing is an incredibly complex and physically demanding sport. It becomes even more so if the coach's workload is increased with the addition of tactical training. Some coaches are prevented in practical terms from including this training because of the many students of which they have charge. A coach with 15 to 20 students cannot include tactics to the necessary degree, however much he might wish to, because of time constraints. If the coach has little time between lessons to relax and gather strength, because the teaching of tactics requires mental alertness, the best he can do is offer the student general advice on tactics. Only the coach with an optimal number of students can create tactical situations and provide concrete assistance on a regular basis.

It is only natural that a coach with a large number of students in his charge is concerned mainly with the teaching of technique. This tendency is magnified by the fact that the fencer can pick up tactics during individual practice such as conventional and methodical loose play while technique can only be learned with the help of the coach.

Other players act as partners in the practising of different variations in team sport. The coach need not join in the activity for even a moment. The case in fencing is different. The coach must be directly involved during the practice of skill or movement drills and thus bears almost as great a physical and psychological load as the student. The individual nature of fencing requires that the coach be personally involved in establishing the fundamentals of tactics.

The level of the coach's participation depends on his age, health and disposable energies. It is also influenced by his views on the teachability and teaching of tactics.

Younger coaches can take a more active role in a physical sense. An older one's physical participation naturally decreases proportionately with age, but this loss is made up in emotional support, direction in actions and sound advice.

Even an accurate reproduction or facsimile of tactics learned in training is insufficient in the actual practice of combat sports such as fencing. The mechanical aspects serve only as the basis. Competition and the art of fencing begin beyond that point. The extent to which a fencer may profit from all the possible variations he has acquired depends on his intellect, practical intelligence and tactical sense.

Tactical sense can be categorized as an ability. It is an integral component of the fencer's talent, a measure of his suitability to the sport and key to success. A good fencer can translate a set of the coach's instructions into several "languages", meaning that he can apply the numerous options learned in practice to many different situations. One fencer is considered more talented than another because of the difference in their tactical sense. Skill which is discovered and becomes evident in the learning of technique is but a fragment of the fencer's talent. It is much more important that he possess a sense of combat and of tactics.

At the time a fencer begins training, it is impossible to tell whether or not he is suited to the sport. In the initial stage he might show some signs of his finesse, cunning, ability to draw conclusions, quick judgement and reaction, and other qualities which relate to the special abilities of fencing. Only when he reaches the stage of bout fencing and free fencing can any certain conclusions be reached as to his real tactical talent. The existence or non-existence of tactical sense remains an enticing question mark for some time and, to a degree, something like a lottery.

The particular character of fencing dictates that prolonged technical work precede the blossoming of the fencer's tactical abilities. Given the appropriate material, correct methods and parallel training in technique and tactics, this period can be somewhat shortened. Having acquired an accurate command of technique and a familiarity with the different variations, the fencer can move on to working out actual tactical combinations. Underdeveloped, simplistic and one-sided technical expertise allows only the most elementary tactical possibilities, even after a prolonged period.

Combat sports such as fencing are somewhat like Janus, the two-headed deity in Roman mythology, because in them it is impossible to separate technique from tactics. Even the simplest actions are imbued with tactics. The question of which action is best suited to a given situation, whether voiced or not, lies behind every technical application, no matter how lacking in tactics and preliminary consideration it may seem to be.

The same reciprocal relationship exists between tactics and technique as between any other two of the fencing abilities. One fencer with outstanding tactical knowledge can compensate for technical shortcomings while another, having a sweeping technical superiority, can often bring the best tactician to his knees.

Tactics synthesize by nature. They rise above rigid theory and bring diametrically opposed schools of thought together under a common denominator. They establish a connection, build a bridge and eliminate the boundaries between individual technical interpretations.

Some coaches are biased towards technique. Their reasons are as follows:

(a) Technique plays an important, though not exclusive, role in the arsenal of fencing. It serves as the basis of knowledge in fencing, a constant factor in the fencer's form and the guarantee of well-balanced, lasting work and consistent results. It is almost the only means of hope for the fencer of moderate competitive ability, a safe harbour for the fencer having an off day, and often the last refuge for a fencer who is indisposed or suffering some temporary crisis. Superficial, shaky or poor technique can negate even the best possible physical abilities.

(b) It is easier to teach and demonstrate technique than tactics. Instruction in tactics is more tiring than instruction in technique and can be taught only in proportion to the coach's own tactical sense. This sense determines the coach's ability to identify with and create in realistic terms the character of a fencing situation.

(c) In terms of mechanics, the coach can do much more for the student's technical development than his tactical training because the great majority of fencers can be taught technique but not tactics. Indeed, technique can be taught successfully to anyone. It is possible to study tactics, but the degree to which they are acquired depends on the fencer's native tactical sense.

A person can only go as far as he thinks possible and wise in relation to tactics. For this reason, a person lacking an inborn tactical sense cannot be taught tactics with much success.

(d) No matter how realistic a fencing lesson tries to be, it can only imitate the actual competitive situation. It must be stressed that it is only similar because the feelings evoked by real combat are missing in the lesson. Only the major elements of combat can be presented to the student in practice situations; all the details and nuances cannot be included. Even situations which seem to be perfectly representative are, in fact, pre-arranged to imitate typical bout circumstances and therefore lacking the natural order of actual competition. This explains why ready-made technical recipes and schemes often fail to work out. Actual bout conditions are generally more diverse, complex, intricate and characteristically unique than those created in a lesson. This makes them extremely difficult to reproduce or repeat and almost impossible to think up in advance. Only assumptions can be made as to what situations might arise, but the actual situations are always more incalculable, unexpected, shocking and extreme than the most realistic conditions ever visualized in a lesson. The level of nervous tension aroused in the competitive atmosphere is one which cannot be recreated even by the most suggestive coach in a bout-like lesson requiring the most intense concentration.

(e) A lesson on tactics produces something like greenhouse flowers; the pure technical elements are difficult to translate into competitive situations as those flowers are to transplant in an outdoor environment. Their viability is suspect because the coach tends to give way to the student in his efforts to teach the fencer, while an opponent would resist and try to counter the fencer's intentions.

(f) The tactics taught are very often variations which can readily be anticipated by the opponent and the necessary counteractions easily planned and built as a result.

(g) The logic of the coach determines the tactical lines to be developed and learned by the student. An opponent, however, does not choose the most logical or most obvious action in many instances.

(h) Risk is a major tactical element in fencing, but it is virtually impossible to teach risk-taking and the sense of risk.

(i) Only concrete elements of tactics can be taught. The instinctive tactical solutions developed in the fencer's mind as a result of a totally realistic situation are basically impossible to teach. It is the student who invariably must breathe life into the movements, thus adding his own inspiration and spirit.

(j) Even the fencer who has learned tactical elements must pay a price. Without independent experience and application, true tactics can never develop.

(k) No matter how much or how intensely a fencer concerns himself with tactics in lessons, his real tactical education can only be completed in bout fencing, an encounter or competitive situation in which more or less is at stake. Even if tactical practice is adjusted carefully to include the most varied conditions, something always remains to be said. The bout proper can assume innumerable forms, and changes can occur in the midst of a movement that originally seemed possible to execute. The most clever and impressive tactical solutions are usually the product of spontaneous recognition.

The native tactical sense of the fencer can be considerably enhanced by the coach's relating of information referring to tactics and by the practice of material of a tactical nature. Only the fencer able to elaborate the knowledge conveyed by the coach and to adjust it to his personality, however, can become a good tactician; that is, a person who can think and act independently in a tactical way, combining what he has learned with his own tactical gifts.

The most important objective, therefore, is to teach the student to be independent. The fencer given a complete tactical cookbook is unlikely to make the tactical efforts of one who is given less tactical education. He does not learn to identify and draw conclusions from situations, processes which are necessary to fencing. The competitor who is not independent enough tends to rely too heavily on his coach and, when competing, has to be told step by step and bout by bout what to do.

The nature of tactics is individually based and so deeply rooted that it is practically impossible to direct a bout from the sidelines. Few coaches can identify themselves so completely with the fencer on the piste that they can virtually score a hit. This does not minimize, however, the importance of competitive tactical advice from the coach which can substantially aid a helpless competitor.

The tactical training of fencers must exist from the outset. Beginners must be immersed in fencing as though it were an intellectual game. As the coach transmits his ideas and programs technical elements, he also sets in motion the student's imagination. A restricted or stifled intellect can never develop fully and, like a caged bird, loses its natural character.

In illustrating the sense and objectives of different actions, and in discussing the methods and conditions of their application, the coach guides his students towards a certain kind of logical action. In teaching technical execution, he gives them the key to using technical details to the utmost advantage. Although unaware of it, the beginner makes his earliest tactical efforts when he faces the master's blade which creates the conditions and background required for these efforts.

The experienced fencer has to practise the same action or movement in different settings. Preparatory movements must change and the action must be executed from various starting positions. The fencing phrase must be built upon reactions which follow in a logical manner, the number of elements being variable and the introductory, middle and closing actions being subject to change. The particular tactical actions can be executed either according to the fencer's own interpretation or as specified by the coach in advance.

Real tactical training in a lesson is based on the coach's ability to see actions in relation to each other, and to transmit that impression to the student, allowing him to combine fencing actions in space within the required plane and to alternate and freely select solutions to a given problem.

Elements necessarily omitted from tactical training or impossible to include in the programme of activities must be passed on orally by the coach to the students.

The coach's statements about tactics and his generalizations concerning the creative management of situations are the student's points of departure. These can be adopted and adapted by the student in keeping with his own practical experience and thought processes. In this way, the fencer is trained not only in the general but also in the extreme, exceptional and uniquely individual movements.

In contrast to the lesson, the actual bout requires that the competitor create and counter-create tactical situations which are adjusted to the particular opponent; he does not apply a general tactical model while fencing a bout. The wide range of technical possibilities and the sudden and unexpected change in circumstances which can arise require that the competitor have in reserve certain particular actions which come into play through the instinctive reactions and quick adjustments of the fencer.

In addition to, or more precisely, through what he has learned tactically, the fencer expresses his true personality. The individual methods and elements arising from that personality coupled with experience always play a role in the effectiveness of the tactics chosen, their texture and variety, and the way in which they are tailored to the opponent.

In giving tactical instruction, the coach takes on the role of a generalized stereotype opponent who uses typical, regular movements to carry out an action. The student stores up these general tactical solutions and then, in actual competition, translates them into practice in accordance with the extent to which they have been drilled.

To achieve maximum tactical effect, the variations of the individual technical elements which occur most often in competitive fencing must be schooled intensively initially, the coach must be a fairly passive opponent, later he must become increasingly active and versatile in his actions. He must, therefore, be more than familiar with all the possible combinations of individual actions and their typical formulations.

At first, exercises are of a technical nature. Gradually practice moves in the direction of tactics, but without compromising the importance of technique, by changing conditions in the exercises. The conditions may be varied through changes in starting positions, options in solving problems, selection of different target areas and alternatives in execution. At the intermediate level of fencing the synthesis of technique and tactics is balanced. With top-class fencers, tactics dominate and account for the most vital part of training.

The first lessons with a tactical character are designed to awaken the student's imagination. Initially only the simplest tactical tricks should be discussed; but, as the different actions are repeatedly practised, new tactical ideas should be included to create a progressively spiralling level of knowledge. At the outset, the coach takes the initiative in actions but eventually allows the student to take over this role.

The different tactical variations must be practised over long periods after they have been introduced and explained to the student. This helps not only in the learning and formal execution of the actions but also in the tactical implications and implementation.

In training his students the coach must be able to take on the characteristics of every possible opponent. At early stages, he should represent an average fencer and recreate situations which are common in fencing. For top competitors, however, he must personify on occasion certain actual opponents. He has to imitate their actions in form and dynamics and their rhythm patterns and speed if he wishes to create the most realistic situations possible. At the start, the coach can give verbal instructions; later he should include the best possible reproduction of the opponent's typical and preferred actions of which he is capable.

Tactical training can be accomplished indirectly, verbally and directly. Situational analysis, the listing of various solutions to a problem, discussion and explanation, and advice—all these take a verbal form. Practical examples, alternative solutions, methods tailored to a particular opponent and his style, and examples of extreme or unusual cases or types, can be brought to life and adapted to practice only through the coach's direct assistance and action.

In fencing any fencer can beat or be beaten by any other. The outcome of any particular bout is never absolutely certain; thus, no fencer should ever feel that comfortable. Even the most familiar of opponents may come up with something new or special in the tactical department. For this reason the fencer is advised to be careful at all times. Every opponent, even one who has been defeated previously, must be taken seriously. No one can run the risk of making a half-hearted effort. A bout taken too lightly and tactics adopted without proper consideration very often fail to pay off.

Tactics are chosen because of several factors, including the opponent's abilities and their relative strengths, his technical standards and physical condition. Only a competitor fully aware of his own abilities and knowing those of his opponent can create and employ efficient tactics.

Sometimes, because the fencer's individual qualities are so well-developed, a new tactical approach can be employed against each opponent and occasionally a number of strategies may be used against one opponent. In his first bout experiences the beginner usually can produce no more than a few conventional tactical solutions. This is due to his natural pre-occupation with the technical needs of the bout. In order to reach his maximum potential in tactical terms, the student must mature, settling in and acquiring the necessary experience. In fencing this takes quite a long time.

i. The concept, essence and theory of tactics

Tactics can be defined as the logical use in combat of movement elements and actions learned in lessons. It is comprised of assessment, decision and execution.

While fencing, the competitor considers, calculates, compares and co-ordinates many things. He dictates movements and adjusts and creates the opportunities for his actions, motivates himself and tries to view all that is happening clearly before taking a decision and acting.

Tactical sense is the ability to evaluate situations realistically, to assess relative strengths, to know his own abilities and intentions, and to discover those of his opponent. He then compares the above factors and any others which might have an influence on the bout, and selects and applies the actions which offer the best chances of success under the given conditions. In short, tactical sense is the ability to synthesize, analyse and draw conclusions from a great number of combat-related factors.

Tactical sense is a complex combination of elements, without which no fencer can become a truly great competitor. These elements include analytic ability, quick recognition of and adjustment to situations, technical expertise, objective judgement, decision-making ability, anticipation and foresight, and the ability to hide or disguise intentions, thoughts and actions.

The theory of tactics is founded upon general laws based on conclusions drawn from practice and universal experiences, and on typical patterns of action. Similar cases are grouped together regardless of the manner of execution and thus bring various formal solutions and methods under a common denominator.

The specific solutions and methods possible in a given situation or a likely situation predicted on the basis of past experience, and the approaches or behaviour constructed from them, constitute the elements of tactical thinking and execution.

The theory of tactics trains the fencer in the natural logic of combat. It facilitates the fencer's finding his own way because essential knowledge is condensed in the theoretical conclusions. It also assists in understanding the opponent, in arranging and elaborating on experiences gained in combat, in properly ordering the individual actions and thus in forming a fencer's personal tactics.

Since no offensive or defensive action can be guaranteed success, risk-taking becomes a greater or lesser component of every tactical plan and execution. How likely an action is to succeed does not overly influence, worry or inhibit the courageous tactician who has calm, controlled nerves. A less bold or more nervous fencer is often prevented by his personality from running any risks.

A natural, comparatively modest degree of risk-taking is necessary in any combat sport. Unjustified and ill-considered risk-taking is nothing but rash behaviour.

III. TASK-ORIENTED AND INDUCTIVE EXERCISES

Task-oriented and inductive exercises are designed to develop the actual abilities and concrete properties necessary to fencing.

These exercises can be varied and expanded proportionately to the coach's imagination and his ability to have the students carry them out. The size of movement, the speed and rhythm of execution and the pauses between individual components of the movement are all elements which can be varied. Symmetrical exercises become asymmetrical through a shift in the rhythm. Those performed with even cadence turn into ones of odd cadence and vice versa.

The combination of several simple exercises creates a compound exercise. They should be designed in a way that directs attention simultaneously to diverse factors as they physically occupy the body.

With certain modifications, adjustments and supplemental elements some task-oriented and inductive exercises can be tailored to illustrate the special needs of fencing, clarify the concept and essence of specific abilities, make them easy to understand, assess those abilities and clearly show how those abilities relate to, are associated with, supplement and substitute for each other in the practice of fencing.

Those exercises which are suited to making the students practise certain movement details under simpler conditions and in simplified form can take the form of inductive exercises.

Different objectives can be met by performing the same exercise under different conditions.

In most cases it is vitally important to perform the exercises exactly as designed. The desired objective can only be achieved by so doing and the students's attention must, therefore, be drawn emphatically to this point. The value of exact technical execution, however, may have less significance in cases where content objectives, such as the practice of cadence and rhythm changes, are the most important considerations.

Task-oriented and inductive exercises can be classified on the basis of very different viewpoints. The simplest and most obvious which categorizes the exercises according to the starting position of the fencer is used in classifying the exercises which follow.

III.1. General gymnastic exercises adapted to fencing

(1) Stride jumps, with no arm movement.
(2) Stride jumps with arm movement.
   The arms are raised laterally to shoulder height each time the feet move to

straddle position. Pace, height and distance between the feet should vary along with the pauses interspersed in the exercise.

(3) Stride jumps with arm movement.

Begun as in (2), on individual choice or at a signal from the coach, the movement is altered at irregular intervals so that the arms are raised when the feet come together. At first the pace is regular but later can vary according to personal taste.

(4) Stride jumps with arm movement.

Begun as in (2), the movement on occasion is executed in three stages, with the arms being raised between two consecutive movements into straddle position. This is done first at a regular then irregular rhythm.

(5) Stride jumps with alternating arm movement.

One arm is raised as the feet return with the other being raised on the next return. Both arms are lowered on the third return.

(6) Stride jumps with alternating arm movement.

One arm is raised to shoulder height as the feet move into a straddle, with the other being raised as the feet return. On the next straddle, the leading arm is raised overhead, with the other arm following on the return. Both arms are lowered to shoulder height on the next straddle and then to starting position on the feet returning.

(7) Stride jumps with alternating arm movement.

Begun as in (6), but the arms return one after the other in conjunction with the feet straddling and coming together until both arms are back to their starting position.

(8) Stride jumps with alternating arm movement.

The dominant arm is raised to shoulder height on the initial straddle. The other arm is raised first to shoulder height and then overhead on the next straddle and return. Both arms then return to the starting position.

(9) Stride jumps with alternating arm movement.

The dominant arm is raised to shoulder height and the other arm overhead on the initial straddle. Both arms return with the return of the feet to starting position. The dominant arm is raised overhead and the other arm to shoulder height on the next straddle. Both arms return with the feet to starting position.

The above exercise should be performed several times at both regular and varied cadences.

(10) Hopping on both feet.

While in the air, the hands clap in front of the body twice, three times, four times in succession.

(11) Hopping on both feet.

While in the air, the hands clap alternately in front of and behind the body twice, three times, four times in succession. Occasionally, while clapping, the ankles tap together or the feet cross.

(12) Hopping with the feet apart.

Land alternately on one foot then the other, bending the knee on landing to take up a semi-lunge position.

(13) Hop on both feet and simultaneously twist the trunk at the hips.

(14) Hopping on the non-dominant foot.

Pull the other knee up in front of the corresponding shoulder and then, turned outwards, pull the knee up beside the body.

(15) Hopping on the non-dominant foot.

The other foot is placed on the knee of the supporting leg and the trunk twists at the hips while hopping.

(16) Hopping on the non-dominant foot.

Circle the other leg forward and backward while in the air.

(17) Hopping on both feet.

At irregular intervals, jump and, while in the air, change the position of the legs three or four times.

(18) Standing on the non-dominant foot.

Lift and move the other foot forward. Jump and, while in the air, tap the ankles together. Land on the non-dominant foot. See Fig. 1.

FIG. 1

(19) Jumping.

Take off on one foot and land on the other. While in the air, cross the feet two or three times in succession. See Fig. 2.

FIG. 2

(20) Hopping on the non-dominant foot.

The free leg is crossed behind the supporting leg and, on occassion, the supporting leg jumps over the free leg either forward or backward.

(21) Holding the dominant foot with the opposite hand, jump forward and backward over the held leg. See Fig. 3.

FIG. 3

(22) Standing on the dominant foot.
The free leg is swung forward and backward with the foot alternately pointed up or down.

(23) Standing on the dominant foot.
The free leg is swung sideways with the foot alternately pointed up or down.

(24) Walk on the heels, toes and outer edges of the feet.

(25) With foot apart, stand on tiptoes and circle at the ankles clockwise and counterclockwise.

(26) With feet together or apart, slowly raise the heels to stand on tiptoes and then lower the heels to the floor and raise the toes.

(27) With feet close together or standing in a slight lunge, raise the heel of one foot and the toes of the other. Alternate at varying speed, first slowly then quickly.

(28) With feet close together or slightly apart, stand on the heels and bend from the hips to touch the toes with the fingers several times. See Fig. 4.

FIG. 4

(29) With feet close together, raise the toes to stand on the heels. Turn the feet outward and return. Resume starting position. See Fig. 5.

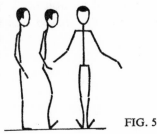

FIG. 5

57

(30) With feet close together, raise the toes and lower them quickly two or three times in succession.

(31) Stand with the toes pointing inwards. Move to one side by pivoting on the heel of one foot and the toes of the other. Alternate heel and toes to move along in one direction. Move in a similar fashion in the other direction. Vary the speed and change directions either on a signal by the coach or at the individual's choice.

(32) Seated on a bench or chair with feet parallel, raise the toes and tap the floor rapidly with both feet, first together and then alternately. Accelerate and slow down the pace on occasion.

(33) Seated on a bench or chair with the legs raised to a horizontal position, rotate the feet at the ankles clockwise and counterclockwise. Alternately point the feet up and down.

(34) Seated on a bench or chair with legs apart and arms raised to shoulder height, raise the legs to a horizontal position and clap the feet together rapidly.

(35) Seated on the floor with legs apart, the sole of one foot is placed on the inside of the opposite thigh. Bend forward several times with the foot on the floor alternately pointed up and down. See Fig. 6.

FIG. 6

(36) Seated on the floor with legs straight and toes pointed up, bend forward several times. While bending, push one foot down so that the outer edge touches the floor. Repeat with the other foot. See Fig. 7.

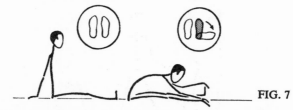
FIG. 7

(37) Seated on the floor with legs bent and the soles touching the floor, push both knees down with the hands.

(38) Kneeling with legs apart and the inside of both ankles touching the floor, sit down and lie back between the splayed legs. See Fig. 8.

FIG. 8

(39) With legs apart and arms extended at shoulder height and palms down, lie supine on the floor. Raise the back off the floor with the ankles making contact with the floor and the toes pointing sideways. See Fig. 9.

FIG. 9

(40) With legs apart and hands under the shoulders, lie on the stomach. Lift the body with a push-up and press the heels to the floor. Vary the pace from slow to fast.

(41) Standing with feet close together, lower to a squat position with arms raised to shoulder height and the heels remaining on the floor. Resume starting position.

(42) With arms extended forward at shoulder height, lift the dominant leg and extend it. Lower to a squat position with the heel of the supporting foot remaining in contact with the floor. Resume starting position. See Fig. 10.

FIG. 10

(43) With arms extended forward at shoulder height, from a squat position stand up on tiptoes. Return to starting position. Alternate between fast and slow executions.

(44) In squat position with feet slightly apart and arms extended at shoulder height, alternately stand on tiptoes and heels. See Fig. 11.

FIG. 11

(45) In squat position, push the knees outward to stand on the outside of the feet. Return and repeat several times. See Fig. 12.

(46) In squat position with hands on knees and elbows pointed outward, bend at the hips and half-stretch the legs with an energetic pushing apart of the knees to put the weight on the outside of the feet.

FIG. 12

(47) In squat position, bend at the hips and half-stretch the legs first with heels and soles remaining on the floor, then hopping at the spot and finally hopping forward.

(48) From a standing position, take a backward step with one foot to take up an attacking position. Bend at the hips and half-stretch legs with the soles and heels remaining on the floor.

(49) With legs wide apart and feet parallel, bend on knee to transfer the body weight to that leg. Stretch the bent leg to transfer the body weight to the other leg. Keep the trunk erect throughout. Repeat several times in both directions. See Fig. 13.

FIG. 13

(50) In squat position with hands supporting, stretch one leg back. Press the heel down by extending and bending the forward leg several times. Change leg positions and repeat.

(51) Leaning against a wall with arms outstretched and one foot ahead of the other, bend and extend the forward leg to press the sole of the rear foot to the floor several times. Change leg positions and repeat. See Fig. 14.

FIG. 14

(52) Rotate the hands at the wrists clockwise and counterclockwise.

(53) With hands held in front of the chest, arms bent and fingertips touching, press the hands together with some resistance from the fingers. Release with a springy motion.

(54) With hands held in front of the chest, arms bent, palms together and fingers

60

pointed forward, rotate the arms inward and then back several times. See Fig. 15.

(55) With hands clasped in front of the chest, arms bent and palms inward, rotate and stretch the arms forward at shoulder height so the palms face out. Return to starting position.

(56) With hands clasped in front of the body, arms lowered, rotate the palms to point out and lift the arms overhead. Return to starting position. See Fig. 16.

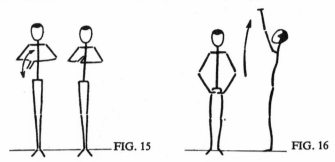

FIG. 15   FIG. 16

(57) With hands clasped overhead and arms extended, pull the arms backward several times.

(58) With hands clasped overhead, arms extended and palms down, rotate the palms up by bending and stretching the arms at the elbows. Repeat several times. See Fig. 17.

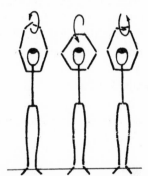

FIG. 17

(59) With feet apart, arms stretched back and palms facing back, swing both arms forward to finish with arms at shoulder height and bent so the palms face up. Return to starting position. See Fig. 18.

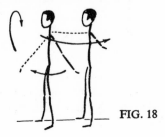

FIG. 18

(60) With feet apart, swing the arms forward and backward. Rotate the swinging arms with the body bent slightly forward.

(61) With feet apart and arms extended in front of the body at shoulder height, drop each arm alternately. As they drop, rotate them rapidly and return them to starting position.

(62) With feet apart, arms extended sideways at shoulder height and palms facing up, bend the elbows and lower the forearms so the elbows are one hand's width from the hips and the forearms are horizontal. Extend elbows to resume starting position. See Fig. 19.

FIG. 19

(63) With feet apart and arms held loosely bent overhead, swing the arms out and down to a lowered position. Return to starting position.

(64) With feet apart, the dominant arm is held one hand's width from the hip with forearm horizontal and palm facing up. The other arm is held out at shoulder height and bent so the forearm is vertical. Stretch the dominant arm to raise it to shoulder height and swing the other arm down to extend obliquely from the shoulder. Bend the dominant arm and swing the other arm up to return them to starting position.

(65) With feet apart, arms extended forward at shoulder height, palms facing up and the outsides of the hands touching, bend both arms at the elbows to lower forearms so that the elbows come into contact. Stretch arms to return to starting position. See Fig. 20.

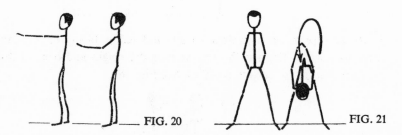

FIG. 20   FIG. 21

(66) With feet apart and hands clasped behind the body, bend at the hips and swing the arms back at the same time. Repeat several times. See Fig. 21.

(67) With feet apart, bend at the hips and touch the outside of the ankles alternately with opposite hand several times.

(68) In a lunge position with dominant arm held in front of the body, bent at the elbow and palm facing down, balance a tennis ball on the back of the hand. Pull the hand away and catch the ball.

(69) As in (68), but slapping the forward thigh or the other hand once or twice before catching the ball.

(70) In a lunge stance with knees slightly bent, slap the forward thigh once or twice before catching the ball as in (68). See Fig. 22.

FIG. 22

(71) As in (70), but slapping the other palm once or twice, or the other palm and the forward thigh, before catching the ball.

(72) In a lunge with the dominant leg leading and knees slightly bent, bounce a tennis ball ahead of the forward foot and catch it by stepping or running forward with the rear leg crossing forward. See Fig. 23.

FIG. 23

(73) With feet apart, roll a rubber ball over the body, shoulders and legs using the fingers and wrist.

(74) In a lunge stance with two or three coins placed on the back of the dominant hand, throw them in the air and catch them one after the other.

(75) Flip a coin balanced on the edge of a table and catch it in the air.

(76) Holding a weapon at the tip with the fingers, use the fingers to crawl up the blade and hold it at the guard.

III.2. Preparatory exercises done in or from the initial position

(1) Alternately hop with the feet in the initial position and with the feet close together.

(2) Hop in the initial position on the spot, forward, backward, right and left, and doing quarter turns either right or left.

(3) Hop in the initial position on the spot. On every other hop, swing the arms overhead.

(4) Alternately hop in the initial position and the on-guard position.

(5) Alternately hop with the feet side-by-side, in the initial position and in the on-guard position. See Fig. 24.

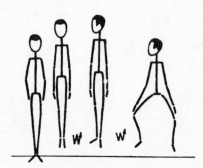

FIG. 24

(6) In the initial position with arms high overhead, jump to the on-guard position with the dominant arm swinging to shoulder height. Jump to the lunge position with the other arm swinging to shoulder height. Return with a jump to on-guard position, swinging the other arm back overhead. Jump back to initial position with the dominant arm swinging overhead. See Fig. 25.

FIG. 25

(7) Hop in the initial position and alternately swing the arms to shoulder height with palms facing up. Return to starting position.

(8) Alternately hop in the initial position and on-guard position with the arms swinging to fencing position.

(9) Hop three times in the initial position and then jump to the on-guard position with the body lowered, the arms swung to shoulder height and the palms facing up.

(10) Hop in the initial position and swing one leg or the other forward several times.

(11) Hop in the initial position and, on a signal from the coach, jump to the on-guard position.

(12) Hop three times in the initial position and jump. While in the air, either kick up the heels, cross the legs or kick the legs forward with feet wide apart. See Fig. 26.

FIG. 26

(13) Hop three times in a right-handed initial position and then jump to a left-handed initial position. Repeat in reverse. See Fig. 27.

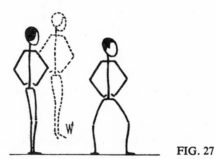

FIG. 27

(14) Jog and skip in the initial position.
(15) Swing one leg then the other forward and backward. See Fig. 28.

FIG. 28

(16) In the initial position, alternately stand on tiptoes and heels several times.
(17) In the initial position, tap the toes on the floor first at the same time and then alternately.
(18) In the initial position, stand on tiptoes and lower the body in stages by bending the knees in three actions. Resume the starting position in the same manner. See Fig. 29.

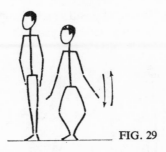

FIG. 29

(19) As in (18), lower to a squat position in stages and resume the starting position. See Fig. 30.

FIG. 30

(20) Lower and raise the body from initial to squat positions slowly and quickly at irregular intervals. Vary the depth of the squat and occasionally hold a position for several seconds.

(21) Squat from the initial position and run forward with the body turned sideways in the direction of movement. See Fig. 31.

FIG. 31

(22) From the initial position, step across the front leg with the rear leg. Bend and straighten the legs, and then step ahead with the front foot. Bend and straighten the legs. Keep the right angle formed by the feet and the knees pushed out.

(23) From the initial position, take a long step forward with the front foot while bending the rear knee. Bring up the rear leg to resume the initial position by straightening the front leg. Take a long step back with the rear leg while bending the front knee. Pull the front leg back while standing up on the rear leg to return to the original spot.

(24) From the initial position, take up the on-guard position by moving either the front leg or rear leg. Bend and straighten the knees three times and then resume the starting position. See Fig. 32.

FIG. 32

(25) Bend and straighten the legs while standing in a slightly bent initial position.

(26) From the initial position lower to a squat. Bend and partially straighten the legs.

(27) In the initial position, jump and pull both knees up. Repeat several times.

(28) In the initial position, jump as in (27) and land with bent knees or in a squat with the feet in the initial position. On occasion, finish with a fleche. See Fig. 33.

FIG. 33

(29) In the initial position, jump and kick up the heels.

(30) In the initial position, jump as in (29) and land with bent knees or in a squat. On occasion, finish with a fleche. See Fig. 34.

FIG. 34

(31) From the initial position, lower to a squat and hop on the spot, forward, backward and to right or left.

(32) Hop in a squat position with the feet in the initial position with the knees first together and then pushed apart. See Fig. 35.

(33) Hop with knees bent in the initial position or on-guard position.

(34) In the squat version of the initial position, raise and lower the heels several times. See Fig. 36.

FIG. 35   FIG. 36

(35) From the initial position, lower to a squat several times by bending and partially straightening the legs. Both soles remain firmly on the floor.

(36) From the initial position, lower to a squat by extending the forward leg. Return to the initial position.

(37) From the initial position, swing the arms to shoulder height and lower to a squat. Straighten the legs while touching the floor with the hands. Repeat several times, then resume the starting position. See Fig. 37.

(38) From the initial position, lower to a squat. Step with either foot into on-guard position. Repeat several times using both movements. See Fig. 38.

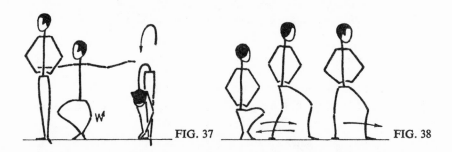

FIG. 37   FIG. 38

(39) From the initial position, lower to a squat. Lunge and resume the initia position by bringing up the rear foot. See Fig. 39.

FIG. 39

(40) From the initial position, lower to a squat. Jump with both feet to on-guard or into a lunge several times and resume the initial position. On occasion, finish with a fleche. See Fig. 40.

FIG. 40

(41) From the initial position, lower to a squat. Lunge and resume the squat by bringing up the rear foot. Repeat several times. See Fig. 41.

FIG. 41

(42) From the initial position, lower to a squat. Take up the lunge by reaching back with the rear foot. Resume the squat by pulling the front leg back. See Fig. 42.

FIG. 42

(43) From the initial position, lower to a squat. Extend the front leg. Resume the squat position and extend the rear leg. Resume the squat position.

(44) From the initial position, lower to a squat position. Extend the front leg. Jump and switch leg positions by pulling in the front leg and extending the rear leg. See Fig. 43.

FIG. 43

(45) From the initial position, lower to a squat. Extend the front leg and alternately raise the toes and heel of the rear foot. See Fig. 44.

FIG. 44

(46) From the initial position, lower to a squat. Extend the front leg and partially straighten and bend the rear knee.

(47) From the initial position, lower to a squat. Extend the front leg and press the toes of the front foot forward. Do the same with the rear leg.

(48) From the initial position, lower to a squat. Move the front leg forward and jump off the rear foot. Tap the rear foot with the heel of the front foot while in the air and land in the starting position. See Fig. 45.

FIG. 45

(49) From the initial position, lower to a squat. Jump and extend both legs while in the air. Land on the heels in the starting position. See Fig. 46.

FIG. 46

(50) From the initial position, lower to a squat position. Jump and extend and pull in both legs while in the air. Land in the initial position.

(51) From the initial position, lower to a squat. Hop and on every other hop extend the front leg to make contact on the floor with the heel of the front foot. Do the same with the rear leg.

(52) From the initial position, lower to a squat. Bend and partially straighten the legs several times. On occasion, jump and straddle the legs and land in the initial position.

(53) From the initial position, lower to a squat with knees slightly bent. Extend the front leg and transfer the body weight to the front foot when it touches

the floor by bringing up the rear leg so the rear foot is immediately behind the heel of the front foot. Advance by repeating this series several times.

(54) From the initial position, lower to a squat. Extend the front leg and transfer the body weight to the front foot to resume the starting position. Extend the rear leg and transfer the body weight to the rear foot to resume the starting position. Keep the centre of gravity low throughout the movement. See Fig. 47.

FIG. 47

(55) From the initial position, lower to a squat. Extend the front leg. Transfer the body weight by rotating the body 180° and extending the rear leg with the toes pointing up. Resume the starting position. Occasionally bend and straighten the knees once or twice following the weight transfer. See Fig. 48.

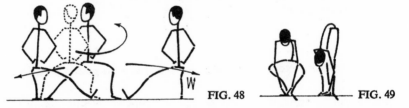

FIG. 48

FIG. 49

(56) From the initial position, lower to a squat with the hands touching the floor. Straighten the legs keeping the hands on the floor. Repeat and then resume the starting position. See Fig. 49.

(57) In the initial position, clasp the hands behind the body and bend forward several times swinging the arms away from the body.

(58) In the initial position, clasp the hands behind the body. Bend forward once in the starting position and once while stepping with the front leg into the on-guard position with the legs straight. Swing the arms away from the body both times. See Fig. 50.

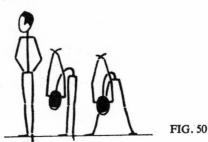

FIG. 50

(59) From a kneeling position, jump and alternately land in a right-handed and left-handed on-guard position. Immediately lower to a squat. On occasion, finish with a fleche. See Fig. 51.

FIG. 51

(60) Lying prone with the arms supporting the body, swing the body forward and backward between the arms by lifting and dropping the hips. Jump into a squat initial position and on occasion finish with a fleche after landing in the squat position. See Fig. 52.

FIG. 52

III.3. Preparatory exercises done in or from the on-guard position

(1) Run and occasionally intersperse two sidesteps in both left-handed and right-handed on-guard positions.
(2) Run and, on a signal from the coach, take three sidesteps alternately in left-handed and right-handed on-guard positions. Lower the body with each sidestep.
(3) Run forward and backward in the on-guard position using crossover steps.
(4) Hop in the on-guard position on the spot, forward and backward.
(5) Hop alternately in the on-guard position and in the lunge.
(6) Hop and occasionally jump, crossing or straddling the legs or pulling up one or both knees while in the air. See Fig. 53.

FIG. 53

(7) Hop forward in the on-guard position three times, lowering the body on each hop. Finish with a fleche after the third hop.

(8) Hop in a squat position, three times with knees together and three times with knees apart. Jump into the on-guard position after the last hop.

(9) Hop in a squat with knees together or apart. Jump into the on-guard position and then into the lunge. See Fig. 54.

FIG. 54

(10) Hop in the on-guard position. Jump with legs straddled and, on landing, finish with a fleche.

(11) Hop on the non-dominant foot. Jump into a low on-guard position and finish with a fleche. See Fig. 55.

FIG. 55

(12) In the on-guard position, alternately raise the toes of the front foot and rear foot at varying speeds and intensity.

(13) In the on-guard position, lift the front toes and rear heel alternately and then simultaneously.

(14) In the on-guard position, raise both heels to stand on tiptoes and return to starting position. Repeat several times.

(15) In the on-guard position, stand on tiptoes. Straighten and bend the legs and then resume the starting position.

(16) In the on-guard position, stand on the heels. Straighten the legs to stand on the toes and then bend the legs to lower the heels into starting position.

(17) In the on-guard position, alternately raise the heels with intensity.

(18) In the on-guard position, straighten the legs and lift the heels to stand on tiptoes. Bend the legs to lower the heels. Repeat several times.

(19) In the on-guard position, lift the toes of the front foot and return them. Swing the front leg forward with the toes pointing up and return it.

(20) In the on-guard position, shift the body weight slightly back and, with short swings of the lower leg, slap the sole of the front foot on the floor.

(21) From the on-guard position, swing the front leg forward from the knee and return it. Lunge and return to the starting position.

(22) From the on-guard position, progressively advance with a series of short swinging movements of the front lower leg into quarter, half, three-quarter and full lunge positions. See Fig. 56.

FIG. 56

(23) In the on-guard position, lift the toes of the front foot, lunge and resume the on-guard position.

(24) From the on-guard position, step with the front foot behind the rear foot and bend at the knees. Return to the starting position. Step with the rear foot in front of the forward foot and bend at the knees. Return to the starting position. On occasion, bend and straighten the legs several times while the legs are crossed. See Fig. 57.

FIG. 57

(25) From the on-guard position, place the front heel against the rear heel and return. Repeat in the reverse manner. See Fig. 58.

(26) In the on-guard position, bend and straighten the legs in different rhythms and to various depths.

FIG. 58

74

(27) In the on-guard position, bend and straighten the legs three times and then jump into the lunge.

(28) In the on-guard position, bend and straighten the legs intensively.

(29) In the on-guard position, bend low at the knees and then straighten the legs.

(30) In a squat on-guard position with heels raised, bend and partially straighten the legs repeatedly and then hop on the spot, forward, backward, to the right and to the left.

(31) As in (30), but with the heels touching the floor.

(32) In a squat on-guard position with the feet flat on the floor, stand on tiptoes. Lower the heels to the floor and resume the starting position. See Fig. 59.

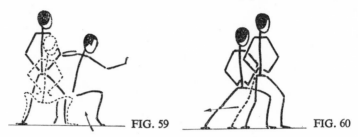

FIG. 59   FIG. 60

(33) In a squat on-guard position, bend and straighten the legs three times, jump into the lunge and finish with a fleche.

(34) From the on-guard position, step back briskly several times with the rear foot and place the entire sole on the floor. See Fig. 60.

(35) From the on-guard position, extend the rear leg to assume the lunge. Bend and partially straighten the front leg three times and resume the starting position.

(36) From the on-guard position, assume the lunge by slowly moving the rear leg backward with the sole of the rear foot slipping along the floor. Return to the starting position.

(37) From the on-guard position, move the rear leg backward gradually with the rear foot alternately supported by the heel and toes. Repeat in the other direction. See Fig. 61.

FIG. 61

(38) From the on-guard position, move the rear leg backward by sliding the rear sole along the floor. When in the lunge position, bend and straighten the front leg twice, then pull up the rear leg to resume the starting position.

(39) From the on-guard position, extend the rear leg backward to assume the lunge. Bring the front leg back to resume the on-guard position so that the backward motion is constant throughout the movement.

(40) From the on-guard position, lunge and bring up the rear foot to resume the on-guard position. Repeat several times in a continuous rhythm.

(41) From the on-guard position, do a half lunge and return. Extend the rear leg backward and return.

(42) From the on-guard position, take forward and backward steps with the body being lowered and raised alternately.

(43) Lying in a prone position supported by the arms, swing the body between the arms by lifting and dropping the hips. Jump and land alternately in left-handed and right-handed on-guard position. Finish with a fleche. See Fig. 62.

FIG. 62

(44) From a prone position as in (43), jump alternately into right-handed and left-handed squat on-guard positions with the hands remaining on the floor for support.

(45) From the on-guard position, bend at the hips to touch the floor while straightening the legs. See Fig. 63.

FIG. 63

(46) From the on-guard position, jump forward on the rear foot with the front leg swinging for balance.

(47) From the on-guard position, jump backward to a low on-guard position, with the front leg swinging back and the front foot landing behind the rear heel. See Fig. 64.

FIG. 64

(48) From the on-guard position, make a long jump and land in a low on-guard position or a squat on-guard position. Finish with a fleche. See Fig. 65.

FIG. 65

(49) From a kneeling position, jump and land alternately in right-handed and left-handed on-guard position. On occasion, finish with a fleche. See Fig. 66.

FIG. 66

(50) From the on-guard position, quickly touch the front palm to the floor at the front foot and finish with a fleche. Vary by touching the front thigh and then the floor in quick succession. See Fig. 67.

FIG. 67

(51) From an on-guard position with one knee on the floor, start to run, on a signal from the coach, at varying intervals or under distracting conditions. See Fig. 68.

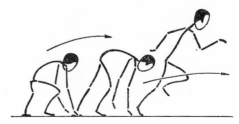

FIG. 68

77

III.4. Preparatory exercises done in or from the lunge

(1) In the lunge, partially straighten and bend the front leg several times. On occasion, finish with a fleche.

(2) In the lunge, bend and partially straighten the rear leg several times. On occasion, finish with a fleche.

(3) In the lunge, alternately bend and partially straighten the front and rear leg. See Fig. 69.

FIG. 69

(4) In the lunge, push off the front foot and lift it as if to resume the on-guard position but, instead of letting the foot come to the floor, repeat the lunge with the front leg starting forward while still in the air.

(5) From the lunge, jump backward to the on-guard position. On occasion, finish with a fleche. See Fig. 70.

FIG. 70

(6) In the lunge, bend and partially straighten the front leg three times and jump backward to the on-guard position. On occasion, finish with a fleche.

(7) From the lunge, execute a fleche. See Fig. 71.

FIG. 71

(8) In the lunge, tap the toes of the front foot quickly on the floor.

(9) In the lunge, tap the toes of the rear foot quickly on the floor.

(10) In the lunge, alternately tap the toes of the front foot and rear foot quickly on the floor.

(11) From a squat, jump into the lunge.

(12) In a squat with fingers touching the floor, partially straighten and bend the legs three times and jump into the lunge. On occasion, finish with a fleche. See Fig. 72.

(13) In the lunge, turn on the heels to take up first the opposite lunge and then return. Repeat several times. See Fig. 73.

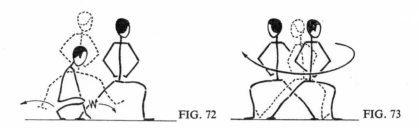

FIG. 72   FIG. 73

(14) Alternately take up the lunge with a half turn and step to the right and to the left. See Fig. 74.

FIG. 74

(15) In the lunge, transfer the body weight from the front leg to the rear leg by an intense bending of the rear leg and return. Repeat several times.

(16) As in (15), but finish with a fleche after resuming the lunge. See Fig. 75.

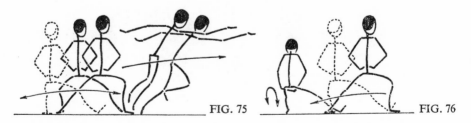

FIG. 75   FIG. 76

(17) In the lunge, transfer the body weight to the rear leg. Bend and partially straighten the rear leg two or three times and resume the lunge. Repeat several times.

(18) In the lunge, transfer the body weight to the rear leg. Lower the rear sole to the floor and then push the body forward by lifting the rear heel. Repeat several times. See Fig. 76.

(19) In the lunge, transfer the body weight to the rear leg. Jump up and touch the rear ankle with the front foot while in the air. See Fig. 77.

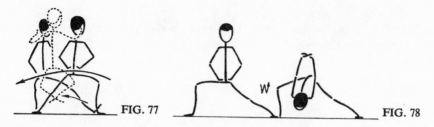

FIG. 77 FIG. 78

(20) In the lunge, bend at the hips between the straddled legs. While in this position, bend and partially straighten the legs with hands clasped and arms extended behind the body. See Fig. 78.

(21) In the lunge, lean the body backward with arms swung overhead. See Fig. 79.

FIG. 79

(22) In prone position with arms supporting, swing the right leg alongside the right hand on the outside and return. Swing the left leg alongside the left hand on the outside and return. See Fig. 80.

FIG. 80

III.5. Preparatory exercises and games done in pairs or in groups

(1) With a partner, lie on the back with legs pulled up to the chest and support the partner. Push the partner forward to land in a squat, initial or on-guard position. The partner finishes with a fleche. See Fig. 81.

FIG. 81

(2) With a partner, stand back-to-back with arms interlocked and hands held overhead and legs straight. Lower to the on-guard position and then resume the starting position.

(3) With a partner, hold hands while back-to-back in lunge position. Bend and partially straighten the front legs several times in the direction of the rear legs.

(4) With a partner, leapfrog to land in the on-guard position. Finish with a fleche. See Fig. 82.

FIG. 82

(5) With a partner, stand toe-to-toe in the on-guard position. Hold hands and try to push or pull the partner out of position.

(6) With a partner, hop on one foot and try to knock the partner off-balance by pushing with the shoulder (cock-fighting).

(7) With a partner, stand toe-to-toe in the on-guard position. Each partner holds his dominant arm in front of the body, one hand's width from the hip; one with palm up, the other with palm down. The partner with palm down slaps the other's hand and turns to run before the other can touch him with a fleche.

(8) As in (7), only stand one foot's length apart. The partner who initiates the action retreats with two steps backward while the other tries to touch him with a lunge.

(9) With a partner, face each other in the on-guard position with arms held one hand's width from the hip. One partner's hand is directly below the other's hand, with the hands in contact. He tries to catch the other's wrist by rotating the forearm before the partner can pull away.

(10) As in (9), only with the hands held back-to-back and touching, try to touch the partner's upturned palm with a quick wrist movement before he can pull away.

(11) With a partner, stand in the on-guard position lunge distance apart with the arms held in normal on-guard position; one with palm up, the other with palm down. Try to hit the partner's upturned palm with a quick lunging action before he can pull away.

(12) With a partner, stand facing each other with arms held loosely in front and hands touching palm-to-palm. The one whose hands are underneath tries to hit the back of the partner's hands with a quick rotation of the hands before the partner can pull away. On occasion, use feints or other distracting tactics, such as talking.

(13) As in (12), but each partner has one hand over and one hand under. Try to hit the partner's upper hand while avoiding the partner's attempts to hit with his lower hand.

(14) With a partner, stand face-to-face with legs straddled. The partner stands with arms bent at the elbows in front of the chest and palms facing each other one hand's width apart. Try to move either hand between the partner's hands without his catching it by clapping his hands together.

(15) With a partner, face one another in the on-guard position. One holds a coin in his hand. The other, with hand palm down and below the hand holding the coin, tries to catch the coin with a quick movement before the partner can close his hand.

(16) Try to catch a glove thrown out front by a partner. Use a fleche from the on-guard position.

(17) Try to hit a glove held to the wall with a straight thrust from short or medium distance.

(18) With a partner who holds a blade by the point perpendicular to the floor, catch the blade when dropped before it hits the floor.

(19) As in (18), but with palm or fingers initially in contact with the blade, catch the falling blade with eyes closed.

(20) With a partner who holds a tennis ball with his palm facing the floor, hold the hand above with palm down and catch the ball when dropped before it hits the floor.

(21) As in (20), only using a ball in both hands, drop one at a time or both together.

(22) As in (21), only each partner holds a ball which the other must catch when dropped.

(23) With a partner, turn a skipping rope and, on a signal or at the individual's discretion, jump into the path of the rope and skip on one or both feet.

(24) With two others turning a long skipping rope, jump in the path of the rope and skip on one foot, in the initial position, in the on-guard position. Leave the path of the rope with a running fleche.

(25) As in (24), only run under the rope to the other side either alone or in a group.

(26) As in (24), only stand on the side opposite to the direction in which the rope is turning. Jump in and hop several times then run out the same way, or run in and out without doing a single hop.

(27) With two others turning the rope, hop backwards and forwards in the on-guard position beside the swinging rope and try to do a running fleche under the rope at the right moment.

(28) With a partner who swings a rope close to the floor in a circle, on a signal or at the individual's discretion move into the range of the rope and jump over it in a specified manner or of one's own choice. This can be done alone or in small groups.

(29) In a group, two parallel lines face each other first at a distance of one metre and gradually reduced to 50 centimetres. One line is designated to try to hit members of the line opposite with a fleche before they can get away. Each line is given a designation by colour or number or other such manner and act on the appropriate signal from the coach.

(30) In a group, two parallel lines face each other at a distance of several metres or at opposite sides of the room. Number each member of each line. When a number is called by the coach, the two who have that number try to retrieve a glove or other object in the centre of the room and return it to their side without being touched by the opposing player, or touch the other player trying to return with the glove to his line. If two players take their time to pick up the glove, the coach can call a second and even third number to involve a number of players at one time.

IV. FOOTWORK

Good footwork has always been one of the major prerequisites to success in fencing. Today, however, because the fencing distance is greater than in previous eras, the fencer approaches and attaches importance to footwork exercises in a different light.

Exceptional dynamism and mobility are needed in order to cope with the increased fencing distance. Classical combinations such as the step and lunge or jump lunge are rarely sufficient to score a hit, particularly in the case of sabre fencing. Often at least one or more movements (a step, a crossover step of a jump) must be added to the sequences mentioned above. Frequently a series of steps or combinations of jumps and steps must be executed to close in on the opponent. Mechanical perfection in the movements is, by itself, not enough to do the job; a wide range of speed and rhythm is also necessary in order to produce the broadest possible variety of movements. The word "athletic" has been taken up by experts to describe today's fencing footwork of continuous high intensity and increased dynamism.

Students must learn the various footwork elements individually since they serve as the base. The final objective, however, is that the fencer be able to combine and connect the individual elements smoothly and effectively.

Footwork both actively regulates the fencing distance and participates in the action which ends in a hit. Steps and jumps are transitional movements. Playing with the fencing distance, the lunge and the fleche lead directly to scoring a hit.

Footwork exercises can be distinguished from each other and classified as either simple or compound.

IV.1. Simple footwork

- step forward,
- step backward,
- crossover step forward,
- crossover step backward,
- lunge and (a) recovery backward to on-guard, or (b) recovery forward to on-guard,
- jump forward,
- jump backward,
- fleche,
- stop-short,
- glide.

i. Step forward (see Fig. 83)

The movement starts with the front foot. With the foot pointing forward and the sole close to the floor, the fencer advances one foot length forward and then contacts the floor, first with the heel and then the entire sole.

At the same moment the front foot contacts the floor, the rear foot should advance. Leaving the floor, it moves forward and carries the body forward with it.

Both feet should cover an equal distance and should finish moving at the same time.

FIG. 83

ii. Step backward (see Fig. 84)

The movement starts with the rear foot. It leaves the floor and moves backward with the front foot pushing to support the movement. Before the front leg is completely extended, the front foot should leave the floor, picking the toes up first and then the rest of the foot to help locate the body in its new position.

Both feet should move an equal distance and should finish at approximately the same time.

The body should be supported in a relaxed manner on the legs. Any body movement before, during, or after a movement of the feet must be strictly avoided.

FIG. 84

The body should move simultaneously with the beginning and ending of the movement of the feet, either in a forward or backward step.

The two phases of a step—the pushing and pulling—should be co-ordinated to ensure that the total movement is smooth and continuous. The feet do not simply take a step but, on making contact with the floor, must stick firmly.

Once the student has overcome any technical problems in taking either a step forward or a step backward, he should concentrate on executing the steps continuously, smoothly, softly and without the slightest noise.

The foot which initiates the movement can move quickly, briskly, slowly, tentatively or in a manner particular to preparatory or reconnaissance actions. The conclusion of the step, should always be as brisk and fast as possible.

Taking a step of maximum length, which should be no longer than one foot length, depends on the work of the thigh and lower leg. A shorter than average step, which is particularly useful for reducing the fencing distance unnoticeably, requires a relaxed and mobile foot.

The longer the step, the longer it takes to conclude and, therefore, the longer the phase of vulnerability to the fencer executing the step. The uncertain balance while in the air provides a longer opportunity for the opponent to take advantage of the tempo offered by the slow-moving step. The longer step also delays the start of any movement to follow.

The crossover variations of forward and backward steps are variations of everyday walking, but done in an on-guard position. They are more natural to execute than the regular fencing step started by the foot placed in the intended direction of movement. At the same time, they are more intense, longer and very often more suggestive than their regular fencing counterparts.

iii. Crossover step forward
The movement starts with the rear foot. It is placed in advance of the front foot and the step completed by replacing the front foot in its original forward position to take up a normal on-guard position.

iv. Crossover step backward
The movement starts with the front foot. It is placed behind the heel of the rear foot and the step completed by replacing the rear foot in its usual position to take up a normal on-guard position.

Again, with crossover steps forward and backward, it is important that the body not move or, more exactly, not move other than with the movement of the feet which carry it.

Experts have developed a number of methods for the teaching of the different steps. The method chosen by the coach depends on his approach and ideas.

Traditionally the so-called partial process has been the favoured method. With it the components of a step are isolated and taught piece by piece. Usually each part of the movement is executed on the command of the coach.

The major flaw in this method is that it cuts the movement into two parts at the most critical points. Students have to stop in positions difficult to hold and rarely occurring in actual practice. For example, in teaching the step forward, students are told to completely straighten the front leg. Such movements make it doubly difficult for beginners because of the problems they cause in maintaining balance. The demand that the step cover maximum distance even on first executions of the steps also leads to many additional errors being committed.

The whole method of teaching, of which there are several variations, eliminates the obvious disadvantages of the traditional approach. With it the beginner becomes aware of the external form and internal sense of the movements in their entirety all at once. It happens without command, in a more intensive manner, through the student's independent experimentation.

Some coaches adopt a method using inductive exercises prior to teaching the actual movement. Others teach half steps or crossover steps to allow the students to acquire the needed fencing steps in the shortest possible time. There are other coaches who have their students march at the spot in an effort to teach forward or backward steps, keeping the students moving and gradually increasing the size of the movement to the required length of the step.

A variation of the method last mentioned above is to have the students execute their first steps from a position in which the legs are only slightly bent and, therefore, the distance between the feet shorter and the on-guard position more relaxed. This approach prevents the beginner from taking too long a step at the outset. In time the fencer can be taught to gradually adopt the optimum on-guard position in terms of depth and width of stance and the proper length of a step as his physical abilities improve.

Most coaches teach the step forward and the step backward separately. Because they have much in common, however, they can be taught at the same time.

As a rule, the teaching of footwork begins with the step forward. Some coaches, however, think that the backward step is less problematic and therefore teach it first.

The traditional approach in teaching the step forward insists from the very beginning that the soles of both feet be placed simultaneously and energetically on the floor, so much so that they make a definite noise. Because this type of execution makes the movement somewhat awkward, the coach is advised to avoid it at the early stages of instruction. The step forward done in a specific rhythm to allow both feet to finish at the same time should be taught later as an inductive exercise in developing the step lunge.

In the case of the fencer who develops the habit of dragging the rear foot in the step forward, a low obstacle of 8 to 10 centimetres in height, a blade or weapon, should be placed on the floor in front of the rear foot. This forces the conscious and somewhat active lifting of the foot while taking a step forward. Where necessary, a blade or other obstacle can be placed in front of each foot.

If the coach wants the student to move both feet an equal distance in taking a

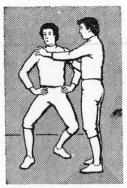

FIG. 85

step, he may mark out the length desired on the floor. Although this goes against principle, the student should be allowed some visual control for a short period. The use of a mirror also lets the student monitor his movements without having to shift his body or head position.

When the student's body moves unnecessarily or is delayed, as often occurs in taking a step backward, the coach or partner should offer immediate and direct assistance by applying a light pressure on the shoulder away from the direction of movement at the moment the step begins (Fig. 85). If necessary, the coach can place one hand on the shoulder opposite the direction of movement and the other hand on the hip leading in the direction of movement to inhibit any body shifts. The hands so placed warn the body of what should be done and make it move in the required direction without delay.

v. Lunge (see Fig. 86)
The lunge is the usual foot movement used to terminate an attack.
This movement starts with the front foot. The toes are lifted and the front swings forward with an extension on the knee. The front heel advances, skimming the floor, as the rear leg pushes with a vigorous extension of the knee. The front foot lands heel first and, as the sole comes to rest, the body's forward and downward motion is arrested. The thigh muscles stabilize the final position.

FIG. 86

It is a must for beginners to accentuate the lifting of the toes and foot at the start of the movement in order to become accustomed to relaxing the front foot and using the related muscles. The coach may tolerate a display of the relevant tendencies in the execution of the movement by advanced fencers and competitors. Only in cases where they tend to begin the movement by lifting the heel should advanced fencers be made to emphasize the raising of the toes.

88

Several methods are available to coaches to help underline and graphically illustrate the essential characteristics of the lunge. One is to place a coin under the heel of the front foot, or a weapon in front of the front leg. On occasion, the point of a blade can be placed on foot or toes.

While practising, the fencer may call on a partner, wall bars or ballet bar to provide extra support (Fig. 87). If practising in front of a mirror, the student should be able to see as much of his sole as possible when starting a lunge, but without lifting his foot too high.

FIG. 87

Finally, to accustom them to a correct start, students should exaggerate the movement, holding it for several counts at the critical point. At such movements the body weight must be supported by the rear leg.

In final position of the lunge the body should be perpendicular to the floor. The front knee is positioned directly over the front foot and the line of the shoulders runs parallel to the floor.

In his longest lunge the fencer's front thigh should be horizontal; that is parallel with the floor. The lower leg stands perpendicular to the floor. A lunge carried beyond this position is of dubious value since it becomes very difficult, if not impossible, to recover to on-guard position in a correct fashion from a lunge which resembles an acrobat's split position.

a. Recovery backward to on-guard (see Fig. 88)

FIG. 88

This movement starts with the front foot. The toes are raised, pushing the body backward as the leg begins to straighten. Before the front leg is fully extended, the front foot leaves the floor with a quick energetic push off the heel. At the same time, the rear leg pulls the body backward with an intense bending of the knee to bring it over the rear foot. This action "sucks" the body into the on-guard position. The movement is completed by the front foot's coming to rest heel first on the floor.

The work of the rear leg plays the dominant role in the backward recovery to on-guard. This must be emphasized well in advance, even during the preparatory phase, by using special gymnastic exercises or other such exercises to introduce the movement to the student. The need for, and feeling of, the pronounced pulling action may be illustrated or aided through the use of an elastic rope (see Fig. 89)

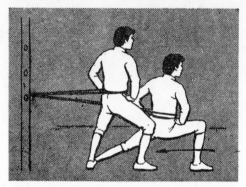

FIG. 89

or by direct intervention of the coach. Standing behind the student, the coach may assist the recovery by holding and pulling the student's rear knee during the movement.

The lunge and recovery to on-guard are closely related movements. For this reason, they should not be separated from each other during the training for any great period of time.

Teaching of the lunge and recovery to on-guard can be done according to the time sequence or vice versa. The former is typical of the traditional approach, while the latter represents the most modern pedagogical theory and practice.

Traditionally it has been the rule for coaches to demand the longest possible lunge from a normal on-guard position from the very start of training. Today, however, a number of coaches allow beginners to execute lunges which are often quite short and recover to an on-guard position in which the feet are quite close together and the legs almost straight. As well as reducing errors, this method has several other inherent advantages as listed below:

- it relieves the fencer of considerable physical strain,
- it effectively prevents the commission of basic errors common to beginners,
- it maintains the principle of gradual progress by moving from the simplest elements to more complicated ones better than the old method. It also

considers the relationship between abilities and skills better in that it starts from the view that, despite careful preparation, beginners do not possess the necessary strength or surplus strength when instruction in the lunge begins which allows them to execute without error a lunge of maximum length on their first attempts,

● it makes the work of the rear leg easier,
● the sole of the foot is less likely to move or leave the floor,
● the rear knee is less likely to turn inwards, an error frequently experienced in first attempting long lunges from a correct on-guard position.

To this end, a number of coaches are experimenting with new methods and changing the traditional sequence of instruction. Some first teach the lunge as a final position. The students stand with feet parallel and approximately three foot lengths apart. They then bend the eventual front knee and turn the corresponding foot with toes raised in the direction of an imaginary opponent. The head also turns in that direction to assume the final position.

Once the students can take up the lunge several times without any problem, and are aware of both the movement and the final position, they can be taught how to recover to on-guard position. When they have a good command of both movements, the students can learn to execute the lunges effectively from the on-guard position.

Whatever method he adopts, the coach should not skimp on the number of preparatory and introductory exercises he employs to present to the students the essence and actual nature of the movements. These eventually pay dividends by making things easier for both coach and students.

b. Recovery forward to on-guard (see Fig. 90)

The recovery forward is used to pursue an opponent who retreats before an attack with lunge.

FIG. 90

The movement starts with the rear foot. It is pulled forward towards the front foot to take up the on-guard position. In the case of the thrusting weapons, the movement of the foot is accompanied by the raising of the rear arm.

The recovery forward is easier to execute than the recovery backward because the rear foot does not carry the body weight. It is, therefore, unnecessary to adopt any other methods than the actual instructions needed to illustrate its execution.

The recovery forward is rarely used on its own. In most instances, it is immediately followed by a lunge, a step lunge, a jump lunge or a fleche.

vi. Jump forward (see Fig. 91)

A jump can be defined as a hop executed close to the ground in which the feet do not begin at the same time but finish simultaneously.

FIG. 91

The movement starts with the front foot. It moves forward with an extension of the leg and is kept as close to the floor as possible. Before the leg is completely extended, it is snapped down to the floor quickly.

At the moment the front leg approaches full extension, the rear leg is energetically accelerated and pulled forward under the body. This should be done so that both feet land on the floor at the same time to complete the movement.

From the above it becomes evident that the first phase of the jump starts slowly and is quite prolonged in contrast with the second phase which is a brief, intense and energetic pull.

Consciously slowing down the start of the jump and intentionally delaying the action of the rear leg and the take-off by holding the front foot in the air longer than usual are special methods used to draw attention to the time difference between the work done by the two feet and the necessary sequence of the two feet needed to execute the entire movement properly.

The length of the jump is the same as that of a normal step.

It must be explained clearly that the jump is not used as a starting step. The student, however, should learn the correct rhythm of the movement under simple conditions, such as executing the jump from an on-guard position with a short distance between the feet or using some external support. Where exercises are used to introduce students to the movement, executions tend to be more characteristic than when students are taught the movement directly.

Jumps used in first intention attacks are usually very typical, obvious, intense and energetic. Jumps are commonly used between other foot movements to fill in any gaps, to manœuvre, or to reach some other tactical objective. For example, jumps designed to force a reaction from the opponent are not always so obvious or dynamic; often they are much more like very energetic steps.

No matter what method is chosen, beginners should avoid the typical dynamic execution in their initial efforts. They should regulate the strength of their actions in such a way as to avoid any excessive insistence and intention to gain the maximum ground possible which leads to the distortion of the form and rhythm.

vii. Jump backward

There are several ways to jump backward, each variation resulting in different lengths.

One variation is the opposite of the jump forward. It resembles the movement used by a shotputter and provides comparatively little gain in the fencing distance. If using the above analogy, the coach should point out the difference in the body position.

The movement starts with the rear foot. It is swung backward, parallel to and slightly above the floor causing the body to lean forward slightly while the front foot bears the weight. In the second phase the rear foot drops to the floor with a slight pulling-in motion. Just before the rear foot drops to the floor, the front foot gives a vigorous push to move the body backward with a hop. Both feet land on the floor at the same time, with the heels making contact last.

The jump variation of the crossover step backward allows the fencer to gain more ground in a more active manner than the normal jump backward.

The movement begins with the body, which leans slightly backward. The front foot gives a quick push and then is swung energetically so that the foot passes behind the rear leg. This accelerates the backward movement of the body and moves it quickly over the supporting rear leg. This throws the fencer into an off-balance position and he is thus forced to take off from the floor with the rear foot.

As a result of the loss of balance and the consequent energetic jump, the fencer becomes airborn for a relatively long time.

The speed of the take-off and the jump as a whole, the trajectory and the length of the jump—all are determined by the movement of the body. For this reason the focus of attention in teaching this jump should be on this point. If the body does not move back a split second before the front pushes off, if it fails to keep up with the foot and puts the movement out of synch, or is slightly delayed even for a moment, then the jump is belated and, as a result, shorter and higher than necessary. The jump can be lower still by keeping the body as low as possible during the movement, in addition to the proper execution as outlined previously.

In order to land in a normal on-guard position without taking any additional steps due to the energy in the backward movement, the fencer should arrange his feet while in the air in preparation for the landing. Thus the on-guard position is taken in the closing stages of flight and the feet firmly planted the moment they contact the floor. Only in this way is it possible to absorb the movement of the body, which is off-balance and travelling at speed, and bring it to a controlled stop instantly in the proper position and without excess motion.

As the feet approach the floor to land, the body must be slowed down and lowered so, at the moment of impact, it drops lower than usual with the intense bending of the knees to absorb the shock. This, too, helps to bring the fencer to a halt.

The longest variation of the jump backward is the crossover jump backward started with a half step backward. This variation adds greater length because it allows a greater swing of the front leg otherwise impossible with an immediate crossover. It also makes the jump easier.

viii. Fleche
The fleche is the most natural of the foot movements, but that does not mean that it is easy to execute well.

Its principal advantage is that it overcomes great distance in a single motion. The disadvantage, on the other hand, is that, if unsuccessful, it leaves the fencer at the mercy of the opponent. This is because the fleche cannot be stopped at a definite point in the same way as a lunge.

The fleche can be executed:
- from the on-guard position,
- from a half step forward or backward,
- from the lunge.

a. Fleche from the on-guard position (see Fig. 92)
The fleche can be defined as a running movement in which the feet crossover and the body is carried forward side first. This body position is maintained until the hit since turning the body to face the opponent would offer too large a target.

FIG. 92

The movement begins with the rear leg which pushes the body forward, keeping it from leaning by pressing down the rear hip, over the front leg and beyond the point where the fencer begins to lose his balance. At this point the front leg

94

vigorously joins in with a pushing motion and the rear leg, having spent its energy, is swung forward in a long crossover step to help regain balance as soon as possible. The body continues to move forward and over the rear leg once it has landed on the floor. The hit should arrive during the crucial crossover phase, with the subsequent movement serving to cushion the landing. The weapon begins to advance as the body starts forward, but the arm is completely extended only when the front foot joins in the pushing action. If very long distances must be bridged, the blade is extended more quickly.

Acting in accordance with the law of action and reaction, the rear arm without the weapon moves downward in the case of the thrusting weapons and upward in the case of sabre to assist in keeping the body in a stable position.

The speed of the fleche depends on the angle of inclination of the body, usually between 45° and 60°, and the impulse of the front leg. The more the body is inclined, the more intensely the fencer must chase it to regain his balance. Also, the more inclined the body, the more help the impulse from the front leg is in pushing it ahead in the direction of the fleche.

The execution of the fleche after a half step forward or backward is identical to the movement described above from a technical viewpoint. The half step backward can be taken with either foot. Regardless of the direction, the step is designed to create a more favourable position from which to attack with strength and speed. This is an important precondition of the attack.

b. Fleche from the lunge (see Fig. 71)

This variation is used in order to continue the offensive. It places a heavy burden on the legs.

The shorter the lunge, the easier it is to start a fleche from it. From a lunge of optimal length the fleche can be executed without any additional foot movement. From a long lunge the fleche must be prepared with some foot movement to reduce the starting distance between the feet to relieve the legs a little and to facilitate the shifting of the body and its start forward. This preparatory movement can be a stop-like movement of varying length either advancing the rear leg or pulling back the front leg.

The fleche must first be taught from the on-guard position.

At first, the student should move forward at a walking pace from an on-guard position in which the feet are closer than usual and the body lower. In the second stage, the pace at which the legs crossover forward should be accelerated gradually and inductive exercise introduced to help build the speed of the fleche, the length it covers and the more pronounced inclination of the body. Exerting pressure on the rear hip with the rear hand helps the fencer prevent his body from standing up during the movement and also forces the rear leg to take a longer and quicker crossover step.

When the student makes his first attempts at executing the fleche, the coach should be close at hand in case the student needs help.

If necessary, the student may be positioned in advance at the best angle of inclination (see Fig. 93) and the fleche subsequently executed from this position.

FIG. 93

Beginners usually prefer the fleche to the lunge. For this reason it is in the best interest of the student that the coach emphasize moderation and begin teaching the fleche only after he has assured himself that the student will not abuse it, especially at the expense of the lunge.

ix. Stop-short
The movement begins with the front leg. It starts in the same way as a step forward but, rather than complete the step, comes to an abrupt stop as though the fencer's foot has been nailed to the floor.

x. Glide
The glide is related to the stop-short. It also starts like a step forward, but differs in that the body weight is transferred almost completely to the front leg. Instead of coming to a halt, the movement continues to advance with what resembles a low hop on the front foot in which the sole skims the floor all the way. The movement concludes with both feet firmly gripping the floor at the same time, much like the finish of the stop-short.

IV.2. Compound footwork

Compound footwork is made up of two or more simple foot movements linked together. With imagination, coaches and students can create a wide variety from the basic movements. The numerous variations are too many to list here, so only two compound movements, the two most classic ones referred to in the literature of the sport, are technically described. They are the step lunge and the jump lunge. Temperament, style and tactical bent of the fencer determine which of the two is preferred.

i. Step lunge

The key to the smooth synthesis of the two foot movements is that the return of the front foot to the floor be delayed, the advance of the body withheld and the quick advance of the rear foot even more accelerated.

Executed in the manner described above, both feet arrive on the floor simultaneously. This may be emphasized in practice by having the feet making a loud noise as they hit the floor. So that the body does not move beyond the front leg, but stays slightly behind it during the step, the front foot is released at the moment the rear foot hits the floor to allow the pushing action of the rear leg in driving the lunge forward energetically. The release of the front foot after the step and its subsequent advance in the lunge must be lively. The step lunge demands that the blade reach the target with a constantly accelerating movement. The arm holding the weapon is extended completely with the planting of the rear foot on the floor.

As in learning many other compound movements, the key to success lies in the fencer's ability to sense the correct rhythm. The step lunge rhythm can be promoted by practising double steps by prior demonstration which imitates the rhythm through the noise of the feet, by tapping the feet while standing in place or by separating the movement and subsequently practising each part. For the student with a natural sense of rhythm, the necessary explanation and demonstration should be followed immediately by execution of the whole movement as though in an actual bout situation.

Tapping the feet in the correct rhythm can be done either in the normal on-guard position or in one with the feet closer and legs straighter than usual. Physical assistance, such as support from a partner or wall-bar, may or may not be used. The starting movement of the front foot which follows the step forward can be illustrated concretely using a pseudo-step forward which gives the rhythm but otherwise remains in place while the rear foot executes its normal action. A minor variation allows the rear foot to knock against the front heel in its move forward and thus push the front foot forward from its original position with the body weight resting on the rear leg.

ii. Jump lunge (see Fig. 94)

This movement covers less distance and gains less ground than the step lunge.

The jump is executed so that the body weight rests mainly on the rear leg and is not too long. This frees the front foot so it is ready to leave the floor at the earliest possible moment and swing into the lunge.

FIG. 94

The arm holding the weapon is completely extended in the last phase of the jump prior to the start of the lunge. The feet assist the weapon in reaching the target through their constantly accelerating movement.

In his first attempts to execute the jump lunge, the student should do the jump in place. Later he should increase the length of the jump until it covers maximum distance so that this first element of the compound movement gains the necessary ground.

IV.3. General observations on the teaching and practice of footwork

Starting from the viewpoint that footwork is the foundation of fencing expertise and without mastering it no one should be allowed to handle a weapon. Beginners were formerly subjected to prolonged periods, even years, of torturing footwork and exercises only. During this time students not only learned the basic movements but also practised and polished all the possible variations. That was years ago; today no one would willingly subject himself to such slavish work.

Without belittling the necessity and primacy of footwork, the methods adopted to teach the secrets of footwork should be based on the theory of comprehensive instruction and according to a spiralling path of progress.

Having learned the on-guard position, the student must acquire the simple foot movements, without which he should not handle a weapon. Giving a weapon to an ignorant beginner is not worthwhile. Some time later, however, the simple foot movements must be practised with weapon in hand.

Foot movements other than the simple ones can be treated effectively as part of the key to or the solution to different situations in conjunction with a dynamically related action; for example, teaching the jump lunge along with attacks on the blade. In other words, they can be taught conveniently with a weapon in hand as the student advances in his overall programme.

The old method of teaching most of the footwork in a block, one movement after another in a rapid succession, should not be used with beginners. Learning compound footwork with weapon in hand poses little problem to an advanced student because these movements are, in fact, no more than variations of the simple movements acquired at an earlier stage.

Footwork can be practised individually, in pairs and in groups. It can be done in front of a mirror. It can be practised on command or other signal, or at the student's initiative. It can be done with weapon in hand or without, the hand being held on the hips, in on-guard position or hanging loosely at the sides. The movements can be performed without any preparatory actions or with some action designed to meet a certain technical objective or to build endurance. Movements can be practised separately or in series, in a predetermined sequence or spontaneously, allowing for the most complex variations imaginable.

Practice conditions can be made easier or more difficult. Difficulty can be increased by using weight belts or the students own body weight as a load by taking up a wider and lower on-guard position than usual.

At more advanced stages of training compound movements should never be broken down and practised as separate components except where the coach wishes to emphasize a certain element to the student or to eliminate a specific flaw.

The global method should always be the preferred method of instruction. Commands should be used only for a brief period in training, not only because verbal stimuli are not necessary at later stages, but also because outside control makes the student too dependent. Once accustomed to commands, he will find it difficult to act without them, thinking they are indispensable. He might also lack the motivation, usually given by commands, to practise footwork, an exercise which is by no means entertaining.

V. FOIL FENCING

The foil is the one sport weapon which has no historical ancestry in combat. It was conceived as a training weapon for épée and developed into an independent weapon. The lighter and more flexible foil with its protective button at the point of the blade served as a practice weapon in preparing for and supplementing the épée, the actual combat weapon used in duelling. It evolved into the primary weapon in the modern sport of fencing because it was the first one used in a sporting manner.

The foil is a thrusting weapon. A thrust scores if it reaches the opponent's target area in a specified manner, with the point clearly hitting the target if only for a split second. Using electrical scoring, the button must hit with a pressure exceeding 500 grams in order to trigger the indicator light.

The hit scored by the thrust is symbolic. This means that the thrust need not be of substantial force to make a valid hit. The most important quality in a thrust, therefore, is not its strength but its precision.

Of the three weapons used in fencing, the foil demands the most patience and technical preparation to acquire accuracy and a wide variety of actions. An épéeist might be ready for bout fencing after learning and more or less automating one or two actions; the foil fencer, however, whose movements are too large and who possesses a limited technical repertory not adequately automated can go nowhere.

The small target area, among other factors, compels the foil fencer to undertake a longer and more thorough period of preparation and learning prior to engaging in bout fencing than the épéeist or the sabre fencer. It is also essential for the foil fencer to develop more defined footwork than the others, and to execute very precise movements.

The foil is a conventional weapon. It is founded upon the observance and uniform interpretation of agreed-upon rules. It is this convention which built, maintains and will ensure the successes of foil fencing.

V.1. The types and parts of the foil

Before the advent of the electric foil, the French and Italian types were the most commonly used. Experts did not consider the orthopaedic, or pistol, grip suited to successfully developing an artistic style.

The orthopaedic grip became increasingly popular with the introduction of electric foil, and gradually replaced the Italian foil which had certain advantages in ordinary foil.

The pistol grip's popularity grew even at the expense of the French foil, and today is used by virtually every competitive fencer. For the Italian, French and pistol grip see Fig. 95.

FIG. 95

Despite the predominance of the pistol grip, it is advisable to begin teaching foil with the French grip. This type of handle makes it easier for students to acquire the skill of using the fingers separately. It also inhibits unnecessary wrist movements and a passive holding of the foil, two errors which frequently occur when using the pistol grip.

To begin training using the pistol grip leads to several errors in the holding, manipulating and feeling of the foil, and causes developmental delays. For these reasons most coaches in the leading fencing nations recommend that the French foil be used in teaching beginners. Switching to the pistol grip at a later stage when the fencer has developed an adequate technique poses fewer problems than those involved when starting from the outset with the pistol grip.

The French foil has a better balance, with its weight always more evenly distributed than the best balanced pistol grip, which tends to be pointheavy.

A plastic foil is effective for the teaching of children in the 10–11-years agebracket. Weight can be gradually increased to ordinary foil, then electric foil weight as the student grows older and wiser by replacing the plastic components piece by piece with metal ones.
The foil is composed of:
- the blade,
- the guard,
- the grip or handle,
- the pommel or locking nut.

The so-called opposition parries of longer duration are executed with the forte, or strong part, of the blade in combination with the guard, which acts to protect the hand holding the weapon.

Beats, engagements and attacks on the opponent's blade are done with the middle of the blade, as are best parries in which the blades make contact at one point only.

The feeble of flexible part of the blade is used for engagements and cutovers employed in reconnaissance and preparation.

In putting together the foil, the blade is bent somewhat inward and downward in relation to the straight line extending in the line of the handle. This bend, which varies according to individual taste, make it easier to:

101

- hold the weapon,
- direct the point almost automatically to the target, providing the weapon is held in a correct manner,
- score a hit from a more favourable and more certain angle.

From time to time the coach should check to see that the student's foil is assembled properly. Since perfect technique needs both a good hand and a properly prepared foil, the role of the coach and the mechanical set-up of the weapon will be constantly emphasized in this treatise.

V.2. The fundamentals of foil

i. The correct grip

The foil is held so that the blade points downward in relation to the straight line through the handle.

When the weapon is held correctly, there is a noticeable space between the handle and the palm of the hand. Pressed firmly in the palm, the handle is difficult to manipulate and unresponsive to the will of the fencer when called upon.

Essential to learning how to grip the foil correctly is the distinguishing of the roles of the different fingers in the grip. The index finger and thumb are the primary manipulators of the blade, with the last three fingers acting to help limit and stop blade movement and to strengthen or loosen the grip.

Co-ordinated fingerwork guarantees:

- the development of a firm grip free from desperate pressure,
- the development of blade manipulation as a separate ability,
- the precise and controlled manipulation of the weapon responsive to the fencer's will,
- the scoring of hits with a secure and accurate point.

In the case of both the French foil (Fig. 96) and the pistol grip (Fig. 97), the grip is taken by placing the index finger on the underside of the handle close to the guard, with the thumb placed opposite on the topside.

FIG. 96   FIG. 97

With the French foil the other three fingers are placed loosely alongside each other. The configuration of the pistol grip positions the remaining fingers automatically, and can be considered a good grip only if it is properly adjusted to fit the fencer's hand.

No matter which grip is used, it should be held in the middle of the palm.

102

It is recommended to teach beginners how to hold the foil using an Italian foil, which is straight and not adjusted to the palm of the hand. This puts the student in direct contact with the blade and, thus, he senses how it behaves when it is moved. This sensing occurs only indirectly with weapons whose handles are adjusted to the palm, which both French and pistol grips are. The flat part of the blade in the Italian foil promotes the correct use of the index finger and thumb in gripping the weapon; the thin neck of the handle, which is not adjusted to the palm, also accustoms the student to not exerting extra pressure and also exercises the fingers quite intensively (see Fig. 98).

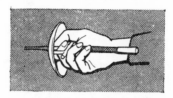 FIG. 98

Some coaches teach the holding of the foil only after students have learned the basic body movements. Others teach the two in parallel or introduce exercises to develop the correct grip of the weapon as early as the stage of preparatory training.

How the foil is held greatly influences technique; therefore the coach must be especially careful to teach the correct grip. Any faults which occur should be corrected and eliminated thoroughly.

Positions of the hand holding the weapon are brought about by rotating the arm along its longitudinal axis. The theory of fencing as regards these positions is treated in:

- the preliminary practice of correct execution of thrusts and parries,
- the establishment of basic points of reference in terms of the blade's position in space.

Italian theory, based on the use of the Italian foil, attached great importance to hand positions. Followers of this school taught hand positions with and without the weapon in hand.

The six basic positions of the hand were determined in relation to the positions of the cross-bar on the handle and the palm of the hand, in actual fact, the positions derive from the various prone (palm down) and supine (palm up) positions of the hand. With French and pistol grips the plane of the blade and the direction in which the fingers point are the determining factors in hand positions because no cross-bar exists.

Today no separate instruction is given in blade position. References are made, however, to hand positions, finger placement, the angle of the blade's inclination and the direction of the edge while teaching the different actions.

ii. Positions of the hand and the blade

The hand can be held in a prone position, with the fingernails pointing inside and the upper side of the blade horizontal, or in a supine position, with the fingernails pointing upward and the upper side of the blade facing obliquely downward and outward. The angle at which each position is held differs by 90°.

A totally supinated position is rarely seen. Only fencers who can maintain a completely relaxed shoulder are able to hold a weapon in this position. Most fencers only try to approximate a fully supinated position, holding their hands half way between it and the prone position. As it has already been mentioned before, this places the upper side of the blade in a position facing obliquely downward and outward.

The supine position makes for a surer, more precise thrust and also facilitates the withdrawal of the elbow.

The extent of rotation in the prone position varies. The least rotation occurs in the on-guard position, with the fingernails pointing inward. In invito, with parries, beats and binds, this rotation can be greater, with the fingernails pointing obliquely downward and inward.

The positions of the blade account for the typical positions of the arm and hand holding the weapon. They are:

- the on-guard position,
- the line,
- the invito or parry.

The on-guard position of the blade can be described as a neutral one, and its characteristics are determined as a matter of convenience. It is an optimum position which allows both offensive and defensive actions to be initiated easily and which closes one line to the target completely. Usually it lies in the sixth line or, less frequently, the second line.

The on-guard position of the blade is an important staging manœuvre done with the hand. As a rule, the fencer manages the bout from this position, initiating reconnaissance and preparatory actions from it.

When taking up the on-guard position, the fencer can hold the weapon with palm and fingers pointing inward or in any stage of the supine position. The totally supinated position, with palm and fingers pointing directly upward, is not recommended even with the French foil. The best position is one in which the fencer lends a supine character to his grip and turns the blade only as much as is needed to have the blade bend slightly outward when the thrust is executed.

The line (see Fig. 99) is an active position of the blade which constitutes a threat to the opponent. It is this position which gives an action conventional priority, and its status and proper method of presentation are spelled out in the rules of fencing.

Theoretically many variations of the line can exist because the point of the foil can be directed toward any part of the opponent's target when the arm is extended. In practice, however, the line is classified as one of two typical situations; the

104

FIG. 99

upper line when the point is directed towards the upper half of the target, and the lower line when the point is directed to the lower area of the target.

In both positions the line must extend along a plane from the shoulder to the hand holding the weapon. In practice students should be told to use either of the two basic lines, the choice being determined by the action to follow.

In actual fact the line deviates somewhat from being absolutely straight because of the bend of the blade as described earlier and the anatomical structure of the arm.

The invito and parry positions are identical hand positions. The difference in terminology expresses a difference in purpose. They give the same appearance, but there are natural functional differences, a situation not uncommon in fencing where movements similar in execution play diametrically opposed roles. The particular role or purpose only becomes clear when in actual use.

The invito exposes the fencer's target. It actually invites the opponent to attack. The parry, on the other hand, deflects the attacking blade from the fencer's target although it physically resembles the invito.

The old fencing theory which makes a distinction in terms of size between movements or positions identical in a technical sense but different in function is not deemed as necessary here. Any possible variations in size of two such movements is not necessarily a criterion for judging the movements from two separate viewpoints. In one instance, the parry may be smaller and the invito bigger; in another, the opposite may be true.

In addition to their functions the invito and parry also differ in the fact that the invito can be seen as a final position while the parry is part of a process.

Invitos can be taken up either in the prone or supine position. Invitos in the supine position include fourth, sixth, seventh and eighth; those in the prone position are first, second, third and fifth. The supine fourth invito corresponds to the prone fifth, the sixth to the third, the seventh to the first and the eighth to the second.

In two of the pairings, fourth/fifth and sixth/third, the blade points upward; in the other two, eighth/second and seventh/first, it points downward.

When the hand is held in the supine invitos, the arm is more extended and the blade more horizontal than when the hand is in the prone positions.

iii. The relation of the blades
The relation of the fencers' blades is described in terms of the positions of the opposing weapons at the time. From this the following possibilities arise:
(a) Both fencers can take up the same position, with the blades:
- on-guard in the same or different positions,
- in line in the same or different lines,
- in invito in the same or different positions.

(b) Both fencers can take up different positions:
- one in on-guard, the other in line,
- one in on-guard, the other in invito,
- one in line, the other in invito.

When the blades make contact, the fencers are standing with blades engaged, in an engaged position neither fencer can dominate the other's blade since no substantial difference exists between the lever arms. In the engagement the contact is made either with the feeble or the middle of the blade.

In a situation where a fencer binds the opponent's blade, however, his weapon dominates the other one. This is done by exerting pressure with the forte or middle of the blade, the choice depending on the fencing distance, to carry the opponent's blade out of its on-guard position or line.

Relations of the blades are fleeting because they are constantly changing and being modified by the two fencers for tactical reasons. Relations of the blades, therefore, must be treated as a variable factor in practice, except in the initial phase of training.

iv. The target area
The fencing target in foil is restricted to the fencer's body and is the most limited of the three weapons. In theory it is divided into four quadrants by dissecting the chest with a horizontal and a vertical line which intersect in the middle of the body. This creates two upper and two lower areas, and two inside and two outside areas.

When the teaching of the parries begins, each individual position is thought of as defending a specific area of the fencing target. All this is simply understood as a theoretical consideration which is only partly in actual practice.

The final position of a parry does, in fact, cover one of the four areas of the fencing target. This, however, does not mean that their only purpose is to deflect thrusts directed at the particular area which they cover.

In contrast to sabre fencing, the parry in foil is not merely a final position but a movement process which performs defensive functions. It is not enough, therefore, for the parry to close the plane threatened by an attack. The attacking blade must be deflected from the threatened area by an active movement.

106

It is obvious that the logic which dictates the whys and wheres of attacks and parries is not solely determined by areas of the target. Arbitrarily dividing up the front of the target and considering the parries as mere positions can lead to some very simplistic conclusions. The directing of attacks to particular areas and the association of parries with respective areas is more important theoretically than practically.

The vulnerability of an area to attack is determined in practice by the situation at the moment, the position of the blades and the fencer's body, the fencing distance and tactical considerations. The fencer's blade may be positioned outside or inside, high or low, in relation to the opponent's weapon; but this does not necessarily mean that the blade is pointed towards the corresponding area of the fencing target.

If the body is turned sideways, a comparatively narrower target is presented and the dimensions considerably reduced, with part of target pulled out of range of attack. Other areas of the target, however, may be exposed. There is no doubt, then, that the vulnerability of particular areas of the target does not always remain the same, nor is an area equally vulnerable from every fencing distance.

Following the principle of attacking along the shortest possible line between two points, the fencer normally executes his thrust to the open target area closest to him. For example, from medium distance, the most frequently occurring distance in foil fencing, he does not try to score a hit on the upper and lower areas of the inside target.

The situation naturally changes if the fencing distance is reduced, if at close quarters, or if the body position changes to facilitate the use of special or infrequently used thrusts. On such occasions, the fencing target literally expands to include areas which usually lie too far away, at unfavourable angles, or are protected by the opponent's blade.

FIG. 100

Fig. 100 shows the target areas to which attacks are directed most frequently because they are less easily defended and the probability of scoring a hit is greater. In a lesson, thrusts are usually aimed at the upper/outer or lower/outer areas of the target.

107

v. The fencing line and fencing distance

The fencing line (see Fig. 101) is the imaginary line which:

FIG. 101

● connects the fencer's heels if he is practising on his own,

● connects the four heels of two people (coach and student or two competitors) facing each other.

It follows that the front foot should be made to sense the fencing line as early as possible in his training. In practice sessions it can be drawn on the floor, or lines already there can represent it. The student must learn not only to stand on this line but also to stick to it as much as possible within the limitations imposed in actual combat.

Moving off the fencing line leads to several technical errors by beginners. It may cause the blade to deviate in an unfavourable direction, dissipate energy mobilized for a quick lunge, reduce the strength available for correctly carrying the body weight and cause it to shift, rock the student off balance which is compensated for by unnecessary movements with the arms and body.

Fencing distance can be divided into three categories: short, medium and long distance. The way to measure the fencing distance is based on a unit comprised of the length of the fencer's arm and weapon, plus the footwork needed to overcome any distance beyond the limit of the outstretched arm.

Short distance is the distance within which the fencer can reach the opponent with his weapon by extending his arm. Medium distance, often called practice distance in foil, is the distance within which the fencer can reach the opponent with his weapon by extending his arm and lunging. Long distance is the distance within which the fencer must use compound footwork and extended arm to reach the opponent with his weapon.

It follows from the above that there are no absolute units for measuring fencing distance. Its measurements and standardization are only made in relative terms.

The individual talents of each fencer make for individual measures of distance. This can cause problems for the student when he begins to engage in bout fencing, but the teaching of distance is no easy job for the coach either.

Keeping the same distance in the early stage of training is the precondition not only for the correct execution of an action but also for forming and developing

108

the student's sense of distance. To reach the level where he can sense and overcome varying distances, the student must learn in a concrete situation how to properly assess distance.

Fencing distance, then, has a major role to play not only in combat but also in training. A coach with a finely tuned sense of distance, who knows his student's disposition at the moment, can make slight compensations in the distance on occasion, always keeping in mind the objectives of training and practice and that distance can be optimal, realistic or excessive.

If the coach wants to assist the student in correctly executing an action, or to reduce the load on a competitor who is returning after an injury or illness, he stands closer than usual in order to shorten the distance. If the desired effect is to have the student extend himself, the coach stands farther away than usual. In working with beginners, the distance described as realistic is used in most instances.

The coach should avoid varying the distance, even in the slightest, when working with beginners. Training with variations of distance included only takes place after the students have acquired a solid technical foundation.

The teaching of thrusts begins from medium distance. The movements are then executed from long distance. Practising thrusts from short distance with only the extension of the arm comes only at the last stage.

Although logic would presumably favour working in the normal sequence, the use of the order of distances recommended in training is as above for the following reasons:

(a) In actual combat, few if any attacks are executed from short distance. Most thrusts are delivered from medium distance.

(b) A thrust from medium distance clearly demonstrates that the hit is scored by the hand with the weapon, but that the foot is the supporting agent in the blade's progress to the target if the limbs are adequately co-ordinated.

(c) If a beginner learns to thrust from short distance, he may not push the point of the blade forward immediately, but rather develop the habit of first lifting the arm and shoulder. He may also commit the added error of leaning in the direction of the thrust. These faults can be avoided when executing thrusts from medium distance.

There are some coaches who consider the thrust executed with a step forward as the first stage, the logical antecedent to the thrust executed with lunge. This, however, runs counter to reality because, under actual conditions, no fencing distance exists which is covered by a step nor any thrust like the one asked for in the above manner of execution. It is another matter if such a method is used during a competitive warm-up in a sequence of lengthening distance or in reducing the load on a competitor in the lesson.

In addition to the three fencing distances described above, there is a fourth one mentioned in fencing literature. It is called close distance, and is the distance within which the fencer at close quarters can score a hit only by bending the arm before executing a short thrust because that is the only way to place the blade in front of, above or below the target. Beginners need only know what close distance is, not how to operate at such a distance.

vi. Determination of the direction of movement

In fencing, direction is described in comparative terms. Comparisons can take into account the fencing line, the chest or back of the fencer as the front and back fencing target, the arm holding the foil or the free arm and the situation of the weapon to which directions are related.

The terms forward and backward are related to the fencing line the direction denoted corresponding to the relationship of that line and the fencer's position.

The terms upper and lower refer to areas of the fencing target lying above or below an imaginary line drawn horizontally across the body.

The terms outward and inward denote the movements of the foil either in the direction of the chest or back of the fencer, as the words indicate.

Finally, the terms outside and inside describe directions always related to the position of the blade.

V.3. The initial, on-guard and resting positions

These three positions are taken up standing along the fencing line.

The initial position (see Fig. 102) is that in which the fencer salutes his opponent

FIG. 102

or coach (see Fig. 103), before and after the bout or lesson.

In the initial position, the two feet are placed at right angles with the heels in contact (see Fig. 104). The body is turned without straining to face along the plane lying parallel with the fencing line and the weight is evenly distributed on both feet.

In the on-guard position, the feet are spread apart and the legs bent at the knees to the extent that the fencer remains stable and mobile. Although the criteria of

110

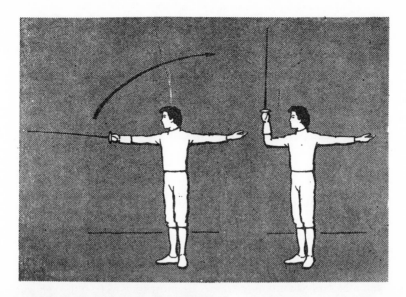

FIG. 103

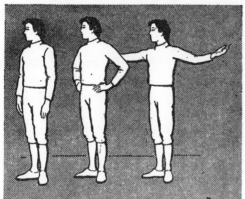

FIG. 104

FIG. 105

stability and mobility seem to contradict each other, they can be harmonized in practice by using the following form without distorting any of its elements.

With the feet spread at an ideal distance, about two foot lengths apart, the legs bent at the knees so that the front knee is placed above the front foot and the rear knee is over the toes of the rear foot. In this position the legs and floor form a pentagon. Any further bending of the knees distorts the pentagon and pushes the knees ahead of the specified lines (see Fig. 105).

The knees must not turn inward. If the front knee deviates inwardly from the fencing line, actions move in the wrong direction.

If the rear knee turns inward in relation to the line perpendicular to the fencing line, it resembles a spring which has been stretched. Even if this does not cause any particular problem in the execution of the lunge, it most certainly may bring about some technical and dynamic distortions in the recovery to the on-guard

111

position. A knee held incorrectly is prevented from bending properly in an oblique backward direction and thus results in an insufficient capacity to pull.

Reformers of the classic on-guard position object to the position of the rear knee on mechanical grounds. They argue that it is unnatural and excessive from a technical point of view to push the knee as far back as possible, and has negative effects in terms of the required effort.

It is their opinion that placing the rear knee in a natural position has both technical and dynamic advantages. With the knee so placed the body can be moved more easily and without delay which, after all, are preconditions for speed and acceleration.

Despite the above arguments it is advised that beginners be taught to hold their rear knees in a slightly exaggerated position. As their movements gradually become more natural and are done with increasing case, the rear knee automatically finds its own most appropriate and convenient position without the coach needing to call any attention to it.

The fencer cannot simply stand on the floor. He must stick to it as though some adhesive were on his shoes. Such a grip on the floor is essential not only for stability but also for mobility; that is, for quickly starting or stopping a movement. The weight is held evenly on both legs.

The body rests naturally on the legs. The plane formed by the shoulders and hips is turned 25° to 30° from the fencing line.

For beginners the line of the shoulders should be horizontal, running parallel to the floor.

The free arm, without the weapon, is held in a natural position. There is no advantage to be gained in pulling the rear shoulder too far back.

Keeping the hand, wrist and fingers of the free arm as relaxed as possible is necessary in order to have an effortless, natural on-guard position and to avoid any signalling of the fencer's intention in advance of his movement.

The fencer also holds his head in a natural position, looking in the direction of the opponent.

The arm holding the weapon is bent at the elbow with the forearm raised and the elbow about one hand's width in front of the hip. The blade is held so that it points slightly upward and toward the opponent's target; that is, with the fist held inside and the elbow outside the fencing line, and the point of the blade deviating inside the fencing line. The hand can be either in supination or in pronation.

When taking up the on-guard position the fencer can easily conform to the requirements listed above. In the course of action, however, it is obvious that to observe those requirements to the letter is impossible since the on-guard position is subordinate to other rules governing the initiation of movements from that position. Any changes of deviations, however, should only be temporary and done in an obviously natural way without disclosing the fencer's next move or intention to the opponent.

112

The constantly changing conditions in a bout, the direction, objective and intensity of a movement can cause changes in the distance between the feet and depth of the body in the on-guard position. Usually the fencer instinctively shortens his stance to increase mobility. In riposting after parrying an attack he normally widens his stance and lowers his body. For such reasons, then, the on-guard position cannot be seen as a standard, inflexibly regular and uniform one.

For each fencer and for every bout situation there exists an optimal, characteristic depth for the body in the on-guard position. It should be held in such a way that the angles at the knees correspond most favourably with the objective of the movement to be executed. In other words, the on-guard position allows the fencer to retain his capacity to act over a long period and without any specific exertion or tendency to stiffen up, and thus always be ready to respond with just the necessary effort.

An on-guard position in which the feet are widely spread and the body correspondingly lower satisfies a need for stability. One in which the feet are closer together and the body correspondingly higher meets the desire for greater mobility. The spread of the feet and the depth of the body, and their relationship, often characterize the style of a fencer; that is, they express whether he is an offensively or defensively oriented personality by nature.

As the fencer moves, his centre of gravity constantly changes position. As a rule, it moves forward or backward according to the movement of the feet. The change in position of the centre of gravity is either a precondition to or a consequence of keeping the fencing distance. A beginner has a difficult time in concealing his intended movement even if he concentrates fully in trying to hide it from the opponent. The smooth and continuous movement of an experienced competitor, however, totally conceals any element which might expose his intention and, to the outsider, the centre of gravity seems to rest equally on both legs without shifting in the least.

It is essential that on-guard position be stable, to provide balance as well as maximum mobility. The on-guard position must allow both forward and backward movements to begin without delay and without revealing the intention to the opponent. It should leave the fencer's muscles in as relaxed a state as possible at all times and limit the danger of their stiffening up. If the above conditions prevail, the on-guard position feels like a natural and unavoidable state of existence.

The classic on-guard serves as the norm to which the student aspires in the course of his training, trying to achieve the maximum development of his abilities, qualities and the conditions necessary to an appropriate on-guard. As the student progresses, personal qualities and anatomical structure have to be considered as factors influencing and moulding individual style. Modern pedagogy recognizes that individual circumstances and abilities play a role in the final determination of the on-guard position.

i. Considerations in teaching the on-guard position

The teaching of the on-guard position can be given in the traditional sequence; that is, following the teaching of the initial position. It can, however, be taught before the initial position. The latter is the more recent approach.

In the traditional method the student takes up the on-guard in two steps on the command of the coach. When the coach says "On-guard position one", the student places his front foot about two foot lengths ahead of the rear foot with the front leg extended and the toes raised. On the command "On-guard two", the student bends both legs and lowers the body to the proper on-guard position, with the front foot being brought energetically to the floor, making an audible noise.

Because the above method:
- makes it difficult to spread the weight evenly on the two legs,
- prevents, or makes it practically impossible, for the soles to make vigorous contact with the floor,

some coaches think it is better for the student to take up the on-guard position which is so essential to fencing in a single motion from the initial position with the sole landing softly on the floor simultaneously with the bending of the student's knees.

Traditionally it was thought best that the fencer place his free hand on the rear hip in the first stages of learning. Today many coaches let the student in on-guard position hang their free arm in a natural, relaxed position alongside the body. This keeps the shoulder girdle in a relaxed state and not bound up as frequently results when the hand is held on the hip. The leg can still move freely since it works independently and thus the on-guard with relaxed free arm position satisfies the need for co-ordinated yet independent action of arm and leg. If the arms are held at shoulder height with palms facing up in the initial position, they are lowered into position as the on-guard is taken up. If the arms are held naturally alongside the body, they are raised into the necessary position. Practice without weapon in hand should not last too long.

If the teaching of the on-guard precedes the teaching of the initial position, the method used is as follows.

The student stands with legs straddled, the feet parallel and a distance of almost two foot lengths apart. Both legs are then bent at the knees with the body remaining erect and the front foot is turned, with toes raised, to point in the same direction as the shoulder on the same side. The head then turns to face the opponent, initially, the arms can be held in a natural way alongside the body or the rear hand may be placed on the rear hip. Having practised this sequence several times, the student then can, from the initial position, step forward with the front foot to assume the on-guard in one motion. This is done by simultaneously bending the rear leg in the initial position as the front foot advances and the appropriate position of the arms is taken up.

To ensure that the weight is evenly distributed on both legs, the following

114

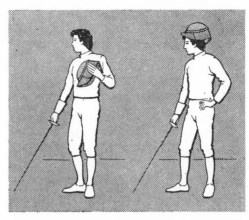

FIG. 106

inductive exercise is recommended. In the on-guard position, straighten the legs to stand on tiptoe and then bend the legs to resume the starting position.

The resting position, the third position in the terminology of fencing, no longer needs to be taken up in so inflexible and strict a manner as before, even in group training situations. Instead, students should be told to relax the muscles and, while some new element is being explained, they should be left to choose the resting position which best relaxes them rather than being told how to stand by the coach (see Fig. 106).

V.4. Foil actions

i. The straight thrust (see Fig. 107)
This is the first action to be learned. It should be practised more than any other action because what appears the simplest of attacking actions is in fact the most

FIG. 107

difficult to execute continuously, with the movements of the arm and feet co-ordinated, at maximum speed and yet concealing the start of the action from the opponent as long as possible.

If beginners learn the fundamentals of the straight thrust, how to initiate it, to co-ordinate the arm and feet and to secure the point as it hits, either using a target or in group training, fewer problems arise in the course of fencing lessons.

Once the point of the blade is directed into the fencing line, the blade approaches the target along a trajectory parallel with and above the fencing line, deviations due to how the foil is assembled and held and the angle needed to hit the target with certainty being taken into consideration. The point of the blade and the guard travel along two different planes while covering the distance to the target. A beginner told to hold his elbow close to the body with the hand and guard lying slightly to the outside and the point lying slightly lower and inward, roughly in the plane of the elbow, does not find it difficult to visualize how to move the blade forward parallel to the plane nor to execute such an action in practice.

When the fencer holds the weapon in the on-guard position with the point very elevated and outside the fencing line, he must be sure to bring the point into a line falling inside the guard when the arm is directed along the fencing line. The same conditions apply when the straight thrust is executed from invito.

The straight thrust is directed towards the opponent's chest at the level of his armed hand. Shorter fencers and beginners may direct the thrust a little lower on the target area.

The blade advances along an unborken line as though the hand, elbow and point of the weapon are pushing something in front of the point towards the target. Hand, elbow and point are held in a horizontal straight line.

The arm holding the weapon is extended before lunging, much in the same way as used in shooting; that is, taking aim precedes the squeezing of the trigger.

The front leg helps to push the point forward just as gunpowder propels a bullet to the target. This analogy often makes it easier for the student to visualize and acquire the correct movement.

On completion of the thrust, the hand holding the weapon finishes slightly to the outside so as to allow the student a sightline to the target along the inside edge of the guard.

A common error among beginners is the tendency to push harder than necessary on the point. This can usually be ascribed to the fact that the movement of the feet does not finish with the arrival of the hit, and the motion in the lunge which is downward and forward continues to press the point on despite the fact that it has already reached the target. This results in a movement which seems to be looking for support or something to lean on, which distorts the distance, the fencer's sense of distance and technique, expecially where this forcing action concludes with the rear foot being dragged forward as is very often the case.

The point must reach the target a split second before the heel of the front foot lands on the floor at the end of the lunge. The contact of the point on the target should cause the student to end his action and apply no more than the needed pressure in the final stage of the thrust.

Usually coaches begin teaching how to smoothly co-ordinate the hand and feet in a phase-by-phase way, using the involved limbs. The lunge begins only after the arm holding the weapon has been completely extended. This is the method used in most instances.

For the student who senses instinctively the natural co-ordination of hand and feet with the foot actually starting to move before the arm holding the weapon has been totally extended, there is no reason to separate the action into phases. The movement is executed slowly in a single motion and the coach gives a verbal cue at the moment when the movements of the arm and feet should be smoothly linked.

If the coach takes up an invito position and does not cue the student when to lunge, the moment to initiate the movement is left to the student. This method promotes practice in the student's own tempo and should be used to practise the straight thrust following adequate physical preparation and thorough explanation.

If the coach wishes to give the student a signal on which to initiate the lunge, he may choose one of two ways; taking tempo from the hand or from the foot.

Tempo taken from the hand may be presented by the coach:

- making contact with the student's blade and then releasing it to take up an invito position,
- taking up different invito positions in alternation.

In the latter, the coach must use cutovers with the blade well elevated when changing positions in order to avoid any contact with the student's weapon.

To give tempo from the feet, the coach uses exaggerated steps, movements which are quite striking, in which both the size and duration differ from the usual. The student must take advantage of the inertia thus created. The thrust starts when the coach's front foot leaves the floor and hits before the coach's front foot lands after the step forward. Only in this way can the principle of taking a tempo from the foot be satisfied in practice.

In teaching the execution of the straight thrust on a tempo from the foot, the distance between coach and student is a fairly long one. The step forward reduces it to medium distance. Once the student can execute straight thrusts from medium distance, he practises the movement from long distance. In the final analysis the student must execute the movement after properly assessing the distance. At this stage the coach varies the distance from the student so that the student uses the necessary footwork to cover the prevailing distance.

The most difficult situation occurs when the student must execute the thrust while trying to maintain the distance between himself and the coach when they both are in motion.

ii. The change thrust

The change thrust (disengagement) is used to carry out an attack on the exposed target area lying closest to the fencer after releasing the blade from the opponent's blade which has initiated an engagement to discover, prepare or disguise an action, and passing the point around the opponent's guard.

The forward spiralling movement which characterizes the change thrust must be executed in different ways suited to different situations. At long distance, the fencer's blade only has to pass around the opponent's weapon. At medium distance, the blade has to pass the opponent's hand and the guard of his weapon. At close distance, the blade may even have to pass around the opponent's arm.

The greater the distance between the fencers, the more the blade must advance at the outset of the change thrust; that is, the arm holding the weapon extends in the initial stage. On the other hand, at shorter distances the rounding movement starts earlier. At long distance, the rounding movement begins when the arm is extended; at medium or close distance, the arm extends when the blade is rounding the opponent's weapon. When the distance is short, the first thing to do is to release the blade from the opponent's engagement. At long distance, the blade can and should advance even if engaged. Both variations can be used when at medium distance.

In rounding the opponent's weapon, the blade travels varying distance depending on the circumstances. The rounding movement is greatest when releasing from engagements in first and fourth positions, and shortest from sixth and eighth.

The change thrust can be executed in two ways. In one, the opponent's weapon is rounded completely. The blade travelling horizontally and the hit landing on the opposite side of the opponent's engaging blade (see Fig. 108). In the other,

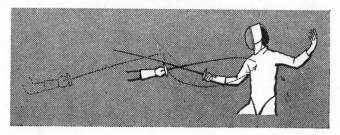

FIG. 108

the rounding movement travels vertically in an upward or downward direction, and the blade therefore need not completely round the opponent's weapon. The hit lands either from above, from eighth engagement, or from below, from sixth engagement, in relation to the opponent's blade (see Fig. 109). The former is used more frequently from fourth and first engagements; the latter, from sixth and eighth.

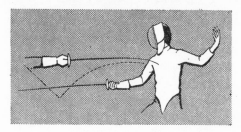

FIG. 109

Naturally, the rounding movement can be executed vertically from the fourth and first engagements, but this option is used less frequently than the horizontal one. For the vertical movement to be effective the fourth engagement must be fairly high and the first engagement low.

The change thrust starts downward from the two upper engagements and upward from the two lower engagements. In finishing the change thrust from the upper engagements, the fencer must consciously and actively lift the point of the weapon. Failure to do so results in the blade's being blocked in the rounding movement.

The situation reverses when rounding a lower engagement. Here the fencer must emphasize the lifting of the blade in a semicircular motion in the first stage of the movement.

In executing a change thrust from medium distance the same considerations apply in co-ordinating the movements of hand and feet as in executing the straight thrust. In the change thrust from long distance the blade advances in the first stage of the step forward past the opponent's engaging weapon and the rounding movement finishes as the rear foot completes the step forward. In the case of advanced fencers or competitors the rounding movement can be delayed and completed with the lunge.

The change thrust can be executed from simple contact of the blades and from engagement. At the start the rounding movement should be taught from simple contact. This is followed by rounding attempted engagements which present increasingly difficult obstacles.

When the coach makes simple contact, which gradually develops into an engagement, with the student's blade, the student must execute the change thrust on cue; that is, in tempo taken from the hand. The change thrust should start the moment the student senses through his blade the coach's attempted engagement.

iii. The cutover (see Fig. 110)

The cutover also rounds the opponent's weapon but, unlike the change thrust, passes above the point of the blade and not around the guard.

Used as an attack, the cutover should start only from an elevated fourth or

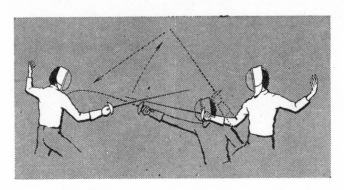

FIG. 110

sixth contact or engagement. Teaching should begin from simple contact. From sixth, the hit should land on the upper part of the opponent's target; from fourth, it may arrive in either the upper or lower target areas.

The cutover can be executed either by lifting the point over or sliding it along to pass over the opponent's weapon.

From medium distance, both forearm and wrist are used in the movement. From long distance, the wrist plays the primary role in execution. At close distance, the trajectory of the attacking blade follows a wider path.

When the cutover comes from medium distance, the lunge starts when the arm is about three-quarters extended as it returns to a horizontal position parallel to the fencing line. From long distance, the attacking blade advances in the engaged line as the front foot begins the step forward and passes over to the other side of the opponent's weapon with the movement of the rear foot.

In the cutover, the blade moves in a plane parallel with the opponent's sixth or fourth position, except if it is executed with a sliding action. If directed to the lower part of the target, the cutover resembles the flank cut in sabre, with the movement of the elbow playing the critical role.

iv. Parries

The parry may be defined as an action which deflects an attacking blade from the target at the exact moment and with a sudden but sure movement of either the middle or the forte of the blade.

Parries can be either supine or prone, depending on the position of the fencer's hand. They can be classified in terms of duration, the longer ones being called opposition parries and the shorter ones, beat parries.

The following parries are determined by hand position and their location:
- fourth (or fifth),
- sixth (or third),
- eighth (or second),
- seventh (or first).

The above pairs of parries are identical in terms of location, but differ in hand position. Those in brackets are held in a prone hand position.

Parries can be categorized by distance covered and method of execution as:
- simple parries,
- semicircular parries,
- diagonal parries,
- circular parries,
- ceding parries.

It is impossible to define absolutely the final position of a parry which would apply to every possible situation. Depending on the fencing distance and the type and direction of attack, the parry may be executed with more or less extended arm and with the blade more or less elevated. All that the theory can offer is a general description and certain guidelines which should always be considered.

Modifications needed for particular situations can only be determined in actual practice.

One general theoretical guideline, for example, concerns the parry done at close quarters. At such times, it is insufficient to form the defence only along the line being threatened. The entire plane must be closed and access to one side completely blocked. This means that the location of the parry must change in every respect, the upper line parries being executed at a lowered level and the lower line parries in a raised position, partly to make a successful defence and partly to create favourable conditions for a riposte.

A parry can be deemed successful if it offers a secure defence of the target and allows the easy and quick execution of a riposte once the parry has been formed. The latter, in addition to expressing the logical unity and interdependence of parry and riposte, sets the allowable tolerances in which the parry may exceed the lateral limits of the actual width of the target.

Another basic principle insists that the parry or any defensive action be executed as far in front of the target as possible. This not only cuts the angle to the target and blocks the path of a thrust more immediately, but also requires a less intensive lateral movement and permits a quicker execution of the riposte.

In the opposition parry, the forte of the blade and the guard combine to block the path of the opponent's advancing weapon. It is used to protect the target against attacks which have gained a certain momentum or which have been divined in advance. Used at the last possible moment, it prevents the opponent from rounding the defending weapon. The strength of the parry is inherent in the difference between the lever arms of the two blades.

Beat parries are used to destroy attacks. This is done by using a beat, similar to an attack on the blade, just as the anticipated attacking action of the opponent begins. The strength of the parry depends on where the beat strikes the opponent's blade.

Two pairs of parries protect the fencing target against attacks to the upper area and two protect the lower target areas.

The fourth, sixth, eighth and seventh parries are executed with the hand in a supine position. For fifth, third, second and first parries, the hand is held in a

FIG. 111

121

prone position. The high sixth and seventh combination used to parry cutovers is executed with the hand in a prone position (see Fig. 111). Whether the hand is held in supine or prone position, the parry must deflect the attack with the edge of the blade.

a. Description of the positions and paths of the various parries
The location of a parry in its final position is related to:
- the position of the hand,
- the distance of the arm and elbow from the body,
- the direction in which the forearm lies,
- the direction in which the blade points,
- the lateral deviation of the blade in relation to the fencer's body,
and can be described in terms of the above.

(1) FOURTH PARRY. The arm is bent at the elbow and held one hand's width from the body at the level of the bottom of the rib-cage. The hand lies in a vertical plane at the inside limits of the body. The blade is directed forward and upward with the point held approximately at eye level. The point may deviate outside the horizontal line from the eye by about one hand's width.

(2) FIFTH PARRY. Fifth parry is similar to fourth except that the hand is held in a prone position. The resulting rotation causes the blade to lie more horizontally with the point lower and more outward. The hand lies in the same vertical plane as in fourth parry.

(3) SIXTH PARRY. Sixth parry is held at a higher level than fourth parry and the arm is more extended. In sixth, the elbow is held in front of and at the level of the hip. The blade continues in the line of the forearm and is directed forward and upward. The hand along with the guard is raised almost level with the shoulder and the point is held at approximately eye level. The point may deviate outside the horizontal line from the eye by about one hand's width.

(4) THIRD PARRY. Third parry is the prone counterpart of sixth parry. It differs due to the rotation of the arm resulting in the elbow being more bent and the hand lower with the blade more elevated and the point directed forward and upward. The point lies at eye level and should not deviate horizontally from the line of the eye by more than a hand's width.

(5) EIGHTH PARRY. The arm is bent at the elbow, which is one hand's width in front of and level with the hip. The hand is held outside the line of the elbow with the point directed slightly inward. The blade points forward and downward in a line through the forearm which is broken at the wrist.

(6) SECOND PARRY. Second parry is the prone counterpart of eighth parry. The hand is held one hand's width below the horizontal line from the shoulder. The elbow is bent and lies outside and above the hand. The point is directed forward and downward one hand's width below and outside the horizontal line from the hip. Arm and blade form a slightly bent arc.

(7) SEVENTH PARRY. The arm is slightly bent at the elbow and is directed forward, inside and slightly downward. The hand is held in the plane of the inside limit of the body with the elbow at the level of the bottom of the rib-cage. The blade slopes downward through a bending of the wrist.

(8) FIRST PARRY. First parry is the prone counterpart of seventh parry. The arm is bent at the elbow and placed horizontally in front of the body. The hand is level with and in line with the opposite shoulder and the wrist bent in the direction of the palm. The blade points steeply forward and downward.

The parries can be executed:
● in a horizontal plane (direct parry); that is, remaining in the same line (upper or lower) but on the opposite side,
● in a vertical plane (semicircular parry), that is, changing line but remaining on the same side,
● diagonally (diagonal parry); that is, changing line and side,
● in a circular motion (circular parry); that is, leaving but returning to the original position.

The following illustrations help to show the execution of the different parries with the hand held in a supine position. Naturally, the parries can be done in much the same manner with the hand held in a prone position.

(1) DIRECT PARRIES
● Sixth from fourth, and fourth from sixth (Fig. 112),
● eighth from seventh, and seventh from eighth (Fig. 113).

FIG. 112

FIG. 113

(2) SEMICIRCULAR PARRIES

● Seventh from fourth, and fourth from seventh (Fig. 114),
● eighth from sixth, and sixth from eighth (Fig. 115).

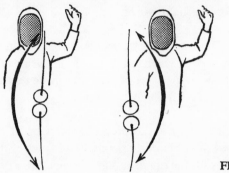

FIG. 114   FIG. 115

(3) DIAGONAL PARRIES

● Eighth from fourth, and fourth from eighth (Fig. 116),
● seventh from sixth, and sixth from seventh (Fig. 117).

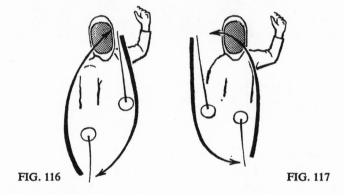

FIG. 116   FIG. 117

(4) CIRCULAR PARRIES

● Circular fourth (Fig. 118a), circular sixth (Fig. 118b),
● circular eighth (Fig. 118c), circular seventh (Fig. 118d).

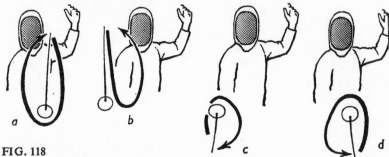

FIG. 118

The various parries can be executed as follows:
- from fourth invito: direct sixth, semicircular seventh, diagonal eighth, circular fourth,
- from sixth invito: direct fourth, semicircular eighth, diagonal seventh, circular sixth,
- from eighth invito: direct seventh, semicircular eighth, diagonal fourth, circular eighth,
- from seventh invito: direct eighth, semicircular fourth, diagonal sixth, circular seventh.

The ceding, or yielding, parries are a particular method of execution used against bind thrusts. The hand makes a funnel-like movement as the two blades remain in contact with the point of contact acting as the tip of the funnel. The blade and point begin to move in a direction opposite than in which the hand acts in executing its funnel-like action.

The ceding parries are:
- ceding high seventh or first parry against sixth bind thrust,
- ceding low fourth parry against eighth or second bind thrust.

Against fencers holding the foil in the opposite hand, ceding high seventh is used against fourth bind thrust and ceding fourth parry against seventh bind thrust. When executed as a ceding parry, the fourth parry, which is in principle an upper line parry, is used against attacks in the lower line. The seventh parry, usually a lower line parry, is used as ceding parry against attacks in the upper line.

v. Ripostes and counter-ripostes

The fencer who is under attack executes a parry in order to regain the right to make a counter-offensive action which takes the form of a riposte. The riposte must follow a successful parry immediately, although the delayed riposte may be used as a tactical variation.

Ripostes can be either simple or compound. They can be executed either with the release of or while remaining in contact with the opponent's blade. The latter are bind thrust and flanconade ripostes.

Simple ripostes include straight and change ripostes, cutover ripostes, bind thrusts and flanconade ripostes.

(1) SIMPLE RIPOSTES FROM FOURTH PARRY

Against an opponent who holds the weapon in the same hand as the fencer, simple ripostes from fourth parry include:
- straight thrusts to the upper area of the target,
- bind thrusts to the upper area of the target,
- flanconade thrusts to the flank of the opponent,
- change thrusts to the upper outside area of the target if the opponent reacts to take up a fourth parry,

- cutovers to the upper area of the target if the opponent reacts to take up a fourth parry,
- cutovers to the lower area of the target or the flank.

Against an opponent who holds the weapon in the opposite hand, they include:
- bind thrusts to the upper area of the target,
- change thrusts to the opponent's flank,
- cutovers to the upper area of the target if the opponent reacts to take up a sixth parry,
- cutovers to the lower area of the target.

(2) SIMPLE RIPOSTES FROM SIXTH PARRY

Against an opponent who holds the weapon in the same hand as the fencer, simple ripostes from sixth parry include:
- bind thrusts to the upper area of the target,
- change thrusts to the lower area of the target,
- cutovers to the upper area of the target if the opponent reacts to take up a sixth parry.

Against an opponent who holds the weapon in the opposite hand, they include:
- straight thrusts to the upper area of the target,
- straight thrusts to the lower area of the target done in pronation,
- bind thrusts to the opponent's flank,
- cutovers to the upper area of the target if the opponent reacts to take up a fourth parry,
- cutovers to the lower area of the target.

(3) SIMPLE RIPOSTES FROM EIGHTH PARRY

Against an opponent who holds the weapon in the same hand as the fencer, simple ripostes from eighth parry include:
- bind thrusts to the lower area of the target,
- change thrusts to the upper area of the target.

Against an opponent who holds the weapon in the opposite hand, they include:
- straight thrusts to the upper area of the target,
- bind thrusts to the upper area of the target.

(4) SIMPLE RIPOSTES FROM SEVENTH PARRY

Against an opponent who holds the weapon in the same hand as the fencer, simple ripostes from seventh parry include:
- straight thrusts to the lower area of the target,
- bind thrusts to the lower area of the target,
- bind thrusts to the upper area of the target,
- change thrusts to the lower outside area of the target if the opponent reacts to take up a seventh parry.

Against an opponent who holds the weapon in the opposite hand, they include:
- bind thrusts to the lower area of the target,

● change thrusts to the upper area of the target if the opponent reacts to take up an eighth parry.

Compound ripostes from the various parries are made up of thrusts which follow simple single feints, circular single feints or simple double feints. In executing compound ripostes, the simple single feints are most often used. The circular single feints and simple double feints are less frequently employed.

Counter-ripostes are, in principle, identical with ripostes. In practice, however, only the simple ripostes usually are employed in the course of a bout as counter-ripostes.

vi. Observations on the teaching of parries, ripostes and counter-ripostes

Only the parries executed in a typical manner need be taught to beginners. The modified versions which are done far in front or close to the body or very low or very high are too difficult for them.

As the students progress, the coach must include instruction in both the supine and prone positions to find which are best suited to them.

Opposition parries should be taught before the beat parries.

Because the opposition parries are analogous from a defensive viewpoint with bind attacks, the simplest way to teach them is through applying pressure to create a counter-pressure reaction. The coach or partner should direct or set a pattern for the movement by applying pressure with the required force and rhythm. This allows an accurate check of the movement and final position through several of the senses.

A similar process can be used to teach the beat parries, with the coach setting the pattern of the movement by executing a preliminary beat.

The teaching of diagonal and circular parries may be effectively aided using blade transfers. The transfer can be executed successfully only if the blade describes a circular movement of fairly large proportion. The constant contact of the blade introduces an element of control, making it difficult for the student to execute the action improperly even if he has an incorrect idea about the movement and inadequate co-ordination. Using this approach helps prevent errors likely to occur in trying to execute diagonal and circular parries solely on the basis of explanation and a few demonstrations on how to locate the blade in the air without some physical intervention or assistance.

Once the individual parries have been learned, the coach can begin to simulate feint attacks to teach the student a wide range of parry combinations. In other words, the student has to develop the ability to execute two or more parries in succession easily, rapidly and within the specified limits. The teaching of combinations can effectively eliminate errors which have previously occurred when attempted parries have met the opponent's half way in the movement and, on encountering this obstacle, have been rendered useless. Such combinations include:

● circular sixth followed by semicircular second,
● circular fourth followed by semicircular seventh,

- circular eighth followed by semicircular sixth,
- circular seventh followed by semicircular fourth.

At first, students should execute parries in a stationary position. Later, they can take a short step backward while parrying. Finally, they learn to parry when closing the distance or while in the lunge. Before being taught these last two forms, the students must learn the modified versions of the various parries; that is, done far from or close to the body, high or low.

The parry executed with a step backward, or a step forward to close the distance, requires a specific co-ordination of the hand and feet. In stepping backward, the parry is taken after the rear foot begins its retreat. With a step forward, the parry starts to form a split second before the front foot begins its advance. The parry taken with a step backward finishes at the same time as the step, the foot which initiates the step acting on its own. A step forward to close the distance is done only behind the cover of a parry already under way. In this instance the fencer holds the final position of the parry longer than usual so that the riposte to follow is secure and the distance has been completely closed.

Ripostes are taught first with a lunge, then from a stationary position and finally with a fleche.

The teaching of compound ripostes with feint follows the teaching of simple ripostes.

The coach should vary the presentation of his blade so that students practise the different varieties of ripostes in succession, either in a predetermined order or at random, and from the same or different parries.

Counter-ripostes can be taught in two ways. In the first, the coach parries the student's thrust. In the second, the coach allows the student's thrust to reach the target and, only afterwards, presents his blade in a way which requires the student to react with a parry followed by a riposte.

vii. Attacks on the blade

An opponent's blade which is held in line must be deflected before the fencer can execute a thrust because such a threat has conventional priority and positional advantage. If not deflected, the fencer might impale himself on it. Attacks on the blade are designed to take the opponent's weapon out of line and can be classified as either binds or beats.

Usually, though not necessarily, binds are used against opponents who tend to hold their weapons firmly or rigidly, thus offering resistance. Beats are more effective against blades which are loosely held.

The bind is an action made with the forte or middle of the blade, depending on the distance, and which catches the feeble of the opponent's blade in order to deflect it. This contact between the blades is maintained for a relatively long time as in the opposition parry and is characterized by a scraping noise caused by the pushing action of the fencer's weapon.

The names of the binds correspond to those of the parries and invitos; they can be identified as fourth, fifth, third, eighth, second, seventh and first binds, respectively.

Binds can be described as the opponent's bind or the fencer's own bind, depending on whose blade has initiated the action.

Theoretically, the bind should take the opponent's weapon completely out of line with the fencer's target. In practice, however, the opponent's blade is rarely deflected one hundred per cent. The fencer's right to attack results not so much from the total completion of the movement but rather because the opponent's blade has been bound to some extent. Judges may disallow or rule against the fencer's attempted bind, but only when it is executed in a manner less than accepted as the norm.

The coach is advised to teach slightly prolonged binds with the blades constantly in contact to beginners.

Beats are executed with an energetic movement. The contact between the two blades, which occurs only at one point, provides a dry, short knock-like sound in contrast to the scraping noise produced by the bind.

Beats, just as binds, are executed with the forte or middle of the blade on the feeble of the opponent's weapon. A beat can be considered successful if it is strong, short, limited and dry.

The conventional advantage of the weapon held in line can only be broken by a beat if it is clearly and noticeably executed with appropriate intensity and power. Executed with a short motion, a beat is virtually impossible for the opponent to avoid or counter. Limited in its movement and stopped at the right position, it allows the fencer to bring his weapon back into an attacking line easily. The term "dry" expresses the fact that contact is made at one point only.

Beats, too, are named in the same fashion as parries and invitos; thus they can be identified as fourth, fifth, sixth, third, eighth, second, seventh and first beats.

Foil rules specify that the fencer is obliged, by beat or bind, to dislodge the opponent's blade in line.

For tactical reasons, however, a competitor is free to use beats and binds against an opponent in on-guard or invito who reveals a certain vulnerability which can be exploited. When used against the neutral on-guard or indefinite invito of the opponent, the beat is designed to loosen the opponent's grip, to open the line to the target and to cause an instinctive reaction on the part of the opponent. Where the opponent's invitos are well-placed and complete, it is not worthwhile to attempt a beat or bind against them.

Beats and binds can be used in combination with each other as well as on their own. Usually the bind is the first element in a combination. The beat preceding the bind is a less frequently used sequence.

Combinations of beats and binds, which may consist of two, three or even more movements, are excellent exercises for developing skills and abilities. They also constitute effective preparations for an attack.

When the opponent holds his weapon in a high line, beats or binds from sixth invito can be executed with:

- direct fourth,
- circular sixth,
- change sixth after a direct fourth contact,
- change fourth after a circular sixth contact.

If the opponent's weapon is in low line, beats or binds from sixth invito can be done with:

- diagonal seventh,
- semicircular eighth,
- change seventh after a semicircular eighth contact,
- change eighth after a diagonal seventh contact.

When the opponent takes a low line, beats or binds from eighth invito can be executed with:

- direct seventh,
- circular eighth,
- change eighth after a direct seventh contact,
- change seventh after a circular eighth contact.

Against the high line of the opponent, binds and beats from eighth invito include:

- semicircular sixth,
- diagonal fourth,
- change sixth after a diagonal fourth contact.

Against a blade held in high line, the fencer can beat or bind from fourth invito with:

- direct sixth,
- circular fourth,
- change fourth after a direct sixth contact,
- change sixth after a circular fourth contact.

When the opponent's blade is held in low line, beats and binds from fourth invito are done with:

- semicircular seventh,
- diagonal eighth,
- change eighth after a semicircular seventh contact,
- change seventh after a diagonal eighth contact.

If the opponent's blade is held in low line, beats of binds from seventh invito include:

- direct eighth,
- circular seventh,
- change seventh after a circular eighth contact,
- change eighth after a circular seventh contact.

Against a high line, beats and binds from seventh invito can be executed with:

- semicircular fourth,

130

- diagonal sixth,
- change sixth after a semicircular fourth contact,
- change fourth after a diagonal sixth contact.

a. Attacks introduced with bind

Attacks introduced with a bind are classified according to their manner of execution as:

- simple binds,
- semicircular binds,
- circular binds,
- change binds,
- transfers,
- bind thrusts,
- flanconades,
- copertinos.

The bind begins by making contact with the opponent's blade. The movement to force it out of line then follows. The advanced fencer may execute the second phase with his blade advancing in the course of the movement. The thrust which follows the completion of the binding action can be straight, change thrust or cutover.

After the bind has deflected the opponent's weapon out of line, the thrust must begin with an oblique movement forward. Only in this way can the bind and subsequent thrust constitute with any certainty an unbroken and continuously advancing process with the various components integrally linked together.

Once the student has learned the individual binds, they can be coupled, with both actions being executed intensely and powerfully and their dynamics and direction being opposite to each other. Many possible transitions exist to link the original contact of the blades to the actual bind.

The use of two successive binds can be done in a continuous, uninterrupted manner. Pauses of varying lengths, however, can be inserted between the two separate actions. In the bind the fencer's blade can be lifted more or less in relation to the opponent's weapon as long as contact is maintained throughout the movement.

The direct, diagonal, semicircular and circular binds move in a manner identical to the corresponding parries and do not have to be discussed here in technical terms. The change binds, transfers, bind thrusts, flanconades and copertines, however, do need special mention.

The change bind is a combination in which the two movements are executed in a circular fashion. The contact between the two blades is momentarily lost while the change is being executed.

The change occurs in the same line, upper or lower, as that of the initial contact; thus the change can be from fourth to sixth or vice versa with the blade passing under the opponent's weapon, or from seventh to eighth or vice versa with the blade passing above the opponent's weapon. It can be executed from the opponent's or fencer's own initial bind or contact.

More often than not the change bind is executed from the fencer's own initial contact. For this reason it should be taught this way before it is taught from the opponent's bind or contact.

If the fencer contacts the opponent's blade with the intention of executing a change bind, he only tries to make contact in the first stage of the combination. To change from one full bind to another is really just dreaming.

The initial bind or contact can be direct, diagonal, semicircular or circular. The following thrust can be a straight or change thrust or a cutover.

After the student has mastered the changing of two consecutive binds, the original combination made up of two elements can be expanded into one composed of three or four stages. The student can insert pauses of varying lengths between individual elements.

Constant change binds are used initially to develop speed. Those done with changes in rhythm and timing promote the development of the student's sense of rhythm. If the latter is executed in combination with keeping the distance, the fencer's sensitivity to and co-ordination of the separate movements of the hand and feet is intensified and developed, and at the same time the ability to divide attention develops. This means that fencing abilities are developed in parallel with technical skills in a comprehensive way.

Transfers are binds which are maintained over a relatively long time using a diagonal or circular movement. Contact between the blades is retained throughout from initial contact to the completion of the transfer.

To execute a transfer successfully, the fencer must have total control of his weapon. The forte of the blade makes contact with the opponent's feeble.

In a diagonal transfer, the blade changes from a high line to a low line, or vice versa. In a circular transfer, however, the blade returns to the original line. Diagonal transfers can be from fourth to eighth and vice versa, or from sixth to seventh and vice versa. Circular transfers follow the same transitions as circular parries and can be in fourth, sixth, eighth and seventh positions.

The initial bind prior to the transfer can be direct, diagonal, semicircular or circular. The thrust which follows the transfer can be a straight or change thrust or a cutover. The wide variety and possible combinations of movements resulting from the above provide a broad range of practice exercises which are colourful and eliminate boredom in training.

Once the separate diagonal and circular transfers have been learned, interesting and exciting combinations can be created to include two or three successive transfers by alternating diagonal and capital movements.

Copertinos are the binds longest in duration and are executed with force. Because the blade finishes farther down the opponent's weapon than it does in other types of binds prior to the thrust, copertinos are best performed in fifth rather than fourth and in third rather than sixth.

132

Bind thrusts are the particular combination of binds and thrusts. Contact between the blades is maintained from the beginning of the bind to the completion of the thrust. The fencer, rather than releasing the opponent's blade after the bind, pushes his weapon forward along the opponent's in the course of the attack, offering opposition with his hand all the time.

The attacking blade must do two things: first, it must keep the opponent's weapon bound and, second, it must execute the thrust while contact is retained. To do this, the attacking blade has to move towards the target and, at the same time, move laterally in the horizontal plane with the point moving forward lying slightly inside the line of the hand. The opponent's blade is thus prevented from reaching the area of the fencer's because it is controlled by the bind and is forced farther out of line by the advance of the attacking blade.

As in the case of transfers, bind thrusts require that the fencer be in complete control of his weapon and that of the opponent.

There are four bind thrusts just as there are four binds, no matter in which hand the fencer holds the weapon. Fourth (Fig. 119) and sixth (Fig. 120) bind

FIG. 119

FIG. 120

thrusts are executed in high line while eighth and seventh (Fig. 121) are done in low line. An excellent lead-up to the second bind thrust is the practice of the thrust with the hand held in second position.

The seventh bind thrust can be done in a high line (Fig. 122) if both fencers hold the weapon in the same hand. If they hold their weapons in the opposite hands, the eighth bind thrust can be executed in high line. The blade does not

FIG. 121

FIG. 122

have to be transferred from seventh to sixth or from eighth to fourth in the above cases. In both instances, the hand remains on the side on which it started, with only the point of the blade being lifted by the wrist to lie over the opponent's blade.

The two outside bind thrusts in sixth and eighth are used frequently when the two fencers hold their weapons in the same hand. Fourth and seventh, the inside bind thrusts, are used more often when the fencers hold their weapons in opposite hands, in the latter, the blades in contact resemble a cross more than in the former.

Flanconade is a bind thrust directed towards the opponent's side. It is done on the same side as the bind but finishes in the opposite line. Where the two fencers hold the weapon in the same hand, the opponent's blade must be transferred or forced from fourth into the low line. If they hold their weapons in opposite hands, the transfer or copertino follows the sixth bind. The binding blade changes from the high to the low line vertically in the plane in which the hand advances. The thrust angles upward with the blade staying parallel to its original line.

Keeping the arm slightly bent at the elbow while attacking helps to locate and hold the hand and arm in the low line and to control the opponent's blade over a relatively long time. Extending the arm can cause the thrust to slip off the target and render the point ineffective through tightness of the muscles, thus negating the fencer's positional superiority.

The blade presentation used in setting the conditions for the student to execute a bind thrust or flanconade is more difficult for the coach than that used in teaching transfers. In exercises for bind thrusts and flanconades, the coach must play several roles including those of:

- an opponent who holds his blade in line too rigidly,
- an opponent whose blade offers resistance but without his arm being stiff or overly contracted.

The resistance offered by the coach through the feeble of his blade provides a track for the execution of the bind thrust, while a slight breaking of the wrist which coincides with the advance of the student's blade ensures the arrival of the hit. This movement deviates from the line of the hit in such a way and at the right moment so as to create the necessary space for the student's point. The coach holds his weapon not quite horizontally in the line of his hand; that is, the hand is held lower than the point when presenting the blade in high line, and higher than the point when presenting the blade in low line.

All the different binds taught or discussed earlier can be done prior to the bind thrusts and flanconades. The ceding or yielding parries are the defensive moves designed to counter bind thrusts.

Ceding parries used to defend against bind thrusts in the high line are executed by lowering the point and, at the same time, raising the hand. Against bind thrusts in the low line, the point is raised and the hand lowered to execute the ceding parries.

The practice of the different parries used against bind thrusts is not easily accomplished in a lesson. This is because the student must be able to present the blade as the coach does when the student practises bind thrusts. He must be able to offer the blade with resistance but without undue rigidity, and with the proper action of the hand in reacting to the bind thrust.

Beats as well as binds can be combined with simple attacks. The following combinations can thus be distinguished:

- beat followed by straight thrust,
- beat followed by change thrust,
- beat followed by cutover.

The beat can be direct, diagonal, semicircular, circular or change beat.

viii. Feints and feint attacks

Feint attacks are called compound attacks. They are composed of the simple elements and movements discussed in the preceding sections.

The feint of a thrust is that most used by a foil fencer. It should be executed in such a suggestive and realistic manner that it draws a parry from the opponent. The fencer then rounds the induced parry to score a hit.

If the fencer rounds only one parry, the attack is a single feint attack. Attacks which round two or more parries are double or multiple feint attacks. In actual practice, double and multiple feint attacks are rarely used.

There is some benefit to be derived from training in the multiple feint attacks even though they are more theoretical than practical. Used in the lesson, they help develop skill and abilities.

The initial action or introduction of the feint can be the simulation of a number of actions, including:

- straight thrust,
- change thrust,
- time degagement thrust,
- cutover,
- cutover degagement thrust,
- bind or beat followed by a thrust.

A defender can react to the feint in several ways depending on the manner of execution of the attack, its location, the initial position of his blade and the relation between the opposing blades. If the attack is in the same line as the invito, the defender is likely to use either a direct or a circular parry. If the attack comes in the line opposite to that of the invito, the most likely parries are the diagonal and semicircular ones. The fencer can only assume what the defensive reaction of the opponent might be, counting on instinctive or habitual movements and reflex parries with which he is already familiar.

The rhythm and duration of a feint or feints is determined by the defender's nervous reaction, his temperament and speed of reaction, and not by the intention of the attacker. If the opponent is passive in nature, only an increasingly progressive attack can draw out defensive reflexes. A more nervous type can be induced to react with the slightest indication or a simulation of a thrust. Obviously, many different types exist between these two extremes.

It is essential that in a feint, the blade approach the target; that is, that the point must advance continuously just as in normal attack. The feint not only poses a threat to the opponent but also helps the fencer close the distance to the target.

The most important element in the feint attack is the time degagement or cutover time degagement thrust. Every feint attack, no matter what type, is based on one of these two actions, or at least a knowledge of them.

Feints can be described and determined accurately by:

- knowing the initial position of the two fencers and the relations between their blades,
- identifying the type of feint used to introduce the attack,
- specifying the line or direction of the final action,
- determining the number and type of parries to be rounded prior to the final thrust,
- specifying in advance the parries to be rounded and from what directions,
- specifying the area of the target to be hit.

Theory is first and foremost for the benefit of the coach and not the amateurs. It is, therefore, unnecessary to confuse students by teaching them complicated definitions.

The coach should simplify matters for the students and communicate this succinct version to them using only basic fencing jargon or, when necessary, terms and phraseology other than the official terminology.

Learning the different technical variations of feint attacks is not that difficult a task for the advanced fencer. What is difficult is the learning, or teaching, of the different types of timing which can be used.

It is extremely difficult to make students sense the slight variations in timing, not unlike the subtle changes in different shades of one colour, and translate them into actual practice.

Teaching should begin with single feint attacks in which each element takes the same time. After being taught with an even rhythm, the action can be executed with different patterns, such as short-short and long-short co-ordinations of the movements.

Once the student has picked up these different methods of timing, practice should begin in executing the movements without the rhythm pattern determined in advance. This develops in the student the idea that the feint attack should never begin with an obvious rhythm which reveals his intention, but that he should choose a timing which certainly misleads the opponent and cannot be seen in advance.

The more elements included in a feint attack, the more complicated the rhythm becomes.

ix. Renewed attacks
Renewed attacks can be executed when the opponent:
- parries the original attack but delays his riposte or fails to riposte,
- parries the original attack but retreats instead of making a riposte,
- withdraws in the face of the attack either with or without parrying.

Renewed attacks differ from initial attacks in several technical aspects. They start from the lunge and not the on-guard position, and the arm is extended, not bent, when the movement is begun.

The footwork which accompanies renewed attacks includes:
- the lengthening of the lunge when the opponent has parried in place or with a short step backward (close distance in terms of renewed attacks),
- renewing the lunge by bringing up the rear foot, or continuing with a fleche from the lunge when the opponent retreats without making a riposte (medium distance in terms of renewed attacks),
- closing distance with a step or jump forward after a forward recovery to on-guard position followed by lunge or fleche when the opponent retreats a great distance (long distance in terms of renewed attacks).

Renewed attacks are most effective when executed with one of the following simple attacking actions:
- change thrust,
- moulinet, or swinging thrust,
- beat followed by straight thrust or change thrust.

If a feint attack is applied as a renewed attack, only a simple single feint attack introduced by a change thrust should be used.

The renewed attacks most often used are the change thrust and moulinet. Beats followed by straight thrust or change thrust, and the simple single feint with change thrust, are executed as renewed attacks only from longer distances. Renewed attacks with beats can be successful not only against the opponent who retreats with his blade in line but also against one who parries but fails to riposte.

Teaching of renewed attacks to intermediate fencers is of limited value. Only the experienced fencer can adopt them successfully.

The riposte, as well as the attack, can be renewed. Preconditions for the execution of a renewed riposte are:

- the opponent delaying or failing to counter-riposte,
- the opponent withdrawing from the fencer's riposte or retreating with or without making a riposte.

Footwork which accompanies a renewed riposte usually consists of a lunge, the lengthening of the lunge, fleche from on-guard position, fleche after a step forward or fleche from the lunge.

Change thrust or cutover are the most commonly used actions employed as renewed ripostes.

x. Counter-attacks (actions built on tempo)

The counter-attack can be described as an active defensive action, the combination of attack and defence.

A counter-attack is successful if:

- the timing is correct; that is, it precludes the opponent's attack by at least one fencing time,
- the thrusting action also acts as a parry, blocking the path of the opponent's blade to the target. (This applies to both the location and the technical execution of the counter-attack.)

Counter-attacks can be simple or compound. They can be executed with simple feint, with or without making contact with the opponent's blade and with any movements which start in a simple way.

Simple variations of the counter-attack are:

- the direct counter-attack, done while the opponent executes a cutover or in the interim phase of a feint attack,
- the time degagement thrust, used against the opponent's attempted preparation by beat or bind and done without any contact between blades,
- the stop thrust, a simultaneous combining of attack and parry executed against the opponent's attempted preparation by beat or bind and done without any contact between the blades,
- the stop thrust, a simultaneous combining of attack and parry executed against the opponent's straight thrust, change thrust, beat or bind followed by straight or change thrust, or in the final phase of the feint attack in which

138

the interim feints have been reacted to with parries, and done with the hand in opposition to the direction of the attacking blade.

Feint counter-attacks are used against second intention attacks.

The counter-attack used against the cutover must begin the moment the opponent lifts his weapon with the intention of making his attack. It should be done with a short step forward. In terms of technical execution, the counter-attack takes the form of a straight thrust.

The counter-attack executed in the interim phase of a feint attack should begin as the opponent starts the feint. It is used instead of a parry by the fencer taking advantage of the time created by the feint.

The counter-attack against a feint attack can also occur when the feint is already in progress; in this instance, the fencer executes the counter-attack following an initial parry reaction to the feint, in the literature it is referred to as executing the counter-attack in the second stage. This method is used against the double or multiple feint attack.

The technical execution of the counter-attack against feints is the same as that of the straight thrust executed from the on-guard position of the blade, from invito and from the line. Depending on the initial position of the blade, it is directed to the upper or lower target area.

The time degagement thrust is based on timing and, used as a counter-attack, should be executed against the opponent who wants to initiate his attack with a beat or bind. The blades should not touch, the fencer rounding the opponent's blade with an accompanying half or three-quarter lunge as dictated by the distance.

The stop thrust, intended as a counter-attack against straight or change thrust and straight or change thrust introduced by beat or bind, must be done with the hand moving obliquely forward in the direction of the advancing blade. This takes the place of a parry, it is most effectively executed when the weapon and arm form a slight angle at the hand rather than being extended in a straight line.

The opposition so offered by the hand is more pronounced in fourth and seventh than in sixth and eighth stop thrusts. The latter two are held in the plane of the shoulder.

Four stop thrusts, corresponding to the four parries, can be identified; that is, fourth, sixth, eighth and seventh stop thrusts. They should be accompanied with a short step forward or short lunge.

A stop thrust can be used against the final movement in a feint attack. The fencer should execute it after he has reacted to all the interim feints, one parry in reaction to a single feint attack, two parries in the case of a double feint attack, and so on. It can be any of the four stop thrusts previously mentioned.

Since the stop thrust replaces a parry and the parry could be either direct or circular, the stop thrust can be a corresponding straight thrust or one circular in its execution. In foil fencing, the straight thrust is the most commonly used; in épée, the circular variation is also quite frequently adopted.

The footwork used in conjunction with stop thrusts in the final phase of a feint attack can either be a step forward or a short lunge.

xi. Second intention attacks, feint counter-attacks (finta in tempo) and renewed counter-attacks (counter tempo)

The fencer's attack is parried by the opponent who follows with a riposte. The fencer parries the opponent's riposte and in turn ripostes. This represents the linear build-up of the sequence of actions in foil fencing. Attack, parry and riposte, parry and counter-riposte—these are the simplest and most obvious movements of two fencers reacting to each other's actions.

The vertical build-up of actions based on compound actions and tactics is formed by reactions to counter-attacks, the actions discussed in the previous section which rely on tempo. From these develop, in sequence, the second intention attack, the feint counter-attack (finta in tempo) thrust against the feint counter-attack.

A classic second intention attack is an action executed against the opponent's counter-attack which the fencer has induced or deduced in advance. It is made up of the parry of the counter-attack and the ensuing riposte.

To correctly execute second intention as described above, the fencer should signal that an attack is coming as he begins a step forward with the front foot, this being done from a long distance. As the rear foot finishes the step, he parries the opponent's counter-attack and ripostes with a short lunge. The footwork in the first stage can also be a jump forward or a sliding advance of the front foot.

Second intention attacks can also be used against the usual parry and riposte of the opponent. In such instances the fencer must parry the opponent's riposte and execute his counter-riposte all while in the lunge.

In parrying in the lunge, the arm holding the weapon is bent so that the blade is very vertical and the location of the parry fairly close to the body.

The next in the sequence of compound action is the feint counter-attack. It is used against an opponent's second intention against the fencer's counter-attack. The counter-attack in this instance is no more than a feint which draws the opponent's parry and which is rounded by the fencer.

In foil fencing, the first feint counter-attacks used are those executed with a time degagement thrust. The coach should also have the students practise feint counter-attacks built on stop thrusts which can be used against feint attacks by including the related exercises in the fencing lesson.

The feint counter-attack with time degagement thrust begins with the thrust being indicated while the front foot takes a short step forward. The opponent's parry drawn by this movement is then rounded to complete the feint counter-attack.

It most cases simple single feints make up the feint counter-attack. Circular single feints are used less frequently.

The stop thrust executed against a feint counter-attack is the highest level of action in the tactical sequence of foil. It is called a renewed counter-attack (counter tempo).

To execute the renewed counter-attack, the fencer first indicates his intention to attack with a short step forward of the front foot. At the same time the opponent begins his feint counter-attack with a short step forward, the fencer executes a stop thrust with a lunge in the expected line of the opponent's final movement, also being done with a lunge. Thus both fencers end up in a lunge in the final position.

xii. Fencing at close quarters

Fencing at close quarters refers to the carrying on of combat at a closed distance, and calls for a special technique and method of fighting.

The extension of the arm holding the weapon to make the thrust is generally not part of the technical execution. In most situations, the elbow must be bent in order to land a hit and the hand rotated at the wrist and moved in the plane of its normal position parallel to the body. Only in this way can the blade find its way under, over or around the opponent's weapon.

The thrusts used at close quarters are the angular, swinging and cutover thrusts as well as a movement akin to that of using a fork.

The shorter than usual distance also necessitates changes in the execution of parries in terms of location, position and form. They are made close to the body with the blade held very vertically in a manner similar to sabre parries in order to block the plane of attack.

Parries are not executed at their normal heights or in their usual lines. Thus fourth and third parries can protect low lines as well as high lines, and second and first parries can defend high as well as low lines.

Areas of the target, normally safe from an attack at longer distance, become more accessible and vulnerable at close quarters.

Body movements play a greater role. Effacing the body, ducking, squatting, stepping sideways and turning away from the fencing line—all help the fencer to avoid being hit by the opponent's weapon, sometimes more effectively than trying to form a parry.

The conventions frequently are observed to a minimum and thus the actions are often no more than a series of successive repeated thrusts.

Most coaches tend to draw a parallel between fencing at close quarters and preparatory, reconnaissance or camouflaging movements of the blade; that is, they tend not to teach these aspects. The feeling is that such things are associated with individual styles and should therefore develop in the course of practice through the students' efforts with some assistance from the coach. After the coach has demonstrated the typical executions and solutions, it is up to the student to practise them as much as possible with partners who like to fence at close quarters.

The ancestor of today's fencing sabre was the curved oriental sword, such as used by the Turks. Although suitable for both cutting with edge and back and thrusting with the point, the sabre is primarily a cutting weapon and most of the basic actions are based on this.

The cut can be made with any part of the edge and the first third of the back of the blade. Thrusts are done with the point, as in foil.

Cuts are directed to the opponent's target which consists of the head, body hands and arms.

The sabre is a conventional weapon like the foil. The validity of a hit depends not on the timing of the arrival of the hits but in terms of specific conventions written in the rules of fencing.

VI.1. The parts of the sabre (Fig. 123)

The sabre is made up of the blade, the guard, the handle and the locking nut or pommel.

The blade, which narrows along its length from the guard to the point, is

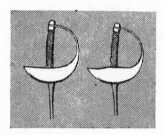

FIG. 123

divided theoretically into three sections: the forte, the middle and the feeble. The edge, the back and the point are also seen as distinct parts.

The forte is used for parrying, the middle for making contact by beat or bind with the opponent's blade and the feeble for cutting.

The point of the blade is used for thrusting. Parries are executed with the edge, while beats and binds can be done with the feeble and back of the blade.

The guard, as the name suggests, protects the fencer's hand. The handle, usually made of wood, fits on the thick end of the blade. The guard, handle and blade are held together by the locking nut.

When fitted together, the blade should be bent downward and inward slightly in relation to a straight line drawn through the handle with the edge facing down.

VI.2. The fundamentals of sabre

i. The correct grip (Fig. 124)

To correctly grip the sabre, the handle should be held between the thumb and index finger, with the thumb on the top, or flat side, of the handle and the index

FIG. 124

finger on the under side opposite the thumb. The handle is held about one centimetre from the guard. The thumb lies as flat as possible along the handle. The remaining fingers, slightly separated, hold the handle flexibly with the little finger pressing it down against the cushion of the palm. There should be a space between the handle and the palm of the hand large enough to hold a walnut.

If held as described above, the weapon and forearm should form an obtuse angle.

A correct grip is the foundation for good technique. It is as essential a precondition for the fencer's development as footwork, for example.

The grip should be fairly relaxed, ensuring an easy hold on the weapon. Pressure should be applied or the grip firmed up only in proportion to the requirements of the different actions and movements. Holding the weapon too firmly causes the fencer's hand to grow tired too soon. The stiffness affects not only the fingers and hand but also the muscles of the arm and shoulder. In turn, the stiffness prevents an easy and quick handling of the weapon.

Holding just the handle helps the beginner to learn the correct grip. From there, holding a shortened or broken blade gradually increases his feeling for the right grip. Finally, the student practises with a complete weapon. In the beginning, the student should practise not wearing a glove in order to get a better feel and awareness of the correct grip.

The highly elastic and flexible handling of the sabre results from an extremely complex use of fingers, hand and arm. The thumb, index finger and little finger are responsible for securing the grip, with the middle and ring fingers playing a secondary role.

More difficult than holding the weapon is learning how to manipulate the handle with the fingers. The fact that the fencer alternates between a looser and a firmer grip depending on the movement in question, with the fingers seemingly opening and closing, allows the handle to move within certain limits as required on occasion.

Although the sabre as practised today does not move only from the elbow, this joint maintains a central role in manipulating the blade, acting much like a control tower. The movements of the elbow are supplemented by the actions of the wrist and fingers, but only to the essential limits.

ii. Position of the hand and guard

The position of the hand and guard are taken up by rotating the forearm. They support and accurately locate the sabre and arm when the various invitos, parries, cuts and thrusts are executed.

The six classic positions of the hand and guard are:
- first, with the thumb pointing down and the palm facing forward,
- second, with the thumb pointing in and the palm facing down,
- third, with the thumb pointing up and the palm facing in,
- fourth, with the thumb pointing forward and the palm facing up in a supine position,
- fifth, with the thumb pointing up and in and the palm facing forward and down,
- sixth, with the thumb pointing up and in and the palm facing in and down.

Ignoring the traditional classification, another sequence can be established if:
- the arm is always rotated in a clockwise direction,
- only those positions of hand and guard are adopted and instructed in a manner in which they actually are used in combat.

In this way no position need be modified when executed in practice. Using the traditional method, for instance, requires a change in the position of the blade when held in second.

From the procedure suggested above, the positions are:
- First position, which is identical to the traditional first position. It also occurs in first and fifth invitos.
- Second position, which differs by 45° from the traditional second position, and in which the arm is rotated around its longitudinal axis with the edge of the blade pointing obliquely up and out and the thumb pointing obliquely in and the palm obliquely out and down. It also occurs in second invito, thrusts, right cheek cut, flank cut and cut to the outside of the forearm and hand.
- Third position, which corresponds to the traditional sixth position, in which the hand rotates 90° with the direction of the edge maintained during the rotation. It also occurs in third invito and with cuts to the arm and hand.
- Fourth position, which is identical to the traditional third in which the blade is turned 45° from the previous position. It also occurs in cuts to the head, upper arm and hand and cuts under the arm with the back of the blade.
- Fifth position, which is identical to the traditional fifth position, and which differs from the previous position by 45°. It also occurs in fourth invito and the initial stage of a chest cut drawn across the target.

● Sixth position, which corresponds to the traditional fourth position, and which differs from the previous position by 45°. It also occurs in cuts to the inside cheek and cuts to the chest and stomach not drawn across the target.

iii. Positions of the blade

Three fundamental positions of the blade exist: on-guard, the line and invito.

The on-guard position offers an equal opportunity for both attacking and parrying actions. It lies approximately the same distance from any part of the target to which an attack can be directed and gives partial protection to the fencer at the same time. Standing in on-guard with his sabre held in front of him, the fencer neither completely closes nor completely opens any line. This makes it possible to defend with equal ease any area of the target offered to the opponent and at the same time execute an attack to any area of the opponent's target which is facing him.

The on-guard position in third best meets the above description. It differs from third invito or parry in that:

● although the edge of the blade faces obliquely out, it is not rotated as much as in the parry or invito positions,

● the point is directed slightly inside the line of the hand, instead of outside as in the parry or invito,

● the point lies slightly lower than in the parry or invito.

These three adjustments result in the sabre being held in a central position. The guard protects the hand and arm while the blade offers cover to the flank and outside cheek. Production against attacks to the head and chest is facilitated by the location of the point slightly inside.

Because of the inherent advantages the third on-guard is the most natural, most obvious and therefore most frequently used position in sabre fencing. Today attacks are rarely executed from second on-guard, something that was common and the fashion in earlier eras.

Some coaches maintain that teaching two third positions, the on-guard and invito or parry, is superfluous and unnecessary. They only teach one third position which can be used universally as on-guard and invito or parry.

The blade is said to be in line when the point is directed towards the opponent's target with the arm extended. The obtuse angle formed by the blade and arm at the wrist, however, should remain.

If the weapon is held in low line, the point is directed at the lower section of the opponent's target; in high line, it is directed to the upper area of the target. This distinction is necessary because attacks on the blade held in low line differ from those used against a blade held in high line.

Although the hand and arm are part of the target area in sabre fencing, the blade held in line should always be directed at the opponent's chest.

Invito is a position in which the blade leaves the target area open from one or several directions. It is designed to draw an attack from the opponent.

In principle, any blade position, other than the on-guard or the line, can be considered an invito regardless of the extent to which the target is exposed to attack, in practice, however, the invitos generally used look the same as and are executed in the same way as the identical parries. In other words, the fencer draws the opponent's attack by using the same movement he would execute to parry an attack directed from the side opposite to which he opens.

Five invitos corresponding to the five parries can be named: first, second, third, fourth and fifth. Their descriptions are given in the section on parries.

The invitos and parries are not differentiated in terms of the scope of their respective movements. In certain instances, however, the fencer should be prepared to execute invitos of a broader and more exaggerated character than the parries in order to draw an attack from certain opponents.

During a bout the three basic blade positions are used and varied to meet the objective the fencer has in mind. Normally he starts from on-guard position. The line is used to fend off aggressive opponents, and the invito to draw the opponent into making an attack.

iv. Relations between the blades

The relations between the two blades are described in terms of their location. The two blades can be held in the same or different positions, with the following variations being possible:

- both blades being held in line,
- both blades being held in on-guard position,
- both blades being held in invito,
- one blade being held in line, the other in invito,
- one blade being held in line, the other in on-guard position,
- one blade being held in invito, the other in on-guard position.

The first three are relations of the same category; the last three relations of different categories.

v. The fencing target

In sabre fencing, the target area includes any part of the fencer's body lying above the imaginary line drawn through the points where the thighs and trunk meet, when in the on-guard position.

The target area can be divided into several sections; namely, the flank or side, outside cheek, head, inside cheek, stomach or belly, arm and hand. These descriptions identify the areas which cuts can hit and determine the direction in which cuts are executed.

vi. The fencing line and fencing distance

The fencing line is defined as the imaginary line which joins the heels of the two fencers facing each other. Deviations from this line can occur because of the fencer's particular stance. To correct this error, the fencer should practise along a line already drawn on the floor. In the old French schools students had to take a lesson standing and moving along a narrow board laid on the floor and so maintain a specified line.

As in foil, three distances can be distinguished in sabre fencing: short, medium and long distance.

The criteria related to these distances are the same as described in connection with foil fencing. Since the hand and arm, which are part of the target in sabre, lie in front of the body in the on-guard position, the fencer is simultaneously at two fencing distances in relation to the opponent. Even if the fencer can reach the opponent's hand simply by extending his arm, he can only hit the opponent's chest by adding a lunge to his arm movement.

Cuts are taught at first from short distance. The execution is improved and polished with a gradual opening of the distance.

As in foil, thrusts first come from medium distance. After, they are practised from long distance and finally from short distance.

vii. Determination of directions

The words forward, backward, high, low, outside, outward, inside and inward, common to foil fencing, are also used in sabre fencing to determine direction. Today, however, the phrases "to the right" or "to the left", which are more natural and self-explanatory, are used instead of the words outside, inside, outward and inward in order to determine direction. Although not the customary ones, there can be no real objection to them since they do not create any confusion and do not have to be learned separately as do reactions to the words outside and inside or outward and inward.

VI.3. The initial, on-guard and resting positions

Today less importance is attached by fencers to the "ceremonial" aspects of fencing; that is, to such things as the initial position and salute to the opponent prior to

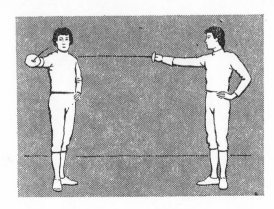

FIG. 125

147

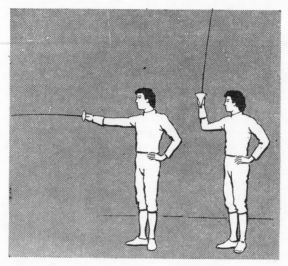

FIG. 126

and at the conclusion of a bout. Competitors virtually ignore the initial position (Fig. 125) and use only a brief form of salute (see Fig. 126).

In spite of this, the initial position has several important roles to fulfil. In the group training of beginners it serves as a means of discipline which breeds controlled movements, identical repetitions of movements and accommodation of the student to fencing.

The initial position is assumed with legs straight and the feet at right angles to each other. The arm which holds the weapon is extended. The guard of the weapon is level with the shoulder and the arm and weapon form an obtuse angle. The point is directed obliquely forward and inside, and the edge of the blade faces the direction of the opponent's target area.

To perform the salute, the forearm is drawn back until it is vertical. At the same time the palm is turned inward to face the fencer. The movement is completed by returning to the initial position.

The on-guard position of the sabre fencer (see Fig. 127) is governed by the same criteria as the foil fencer's on-guard position and which are described in the

FIG. 127

148

chapter on foil fencing. The specific conditions and requirements of sabre cause the on-guard position to differ from the foil position in several details in that:

● the stance is narrower; that is the feet are closer together,
● the position of the rear knee is more natural,
● the angle formed by the feet is usually less than 90°,
● the effacing of the body to reduce target area is less necessary than in the case of both thrusting weapons.

Notwithstanding the above differences, the student should be taught to take up the on-guard position according to the theoretical standards. It is all the more important because abilities and skills moulded and formed hand-in-hand with the teaching of the on-guard position and which become extremely useful at later stages directly or indirectly cannot be discarded by the coach's not giving instruction based on the standards.

The adjustments needed to make the sabre fencer more mobile come about almost automatically without any deliberate or exaggerated effort in the course of practice. It is in this way that the on-guard is shaped to meet the image required by sabre fencing.

In the on-guard position the arm holding the weapon is bent at the elbow and the forearm held almost horizontally about one hand's width from the hip. The blade is either in third on-guard or in third invito. The free hand is placed on the rear hip while taking up the on-guard position, but leaves this position and takes an active part in helping the fencer maintain balance as he moves forward and backward. This is done without any deliberate control or guidance on the part of the fencer.

The teaching of the on-guard position in sabre is done in the way described in the chapter on foil fencing, with the necessary modifications being taken into account.

Figure 128 presents a possible variation of the resting position which can be taken up from the initial or on-guard positions. Today sabre fencers strictly observe the taking up of the resting position only in exhibitions.

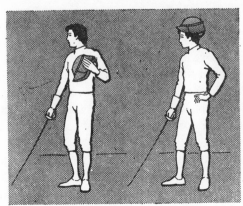

FIG. 128

VI.4. Sabre actions

Attacks in sabre are executed with cuts or thrusts. They can be directed to the opponent's head, body, arm or hand. Attacks can be simple or compound and can be coupled with beats or binds. There can be genuine attacks, false attacks, first or second intention attacks, renewed attacks and all forms of counter-attacks.

The principle form of attack is the cut, which begins with a rotation of the blade to place the edge or back in the direction of the opponent's target. The blade should travel the shortest possible route to the target, describing a larger or smaller arc depending on the prevailing situation and conditions.

The height at which the cut is delivered can vary. The guard can advance oblique-ly forward, upward or downward, as though on a slope. No matter what path it follows, however, the movement of the weapon should never reveal in advance the intended action and thus betray it.

Most cuts are executed with the hand and guard being moved in the plane in front of the shoulder. In the final stage of the cut there may be a slight outward movement, but to an insignificant, almost unnoticeable extent. For chest and belly cuts not drawn across the target, or cuts executed outside and high on the hand and arm in an angular fashion, hand and guard automatically switch to the other side. Maintaining the obtuse angle formed by the blade and arm almost automatically places the guard in the necessary position. It should be stressed that the guard not move sideways in the direction of the cut since this is an unnatural movement.

Cuts must start from a position of the fencer's intention. The movement starts with an easy motion of the hand and arm, and the pace gradually accelerates as the target is approached, finishing energetically and vigorously. When executed from medium distance, the arm holding the weapon is extended a split second before the front foot starts the lunge. Where necessary, beginners may be permitted to start with a more intense arm movement than usual. The front foot follows the arm movement immediately to avoid any possible interruption of the attack. When the on-guard position is resumed, the hand and arm begin to move just before the movement of the foot.

When executed from long distance, the arm holding the weapon is extended only as the rear foot completes the step forward.

The actual cutting movement of the blade is executed by a pushing and pulling action of the thumb and little finger done simultaneously and with a firm but limited forward push of the wrist. When the wrist is used to the maximum in the correct way, the blade bounces off the target when it hits, giving a characteristic sound. If the wrist is used too much, control of the weapon is lost and cuts cannot be properly limited.

The extension of the arm holding the weapon and the action of fingers, thumb and wrist finish at the moment the blade hits the target. The hit should arrive just before the heel of the front foot arrives on the floor in the lunge.

Even in the final position of the cut, the obtuse angle formed by the blade and arm is maintained. The magnitude of the angle may vary within certain limits but it should never become a straight angle (180°).

After each cut the student resumes third on-guard or third invito position. To prompt the student to start the return to on-guard with the arm, the coach should threaten the third line after each hit executed by the student.

If the student's blade tends to stick in the cut rather than return the arm after the cut because he presses the edge onto the target, he should execute two or three cuts in succession at the target with the arm extended so that he feels and understands how the fingers, thumb and wrist work in the final stage of the cut.

Although thrusts are secondary in importance to cuts in sabre fencing, they nevertheless have a major role to play. Executing a thrust with the sabre is much more difficult in terms of technique than a thrust in foil or épée. This is because of the angle formed by the blade and arm. In foil and épée, the weapon and arm are held in a straight line except in some special cases. For the above reason and because the sabre is a cutting weapon, the student is first taught several cuts before being introduced to the way in which to execute a thrust.

Thrusts in sabre invariably are executed with the hand and guard in second position, which maintains the obtuse angle and places the edge facing obliquely outward and upward, and held in most cases at the level of and slightly outside the line of the shoulder. An exception is the inquartata or turning away from the fencing line in which opposition is given by placing the hand on the opposite side. The point should reach the target just before the heel of the front foot arrives on the floor in the lunge.

Thrusts usually are not directed to the opponent's hand, arm or head although such actions are possible.

The same principles apply to the co-ordination of the hand and feet in executing thrusts as in executing cuts. The fencer therefore resumes the third on-guard or invito position after concluding the thrust.

i. The simple attacks
The simple attacks possible in sabre are:
- simple cuts directed to the major areas of the target which include the head, flank, outside cheek and chest,
- straight thrust,
- change cut or change thrust,
- angular cut,
- simple cuts directed to the hand and arm, from above and below with the edge, from below with the back, from outside or inside by drawing the blade across.

a. Direct cuts to the major areas of the target

Regardless of the distance travelled by the blade or the arc it describes during the cutting action, the cut is considered as straight if the blade moves from its starting position to the target without encountering any obstructions:

(1) THE HEAD CUT (Fig. 129) The head cut from third on-guard or third invito is executed by rotating the edge in the direction of the intended cut while maintaining the obtuse angle and then extending the arm. The guard remains in the

FIG. 129

plane of the shoulder when in the final stage of the cut. Breaking the weapon slightly inward from the line of the arm ensures a more certain landing of the hit on the target.

In executing the head cut from fourth invito, the blade moves obliquely forward and outward as the arm extends to travel along the same line as described in the preceding paragraph. Technically it is identical to the cut executed from third on-guard or invito.

From fifth invito the head cut is executed by rotating the blade in the direction of the intended cut, with the elbow making a counter-clockwise circular movement which begins by moving backward. The obtuse angle is maintained. The blade passes the free arm and opposite side of the body. The hit should land on the target at the moment the arm reaches its full extension and in the manner described in the head cut executed from third on-guard or invito.

(2) THE FLANK CUT (Fig. 130) The flank cut is executed from the third on-guard or invito by rotating the blade inward so that the hand slopes obliquely inward with the obtuse angle maintained. The arm is extended at the same time. In the final position of the cut, the edge is directed obliquely forward and upward.

FIG. 130

152

From fourth invito the flank cut is executed by simultaneously extending the arm and rotating the blade. As this is done, the guard moves obliquely forward into the plane of the shoulder. The edge faces obliquely forward and upward in the final stage.

The flank cut is executed from fifth invito by lowering the blade and arm to the height at which the cut is to be delivered. This is done with the forearm moving downward and backward in a semicircular manner. The arm is then extended and the final stage of the movement taken up as described previously.

(3) THE CUT TO OUTSIDE CHEEK (Fig. 131) This cut is executed technically in a manner similar to the flank cut. It differs from the flank cut in respect to the

FIG. 131

height at which it is delivered, in the final stage of the cut to outside cheek, the edge faces obliquely forward and upward.

The cut to outside cheek should be taught first from third on-guard or invito, and then from fourth invito and second invito.

(4) THE CHEST CUT The chest cut can be executed either by hitting the target with the edge so that it bounces off after contact or by drawing the blade across the target.

(a) with the edge (Fig. 132) From third on-guard or invito, the edge is directed diagonally towards the opponent's chest by rotating the arm outward. The hit

FIG. 132

is scored with the blade maintaining this position, with the edge facing obliquely inward and downward. In order to keep the obtuse angle, the guard is turned as the arm extends so that it faces inward at the finish of the cut.

The second stage and final stage of the chest cut with the edge are executed in the same way as above from the other invito positions. The differences which occur arise from those already discussed.

(b) drawn across the target The technical execution of the drawn chest cut differs considerably from that done with the edge and also from the general theory of cuts in that:
- the cut does not begin with a direct rotation of the edge,
- the wrist plays a more important role than in other cuts,
- the blade rotates around its longitudinal axis during the execution of the cut,
- the peripheral speed which results in greatly accelerating the point and blade,
- the wrist describes a small loop and returns to lie in the line of the arm at the end of the cut,
- the arm holding the weapon follows the wrist and moves with a funnel-like action,
- the hit can land on the target with either the edge or the back of the blade. The point moves forward as if on its own while the wrist, acting with a characteristically firm and effective motion, brings the cut to a successful conclusion. If the action of the wrist is ignored or is done in too casual a manner, its advance is broken and hesitant and does not lead the cut as it should. Consequently the cut is abortive and comes to a stop halfway.

Executing the drawn chest cut is more difficult than the other types of cuts and should therefore be the last one taught. The method recommended for its instruction is as follows.

The student stands so that he can reach the coach even if his arm is bent.

The student places the edge or flat of the blade on the target and, after bouncing a light and then more intense hit off the target, tries to draw it across the chest. The fingers and wrist are actively involved in the repeated hitting of the target. The student should also try to draw the cut across the chest without first bouncing the blade off the target. As the blade is drawn across the chest, the point describes a slightly distorted ellipse on the target with the hand and arm following a similar path.

Once the student has succeeded in executing the exercise several times, the fencing distance is opened gradually so that the student do the cut with an extension of the arm.

The belly cut, which is executed a little lower than the chest cut, is rarely taught separately today. If the coach feels that a distinction should be made between chest and belly cut, he should have the student rotate his hand into fourth position, a supine guard, in order to execute the cut with the edge and to ensure its accuracy.

The belly cut is drawn across the target horizontally rather than diagonally. This is because it hits close to the lower limit of the target area.

b. The straight thrust (Fig. 133)

The straight thrust is most often executed from third on-guard or invito. As the arm is rotated inward, the point is lowered and the arm extended. The obtuse angle is maintained throughout the movement and in the final position of the thrust, with the edge facing obliquely upward and outward.

FIG. 133

If the opponent attempts to cover his target with a bind of the fencer's blade, a thrust or cut can be executed by rounding the binding blade. This rounding can be done either by passing the opponent's guard or passing over the opponent's point. The former results in change thrust or cuts while the latter is done by angular of thrown cuts, the thrown thrust being a theoretical possibility but practically never used.

c. The change cut (Fig. 134) and change thrust (Fig. 135)

In rounding the opponent's blade the fencer follows the shortest possible path to the target. Against fourth and third binds the fencer rounds the opponent's blade underneath the guard; against a bind in second, the opponent's blade is rounded from above. It is of little value to practise change cuts and thrusts against binds in fifth and first positions.

When a change is executed from medium distance, the first stage is to break the contact between the two blades. With an action of the wrist, the fencer makes

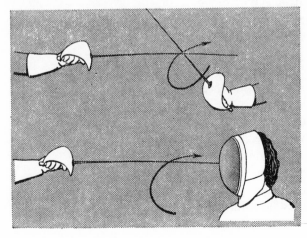

FIG. 134

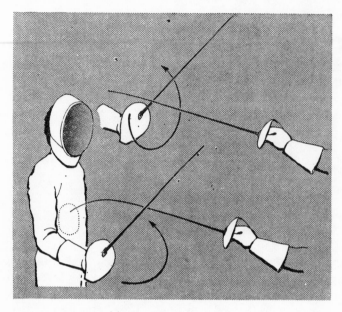

FIG. 135

a semicircular movement of the point to round the opponent's guard and carry out the hit. During the rounding movement the hand moves forward towards the target with the extension of the arm, giving the movement a spiralling trajectory.

When the change cut or thrust is executed from long distance, the blade begins to advance on the side which has been bound and this advance is prolonged until the lunge is initiated. The fencer rounds the opponent's guard in the final stage of the lunge. No matter how close the distance has become, the fencer must not pull back his arm when rounding the guard.

Aspects of the change cut or thrust other than those described above are governed by the general principles which apply to direct cuts and straight thrusts.

Against a bind in third, the possible attacks are:

- change flank cut,
- change cut to arm or hand,
- change thrust.

Attacks against a fourth bind include:

- change cut to arm or hand,
- change cut to outside cheek,
- change head cut,
- change thrust.

Attacks against a second bind can be:

- change cut to arm or hand,
- change cut to outside cheek,
- change head cut,
- change chest cut with edge,
- change thrust.

156

d. The angular cut (Fig. 136)

In executing a thrown or angular cut, the fencer must round the opponent's blade by passing over its point. A co-ordinated action of the fingers, thumb, wrist and forearm lift the fencer's blade just to the extent which allows his blade to pass the opponent's point with minimal clearance.

Angular cuts are effective only against third or fourth binds. They are impractical against the other three binding actions and thus should not be included in the lesson even as exercises in controlling and handling the weapon.

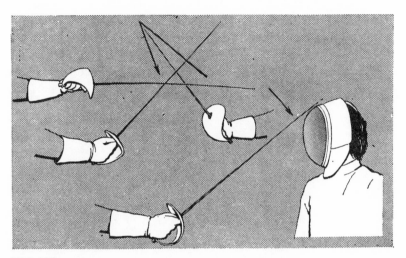

FIG. 136

Angular cuts can be executed:

● to the head or to the chest against third bind,

● to the head, the outside cheek or to the flank against fourth bind.

The same principles which govern the final stage of direct cuts and were previously discussed in the technical execution of direct cuts are also valid for the final stage of angular cuts.

e. Cuts to the arm and hand

Cuts to the opponent's arm and hand are designed to hit the most advanced areas of the target and, therefore, can reach the target with a lunge even when the opponent's body is a considerable distance away. This is the main advantage to be gained in directing cuts to the arm and hand of the opponent.

The disadvantage is that more accuracy is needed and the blade must be handled more precisely because the target concerned is very mobile and small in size. Also, the parries used against cuts to the arm and hand are reduced in size since a simple turning of the hand can offer the needed protection. Because of these difficulties the fencer should only risk executing a cut to arm or hand when a full tempo is created following appropriate preparation and only then with a direct movement.

Cuts to the arm and hand are rarely used today as attacks. They are, however, frequently done as renewed attacks or counter-attacks.

Notwithstanding the above points, it is worthwhile to teach these cuts as attacks because the skills and abilities acquired stand the student in good stead when learning renewed attacks and time cuts.

Four cuts to the arm and hand can be identified in terms of the part of the target to which are directed. They are:

- cut to under arm or hand,
- cut to upper arm or hand,
- cut to outside arm or hand,
- cut to inside arm or hand.

(1) CUT TO UNDER ARM OR HAND (Fig. 137) The cut to under arm or hand can be done with both the edge and the back of the blade. The hand is held in a low position.

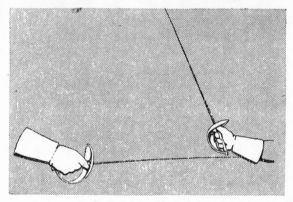

FIG. 137

(2) CUT TO UPPER ARM OR HAND (Fig. 138) The cut to upper arm or hand can be executed either from inside or outside the opponent's blade. In the latter the hand is bent in an exaggerated way at the wrist. In both cases the cut is executed with the edge and in a way that resembles a head cut.

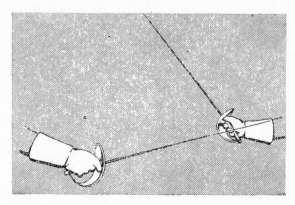

FIG. 138

158

(3) Cut to outside arm or hand (Fig. 139) The cut to outside arm or hand is done with an action that is similar to the flank cut, but in a low plane and from the outside.

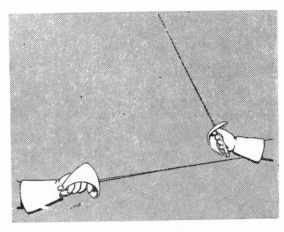

FIG. 139

(4) Cut to inside arm or hand The cut to inside arm or hand can be executed either with the edge bouncing off the target or by drawing the edge across the target in the manner of a chest cut. The latter is more frequently used but is more difficult to do.

A characteristic feature of cuts to the arm and hand is the bent position of the hand, much like the position used in épée, designed to avoid the cut running into the opponent's guard. The angle formed at the wrist is always formed in a direction opposite to the direction of the cut and while moving away from the opponent's blade. For the cut to upper inside arm or hand, therefore, the guard is held outside the fencing line; for the cut to upper outside arm or hand, the guard moves inside the fencing line, and so on.

The teaching of the upper and inside cuts to the arm and hand is done from the third on-guard or invito or the fourth invito. The cut to under arm or hand is practised from second invito, while the cut to outside arm or hand is taught from fourth or second invito.

Initially, cuts to the arm or hand are executed with the edge. This can be followed by practising the cuts with the back of the blade. The teaching of the cuts which are drawn across the target should be the last ones introduced.

The fencer resumes the on-guard or invito after executing a cut to the arm or hand.

ii. Parries
As in foil, there are several methods the sabre fencer can adopt to counter an opponent's attack. They include:
- parries,
- time counter-attacks,

● opening the fencing distance, used more often to keep the arm and hand out of the opponent's reach than to retreat before the opponent's blade or to evade the attack by moving the body out of its path.

The most important of the defensive actions is the parry which gives the fencer the right to riposte in accordance with the conventions of sabre.

In theory, a parry done in a stationary position is sufficient to prevent a cut by the opponent from reaching the fencer's target. In order to deflect a thrust from the target, the parry must be a moving one.

When parrying a cut, the blade is placed between the fencer's body and the attacking blade in a way that blocks the path to the target and halts the cut. If the opponent attacks with a thrust, the fencer uses an opposition or beat parry to deflect the incoming blade off-line. In either case the defensive movement must be an effective one.

Whether the attack is done with cut or thrust, only a parry begun in good time and done with a firm but limited movement of correct proportions can succeed.

Parries can be categorized as opposition parries, beat parries or mixed parries, a combination of opposition and beat parries.

Opposition parries are done with the forte of the blade and the guard in contact with the opponent's weapon over a relatively long time. Beat parries are of shorter duration and done by energetically contacting the opponent's weapon with the middle of the blade in order to deflect it off-line.

The combination of opposition and beat parries serves a double purpose; first, to parry the attack and, second, to loosen the opponent's grip on his weapon. To do this, the mixed parry must be executed with an intense movement. The danger in using this type of parry lies in the fact that, if it fails to find the opponent's weapon, it exceeds the effective limit of the parry because of the inertia developed. This delays or prevents the formation of a subsequent parry. It should be used, therefore, against attacks induced or deduced in advance because the risk the fencer runs is less in this instance than when it is used at random.

The parry is done with the edge facing the direction of the incoming cut in order to meet it. This ensures that the parry is firm enough because the blade is supported by the thumb and little finger.

Five parries, corresponding to the five invitos, are taught in sabre fencing. They are first, second, third, fourth and fifth parries (see Fig. 140).

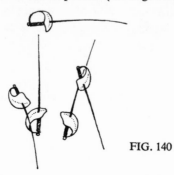

FIG. 140

Two of the parries protect the body, two protect the arm and hand, and one protects the head. The parries which protect the flank and chest are positioned almost vertically, while that which protects the head lies in an almost horizontal position.

a. Description of the positions and paths of the various parries

(1) FIRST PARRY The hand holding the weapon is held in the plane of the opposite shoulder. The forearm lies roughly horizontally across the body and forms an obtuse angle with the upper arm at the elbow. The blade points obliquely forward and downward with the edge facing obliquely forward. This parry protects the fencer's chest.

(2) SECOND PARRY The upper edge of the guard is held just below the level of the shoulder and about a hand's width outside the line of the shoulder. The arm is slightly bent at the elbow and the blade is directed obliquely downward with the point at about knee level. The edge faces obliquely outward. This parry defends the fencer's flank.

(3) THIRD PARRY The elbow of the arm holding the weapon is held bent about one hand's width from the hip with the forearm almost horizontal. The blade points obliquely forward and upward, and the edge faces obliquely forward and outward. This parry protects the outside cheek and flank.

(4) FOURTH PARRY The elbow of the arm holding the weapon is held in front of the hip and bent so that the forearm lies across the body in front of the stomach and is somewhat sloping. The hand and guard are held in line with the inside hip. The blade points obliquely forward and upward with the edge facing obliquely forward. This parry defends the chest and stomach.

(5) FIFTH PARRY The hand and guard are held a hand's width outside the plane of the temple above and in front of the head. The upper arm lies almost horizontal and the forearm is inclined outward and forward slightly off the vertical. Both the blade and edge point obliquely forward and upward with the point of the blade held higher than the guard. This parry protects the fencer's head.

Beginners should be taught the final positions as described above. Later the students may deviate from the typical formation of the parries because a defensive movement must be adjusted to the opponent's attacking action. If cuts or thrusts are being directed at varying levels, the plane of the parries must be raised or lowered accordingly.

Parries can be classified according to the paths followed by the blade and the guard into the following types:

● direct parries,

● semicircular parries,

● circular parries.

The movement of point, blade and guard must be co-ordinated along with those of the forearm and elbow so that they all reach the final position of the parry together and stop at the same time.

(1) DIRECT PARRIES Both the point and guard move from one position to another along the shortest possible route in either a horizontal or vertical plane. The fencer executes a direct parry when he:

● parries fourth from third or vice versa (see Fig. 141) with the guard moving in a horizontal plane,

● parries fifth from third and vice versa (see Fig. 142) with the guard moving in a vertical plane,

● parries first from second and vice versa (see Fig. 143) with the guard moving horizontally,

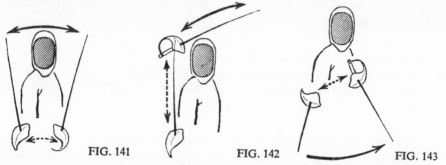

FIG. 141   FIG. 142   FIG. 143

● parries second from third and vice versa (see Fig. 144) with the guard moving forward and downward to second and upward and backward to third along an inclined plane,

● parries fifth from fourth and vice versa (see Fig. 145) with the guard moving diagonally,

● parries fifth from second and vice versa (see Fig. 146) with the guard moving backward and upward to fifth and forward and downward to second along an almost vertical plane.

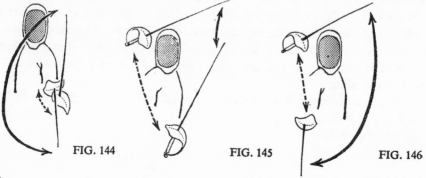

FIG. 144   FIG. 145   FIG. 146

(2) Semicircular parries The point of the blade describes an arc, not a straight line, as the parrying movement follows a semicircular path from one position to another. The fencer executes a semicircular parry when he:

- parries second from fourth and vice versa (see Fig. 147) with the point moving inward and downward to second and upward and outward to fourth,
- parries first from third and vice versa (see Fig. 148) with the point moving outward and downward to first and inward and upward to third,

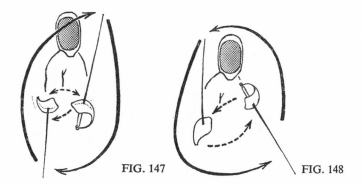

FIG. 147   FIG. 148

- parries fifth from third (see Fig. 149) with the point moving outward and downward as it begins to travel a semicircular path,
- parries first from fifth (see Fig. 150) with the point moving outward and upward along a semicircular path and the guard being lowered.

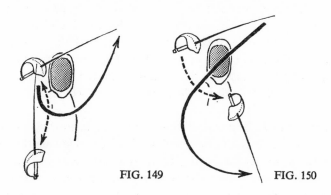

FIG. 149   FIG. 150

(3) CIRCULAR PARRIES The point of the blade describes a circle during the movement while the guard remains in the same position. The blade finishes in the same position as that from which it started.

Theoretically it is possible to execute a circular parry from any of the five positions. In practice, however, only circular parries from third, fourth and second are used to parry thrusts (see Figs. 151, 152, 153).

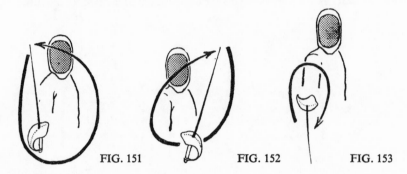

FIG. 151   FIG. 152   FIG. 153

The wrist does the major part of the work in executing a circular parry. Its action is complemented in the second stage by a movement of the forearm which completes the circle.

Cuts directed at the body must be parried with a complete movement. Executing a half parry or just turning the edge in the direction of the attacking blade can be sufficient to defend against cuts to the arm and hand.

Cuts to the upper arm can be countered with third, fourth and fifth parries. Cuts to the under arm with the edge or the back of the blade can be parried by second parry, while cuts to the outside or inside of the arm with the edge or drawn across the target can be countered by third and fourth parries respectively.

The type of parry most effective against bind thrusts is the ceding or yielding parry. Against a bind in third, ceding first parry is used. Against a bind in second, ceding fourth is executed.

Cuts preceded by a beat with the back of the blade are difficult to parry because the opponent's blade lies inside the fencer's blade following the beat, a position which threatens the fencer greatly. To counter such actions, the fencer often uses ceding parries. They are executed by letting the blade continue in the direction of movement brought about by the beat but at the same time moving the guard towards the opponent's blade along the shortest possible route. Thus the point describes a semicircle but the guard travels a much shorter path.

A back edge beat against first invito followed by a chest cut is parried with ceding fourth. Ceding third parries a flank cut which is preceded by a back edge beat against second invito. A back edge beat against fourth followed by a cut to inside cheek is parried by ceding first. A back edge beat against third on-guard or invito and subsequent cut to outside cheek is countered by ceding seventh parry, which is an emergency parry.

164

Executing a riposte from a ceding seventh parry is extremely difficult because the position which results is not favourable to the possible execution of any particular cut.

b. Defensive systems

The defensive system based on the line offers one major advantage in that the related first, second and fifth parries can be executed within a limited space close to the fencing line (see Fig. 154). The distance covered in moving from one position

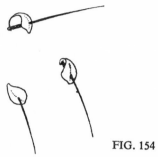

FIG. 154

to another is therefore quite short. Also, because the parries are formed in front of the body, the opponent loses much of the effectiveness of his blade.

The disadvantage in the system lies in the fact that the fencer's arm is held in a somewhat extended position and thus is more exposed to the opponent. It also leaves the fencer's blade close to the fencing line and vulnerable to attacks on the blade.

The system known as the triangular system has the advantage that the related movements are more natural and therefore easier to execute. These positions are not supported as much by the shoulder and elbow as the arm is not as extended, and thus the fencer's arm and hand become less vulnerable because they are farther from the opponent.

The system based on the line can be rounded only from above. A blade following the triangular system can be rounded from both above and below; that is, over the point and under the guard.

A fencer using the system based on the line reacts to the opponent's feint movements during the course of the action. If the triangular system is used, the fencer waits for the opponent's final cut without reacting to any feint movements and tries to parry in the final stage of the cut.

Today competitors rely mostly on the triangular system composed of third, fourth and fifth parries (see Fig. 155).

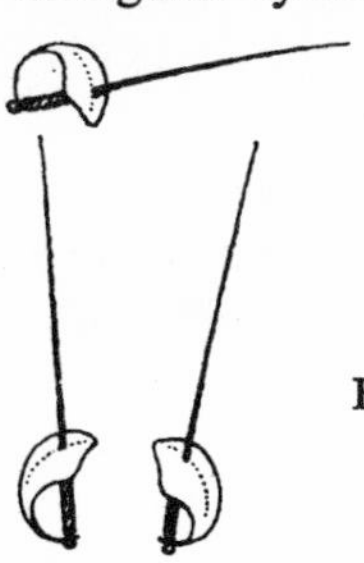

FIG. 155

Occasionally they complement it with second and first parries from the system based on the line. Combining the two defensive systems gives a wider choice of parries to the fencer, five being available instead of just three. Also, the number of transitions and transfers of position is proportionately increased.

Parrying an attack is more difficult in sabre than in foil fencing because:
- the foil target is smaller than the sabre target,
- the parrying movements are smaller in foil than in sabre,
- hits in foil are scored only with thrusts, and not both cuts and thrusts as in sabre,
- the arm and hand, which lie closer to the opponent, are not part of the foil target as they are in sabre,
- the various sections of the foil target are all about equally vulnerable, whereas the advanced areas of the sabre target are more vulnerable than the other areas,
- in foil, all thrusts are directed in a certain plane no matter what their point of origin and the distance covered, and finish in almost the identical line except in the case of a few special types of thrusts; in sabre, cuts are executed in all directions and, regardless of their starting position, can reach the target from any direction and the direction of the cut can be changed even in its final stage,
- the parries in foil do not have to be adjusted to suit particular attacks because several parries can counter a given thrust; in sabre, parries are specific in purpose and, if chosen incorrectly, lead to a hit being scored on the fencer,
- there are more parries possible in foil than in sabre because each direct parry in foil has a corresponding circular parry, doubling the defensive possibilities.

The fencer can execute a parry while standing in place or with a short step backward. The latter is most frequently used. Parrying with a step forward should only be used when the fencer is absolutely certain to which target area the opponent intends to direct his attack.

To properly execute parries in sabre, the fencer needs sharp eyes, sang-froid, quick reflexes and the ability and dexterity to handle his weapon precisely.

Initially, fourth, third and fifth parries are taught and in that order. Second and first parries are instructed at a later stage.

Students should be taught first how to parry cuts to the body and head, followed by parries to counter cuts directed to the arm and hand, and finally how to parry thrusts.

iii. Ripostes and counter-ripostes

Ripostes in sabre fencing can be executed by cuts to the opponent's body and head, hand and arm or by thrusts to the chest. Two types of ripostes exist: simple and compound or feint ripostes.

166

Simple ripostes executed with cuts can take the form of:

- direct cuts,
- change cuts,
- angular cuts.

Simple ripostes done with thrusts can be:

- straight thrust,
- bind thrust,
- change thrust.

Compound ripostes usually take the form of a single feint riposte. Under actual bout conditions double feints are rare, but they are useful to practise in lessons in order to develop the manipulation and handling of the weapon.

In most instances, ripostes in sabre fencing are executed by cuts. Thrust ripostes are less frequent and even rarer in compound actions.

The execution of ripostes follow the same principles which govern the execution of simple cuts and thrusts. Feints are made with the arm bent at the elbow because of the short distance from which ripostes usually are delivered.

From first parry, the simple ripostes which can be done include:

- angular head cut,
- angular chest cut,
- straight thrust (used infrequently),
- flank cut.

From second parry, simple ripostes can be:

- cut to outside cheek,
- change cut to hand or arm,
- change thrust,
- bind thrust.

Simple ripostes from third parry can be:

- head cut,
- flank cut,
- angular chest cut,
- bind thrust,
- change thrust,
- cut to outside arm (used infrequently).

From fourth parry, simple ripostes include:

- head cut,
- cut to outside cheek,
- cut to upper arm,
- change cut to flank,
- chest cut.

Simple ripostes executed from fifth parry can be:

- cut to arm or hand,
- flank cut,
- angular head cut,

167

● angular chest cut,

● straight thrust.

From all parries, compound ripostes are ripostes with a single feint.

The same possibilities which exist for executing an initial riposte also exist for counter-ripostes.

Normally, however, counter-ripostes take the form of direct cuts.

a. Indirect ripostes

When the fencer holds a parry a little longer than usual, even if only for a split second, the opponent often reacts automatically with a parrying movement to counter an anticipated riposte. In changing his position, the opponent exposes an area of the target which otherwise would have been protected. If the fencer executes a riposte to the area which has been uncovered by the opponent's reaction, this riposte is called indirect.

iv. Attacks on the blade

An attack coupled with a bind or beat must be executed against an opponent holding his blade in line. The bind or beat removes the conventional priority given the blade in line which threatens the target area.

Generally speaking, the bind should be used against a blade held firmly or rigidly in line. Against a more loosely held blade the beat is effective.

The bind puts pressure on the opponent's blade in order to carry it out of line. The beat deflects the opponent's blade in line from the target and is done with a short, strong and energetic action to successfully dislodge the opponent's weapon.

A bind or beat is required against a blade in line. A beat may also be used against an opponent in on-guard position or in invito. A bind is never used against invito. A beat used in the above instance is designed to loosen the opponent's grip on his weapon and make his defensive actions more difficult, to open an area of the target even farther away, to gain time, to cause the opponent to react reflexively, to discover the opponent's intentions and make reconnaissance, to prepare an action, to distract the opponent's attention and to camouflage the fencer's intentions.

Attacks on the blade are less frequently used today than in earlier eras. This is due to the fact that:

● sabre fencers rarely hold the blade in line,

● the fencing distance in sabre is much greater than in either foil or épée.

a. Simple actions executed with a bind

Binding the opponent's blade is an action rarely used in sabre fencing. Nevertheless students should practise such movements to enrich their technical repertory and to develop their abilities to manipulate and handle the weapon.

The bind is executed with the forte or middle of the blade making contact with the middle or feeble of the opponent's blade. Binds in third or second act against the edge of the opponent's blade with a gliding pressure. In fourth and first, binds make contact with the back of the opponent's blade.

In theory, five binds corresponding to the five positions do exist. In practice, only second, third and fourth binds are used.

Binds can be classified as:

- direct binds,
- semicircular binds,
- circular binds,
- change binds.

The direct and semicircular binds are used much more often than the circular ones. Change binds are usually used only in lessons as exercises to develop the handling and control of the weapon.

The bind begins with the two blades coming into contact. The objectives are twofold; first, to determine how firmly the opponent grips his weapon, and second, to prevent the opponent from avoiding the fencer's ensuing movement.

The paths described by the direct, semicircular and circular binds are identical to those of the direct, semicircular and circular transitions or parries.

The change bind is a movement executed in a way that transfers the blade from one bind to another with a circular movement of the wrist. Contact between the two blades is lost briefly. The change bind establishes contact in the same line, upper or lower, as the original contact but on the opposite side. The change bind, therefore, can be from third to fourth and vice versa, passing under the opponent's guard, or from second to first and vice versa, passing over the opponent's guard.

The initial contact prior to the change is just a pseudo-bind, a light contact.

Either a cut or a thrust can follow the execution of a bind. Cuts can be direct or round the opponent's blade from above or below. Thrusts can be executed either with the blades remaining in contact or by releasing the opponent's blade. The former are known as bind thrusts.

Bind thrusts should be used against an opponent who holds his hand higher or lower than the point of his blade and offers resistance through the blade.

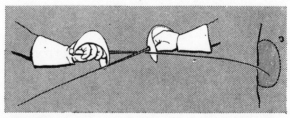

FIG. 156

Such a blade acts as a track along which the bind thrust can act. When the hand is held high, a bind thrust in second (Fig. 156) is effective; if the hand is low, then a bind thrust in third (Fig. 157) can be done.

FIG. 157

169

The following are examples of simple actions combined with a beat.

(1) Against an opponent who holds his blade in high line:

- from third invito, the fencer executes a direct fourth bind followed by a head cut or chest cut either with the edge or draw across the target,
- from second invito, the fencer executes a semicircular fourth bind followed by a head cut or chest cut,
- from fourth invito, the fencer executes a circular fourth bind followed by a head cut or chest cut,
- after making contact in third, the fencer executes a change bind in fourth followed by a head cut or chest cut,
- from fourth or second invito, the fencer executes a direct third bind followed by a head cut or flank cut or bind thrust to the upper area of the target,
- from third invito, the fencer executes a circular third bind followed by a head cut or flank cut or bind thrust,
- after making a contact in fourth, the fencer executes a change bind in third followed by a head cut or flank cut or bind thrust.

(2) Against an opponent who holds his blade in high line and reacts to the fencer's bind with fourth parry:

- from third invito, the fencer executes a direct fourth bind followed by a flank cut passing over the opponent's weapon or cut to outside cheek rounding the opponent's guard,
- from second invito, the fencer executes a semicircular fourth bind followed by a flank cut or cut to outside cheek,
- from fourth invito, the fencer executes a circular fourth bind followed by a flank cut or cut to outside cheek,
- after making a contact in third, the fencer executes a change bind in fourth followed by a flank cut or cut to outside cheek.

(3) Against an opponent who holds his blade in high line and reacts to the fencer's bind with third parry:

- from fourth or second invito, the fencer executes a direct third bind followed by a chest cut passing over the opponent's weapon or a change thrust rounding the opponent's guard,
- from third invito, the fencer executes a circular third bind followed by a chest cut or change thrust,
- after making a contact in fourth, the fencer executes a change bind in third followed by a chest cut or change thrust.

(4) Against an opponent who holds his blade in low line:

- from third invito, the fencer executes a direct second bind followed by a cut to outside cheek or thrust to the upper area of the target rounding the opponent's guard or bind thrust to the lower area of the target,
- from fourth invito, the fencer executes a semicircular second bind followed by a cut to outside cheek or thrust to the upper area of the target or bind thrust,

- from second invito, the fencer executes a circular second bind followed by a cut to the upper area of the target or bind thrust,
- after making a contact in first, the fencer executes a change bind in second followed by a cut to outside cheek or thrust to the upper area of the target or bind thrust.

b. Simple actions executed with a beat

Beats make up the other major group of attacks on the blade. They are used more frequently than binds in sabre fencing.

Beats should be done with the forte or middle of the blade on the feeble or middle of the opponent's blade. Either the edge or back of the blade can be used and the beat can be executed against the edge or back of the opponent's blade.

The beat should be limited in size and stop in the place previously occupied by the opponent's blade before it was dislodged. The beat should also be executed quickly to take the opponent by surprise and prevent him from avoiding it. Finally, the force of the beat must be sufficient to displace the opponent's blade from its threatening position.

Beats can be either dry or grazing. The dry beat makes contact with the opponent's blade at one point only, giving it an energetic smack. In the grazing beat, the blade slides down the opponent's blade after contact is made and makes a scraping noise. It can be described as a combination of bind and beat.

Although five beats can exist to correspond to the five positions, only three, the second, third and fourth beats, are actually used.

Beats can be classified as:

- direct,
- semicircular,
- circular,
- change beat.

The beats most often used are the direct and semicircular. Circular beats are less frequent, and change beats are taught mostly as exercises to develop and polish the student's ability to make proper contact with the opponent's blade.

The paths followed by direct, semicircular and circular beats and related movements are identical with those of direct, semicircular and circular transfers or parries.

Points related to the execution of change beats are the same as those related to the execution of change binds.

Either a cut or thrust can follow the execution of a beat. Cuts can be directed to the body, head, hand or arm but are most often used to score hits on the body and head. Cuts hit directly or after passing over or rounding the opponent's weapon. Thrusts can be straight or done by rounding the opponent's guard, this actually being a change thrust.

The following are examples of simple actions combined with a beat.

(1) Against an opponent who holds his blade in high line:

- from third invito, the fencer executes a direct fourth beat followed by a cut to outside arm, cut to outside cheek, head cut or chest cut,
- from third invito, the fencer executes a circular third beat followed by a flank cut or head cut,
- from fourth or second invito, the fencer executes a direct third beat followed by a flank cut or head cut,
- from second invito, the fencer executes a semicircular fourth beat followed by a cut to outside arm, cut to outside cheek, head cut or chest cut,
- from fourth invito, the fencer executes a circular fourth beat followed by a cut to outside arm, cut to outside cheek, head cut or chest cut,
- after making a contact in third, the fencer executes a change beat in fourth followed by a cut to outside arm, cut to outside cheek, head cut or chest cut.

(2) Against an opponent who holds his blade in high line and reacts to the fencer's beat with fourth parry:
- from third invito, the fencer executes a grazing beat followed by a flank cut passing over the opponent's weapon,
- from third invito, the fencer executes a direct fourth beat followed by a change cut to outside cheek,
- from second invito, the fencer executes a semicircular fourth beat followed by a change cut to outside cheek,
- from fourth invito, the fencer executes a circular fourth beat followed by a change cut to outside cheek,
- after making a contact in third, the fencer executes a change beat in fourth followed by a change cut to outside cheek.

(3) Against an opponent who holds his blade in high line and reacts to the fencer's beat with third parry:
- from second invito, the fencer executes a grazing third beat followed by a chest cut,
- from fourth invito, the fencer executes a direct third beat followed by a change thrust to the upper area of the target.

(4) Against an opponent who holds his blade in low line:
- from third invito, the fencer executes a direct second beat followed by a cut to outside cheek,
- from fourth invito, the fencer executes a semicircular second beat followed by a cut to outside cheek,
- from second invito, the fencer executes a circular second beat followed by a cut to outside cheek,
- from third invito, the fencer executes a semicircular grazing first beat followed by an angular head cut.

(5) Against an opponent who holds his blade in low line and reacts to the fencer's beat with second parry:
- from third invito, the fencer executes a direct second beat followed by a change thrust to the upper area of the target,

- from fourth invito, the fencer executes a semicircular second beat followed by a change thrust,
- from second invito, the fencer executes a circular second beat followed by a change thrust,

c. Beats executed with the back of the blade

Actions introduced by a beat with the back of the blade, or by a beat with the edge finished with a cut using the back of the blade, against the back of the opponent's blade are described as attacks with the back of the sabre.

The beat can be done with:

- the back of the blade against the back of the opponent's blade finishing with a cut using the edge,
- the edge against the back of the opponent's blade finishing with a cut using the back of the blade.

A beat with the back of the blade is designed to loosen the opponent's grip on his weapon and also to inhibit his ability to parry. Such an action is effective against an opponent who holds his blade in a very vertical invito position.

The following are examples of actions done with the back of the blade.

(1) Against an opponent who holds his blade in third invito, the fencer from third invito executes a beat with the back of the blade against the back of the opponent's blade followed by a cut to outside cheek.

(2) Against an opponent who holds his blade in fourth invito, the fencer from fourth invito executes a beat with the edge against the back of the opponent's blade followed by a cut with the back of the blade to inside cheek.

(3) Against an opponent who holds his blade in second invito, the fencer from second invito executes a beat with the back of the blade against the back of the opponent's blade followed by a flank cut.

v. Feint attacks

The feint is a movement which gives the impression that an attack is being launched, and can simulate either a cut or a thrust. It is designed to provoke the opponent's instinctive reaction to parry. The fencer then rounds the parry and executes a cut or thrust to an area of the target other than the one threatened by the feint.

To induce the opponent to react instinctively with a parry, the feint must be done with a clear and suggestive movement which gives a realistic impression. Both the feint and the final action can be done with a cut or thrust.

Variations of single feint actions include:

- feint cut followed by a cut,
- feint cut followed by a thrust,
- feint thrust followed by a thrust,
- feint thrust followed by a cut.

Double feint actions are composed of three movements and, because of the addition of a third element, present many more possible variations in execution. This extra interim movement can be a simulation of either a cut or a thrust.

The first element of the feint attack can indicate an attack to any area of the opponent's target. The finishing movement should be directed to the body or head of the opponent.

The interim movement and final element of a double feint action must always be a time degagement cut followed by a thrust or angular time degagement cut.

Sabre feint actions are easier to describe than foil feint actions because the former are classified according to the area of the target to which they are directed. They can be described as in the following examples:

● feint to head followed by flank cut,
● feint to flank followed by head cut,
● feint to head and flank followed by head cut,
● feint to head followed by a thrust, etc.

In most cases, only simple feint actions designed to deceive simple parries are used in sabre fencing. Circular feints are rare because circular parries are used infrequently.

The long fencing distance between the two fencers and the vertical position of the opponent's weapon mean that most feint actions are executed without any contact between the blades. Feint actions done without making contact can start with the indication of:

● a direct cut or straight thrust,
● a change cut or change thrust,
● a time degagement cut or a time degagement thrust,
● an angular cut.

The majority of feint actions done with an initial contact between the blades are introduced with a beat. The coach, nevertheless, should have the students practise feint attacks begun with a bind to develop and polish their handling and controlling of the weapon.

Beats and binds used to introduce feint attacks need not be as strong and intense as those introducing simple actions.

Against a nervous opponent the feint is executed with a brief movement. A more prolonged movement is used against an opponent of a calmer and quiter nature.

The following are examples of single feint actions.

THE OPPONENT:

(1) holds his blade in third invito and reacts to the fencer's feint with semicircular fifth parry,

(2) holds his blade in fourth invito and reacts to the fencer's feint with fifth parry,

(3) holds his blade in second invito and reacts to the fencer's feint with fifth parry,

(4) holds his blade in fifth invito and reacts to the fencer's feint with second parry,

(5) holds his blade in fifth invito and reacts to the fencer's feint with fourth parry,

(6) holds his blade in fifth invito and reacts to the fencer's feint with second parry,

(7) holds his blade in fourth invito and reacts to the fencer's feint with third parry,

(8) holds his blade in fourth invito and reacts to the fencer's feint with third parry,

(9) holds his blade in third invito and reacts to the fencer's feint with fourth parry,

(10) holds his blade in second invito and reacts to the fencer's feint with first parry,

(11) holds his blade in low line and reacts to the fencer's feint with third parry,

THE FENCER:

● from on-guard, executes a feint to head followed by a flank cut after rounding the opponent's fifth parry,

● from on-guard, executes a feint to head followed by a chest cut after rounding the opponent's fifth parry,

● from on-guard, executes a feint to head followed by a thrust to the body after rounding the opponent's fifth parry,

● from on-guard, executes a feint to flank followed by a head cut after rounding the opponent's second parry,

● from on-guard, executes a feint to chest followed by a head cut after passing over the opponent's fourth parry,

● from on-guard, executes a feint to chest followed by a cut to cheek after rounding the opponent's second parry,

● from on-guard, executes a feint thrust to chest followed by a head cut after passing over the opponent's third parry,

● from on-guard, executes a feint thrust to chest followed by a thrust to chest after rounding the opponent's third parry,

● from on-guard, executes a feint to upper arm followed by a cut to outside cheek after rounding the opponent's fourth parry,

● from on-guard, executes a feint to chest followed by a flank cut after rounding the opponent's first parry,

● from on-guard, executes a beat in second with feint to outside cheek followed by a thrust to chest after rounding the opponent's third parry,

THE OPPONENT:	THE FENCER:

(12) holds his blade in high line and reacts to the fencer's feint with semicircular fifth parry,

● from on-guard, executes a fourth beat with feint to head followed by flank or chest cut or thrust to chest after rounding the opponent's fifth parry,

(13) holds his blade in high line and reacts to the fencer's feint with fourth parry,

● from second invito, executes third bind with feint of change thrust followed by a cut to outside cheek after rounding the opponent's fourth parry,

(14) holds his blade in low line and reacts to the fencer's feint with third parry,

● from on-guard, executes a second bind with feint of change thrust to the upper area of the target followed by a thrust to chest after rounding the opponent's third parry.

The following are examples of double feint actions.

(1) holds his blade in third invito and reacts to the fencer's feints with semicircular fifth parry followed by second parry,

● from on-guard, executes a feint to head and feint to flank after rounding the opponent's fifth parry followed by a head cut after rounding the opponent's second parry,

(2) holds his blade in third invito and reacts to the fencer's feints with fourth parry followed by third parry,

● from on-guard, executes a feint thrust to chest and feint cut to outside cheek after rounding the opponent's fourth parry followed by a thrust to chest after rounding the opponent's third parry,

(3) holds his blade in low line and reacts to the fencer's feints with third parry followed by fourth parry,

● from on-guard, executes a second beat with feint to outside cheek and feint thrust after rounding the opponent's third parry followed by a cut to outside cheek after rounding the opponent's fourth parry,

(4) holds his blade in third invito and reacts to the fencer's feints with semicircular first parry,

● from on-guard, executes a feint to chest and feint to flank after rounding the opponent's first parry followed by a head cut after rounding the opponent's second parry.

vi. Renewed attacks

Renewed attacks in sabre follow the same theoretical principles as described in the chapter on foil fencing. The footwork and blade action chosen by the fencer depend on the opponent's reactions and the fencing distance at the moment in question.

If the opponent parries in place and fails to riposte, the renewed attack is executed with a simple action such as a change cut to hand, arm or chest with appel.

If the opponent steps back with his parry, the fencer can pursue by resuming the on-guard position and renewing the attack with lunge or fleche. The attack should be a feint attack because the fencing distance has been opened.

If the opponent retreats, with or without parrying, by taking several steps to take himself out of range, the fencer can only reach with a renewed attack by recovering forward to on-guard position and pursuing the opponent with a step forward or jump preceding the lunge or fleche.

If the opponent retreats with his blade in line, the fencer must introduce the renewed attack with an attack on the blade to remove the opponent's conventional advantage.

vii. Counter-attacks

The counter-attack with either cut or thrust which prevents the opponent's action from scoring and which is executed during the opponent's attack is called a time counter-attack. It should be done at least one fencing time before the opponent's action.

Time counter-attacks can be executed with:
- time degagement cut or thrust,
- time cut,
- stop thrust.

a. The time degagement cut or thrust

This action is most effective against opponents whose attacks on the blade with bind or beat are technically incorrect, being too large and too obvious. It is executed in much the same manner as the change cut or thrust, with the fencer rounding the opponent's attempted bind or beat with his blade tracing a spiralling path forward. The opponent's blade is passed around the guard and the final cut directed to chest, arm or hand.

The following are examples of the time degagement cut or thrust used as a counter-attack.

THE OPPONENT:	THE FENCER:
(1) takes a step forward from long distance and attempts a bind in second,	● avoids the opponent's bind and executes a cut to outside cheek or thrust to chest with a lunge,

| (2) takes a step forward and attempts a bind in third, | ● avoids the opponent's bind and exexutes a time degagement thrust to the chest, |
| (3) attempts a bind in fourth, | ● avoids the opponent's bind and exexutes a time degagement cut to the hand or arm. |

b. The time cut

The cut executed to the opponent's arm as his attack is in progress is called a time cut. Its success depends on the fencer's technical ability and sense of tempo and, even if done correctly, it may fail. As a safety measure, therefore, the fencer should parry with either a step or jump backward after the time cut in order to remove himself from the range of the opponent's attack.

The cuts are executed in the same way as described in the execution of cuts to the hand and arm.

The following are examples of the time cut.

THE OPPONENT:	THE FENCER:
(1) executes a feint to flank followed by head cut,	● executes a time cut to upper arm in the opponent's feint and steps or jumps back with fifth parry.
(2) executes a feint to head followed by flank cut.	● executes a time cut to inside arm on the opponent's feint and steps back with third parry.

Time cuts can be executed against ripostes as well as attacks if the movement is too large, too slow or done with a feint. The time cuts against ripostes should be done the moment the fencer's initial action has terminated or been parried. For example, the fencer's initial attack is parried with a fifth parry by the opponent, who begins a riposte to chest with a wide movement. At the moment the riposte begins, the fencer executes a time cut to the opponent's hand and steps back with his own parry.

c. The stop thrust

The stop thrust is a time counter-attack which anticipates and intercepts the opponent's attack and renders it ineffective; it can be described as both an offensive and defensive action done at the same time. If the stop thrust is executed during a feint in a feint attack, it need not intercept and neutralize the opponent's final movement.

Stop thrusts are done energetically and with a short lunge. The guard offers strong opposition in the direction of the expected position of the opponent's final action.

If the fencer is in a low position at the time he executes the stop thrust, the movement is carried out in low line; if it is done from a high position, the stop thrust is directed in the high line.

viii. Second intention attacks, feint counter-attacks (finta in tempo) and renewed counter-attacks (counter tempo)

A second intention attack is a movement executed against a habitual action of the opponent, such as a tendency to riposte to the same target area, or against an action induced or deduced in advance, such as a planned counter-attack by the opponent.

Against the habitual riposte the fencer executes a second intention counter-riposte. A second intention parry and riposte is effective against the opponent wishing to use a time counter-attack. No matter which action is chosen, the real intention cannot be revealed. Second intention actions which are hesitant or not firm enough have little chance of success.

In sabre fencing second intention attacks can be executed against all three variations of the time counter-attack; that is the time degagement cut or thrust, the time cut and the stop thrust.

The following are examples of second intention attacks against the various time counter-attacks.

(1) Against the time degagement cut or thrust:

the fencer steps forward and indicates a fourth bind but completes the step with a parry in third and ripostes with the necessary footwork,

● the opponent reacts by rounding the fencer's indicated fourth bind with a time degagement cut to outside cheek or time degagement thrust.

(2) Against the time cut:

the fencer steps forward and indicates a head cut with slightly raised arm but completes the step forward with a parry in third and ripostes with the necessary footwork,

● the opponent reacts to the fencer's indicated head cut with a time cut to the arm.

(3) Against the stop thrust:

the fencer starts with a feint to head but completes the movement with a parry in second and ripostes,

● the opponent reacts to the fencer's feint with a stop thrust.

Feint counter-attacks (finta in tempo) are actions used by the fencer on the defensive against the opponent's second intention attacks. They are done by executing a feint time counter-attack on the opponent's initial action and avoiding the opponent's second intention parry to finish with a cut or thrust to an area of the target not originally threatened. For example, the fencer feints a time degagement cut to outside cheek on the opponent's indicated second beat and executes a time degagement thrust to avoid the opponent's second intention third parry.

The renewed counter-attack against a feint counter-attack (counter tempo), as the name suggests, is usually in the form of a time cut against the opponent's feint counter-attack. If the fencer discovers or deduces that the opponent is preparing a feint counter-attack because it has not been properly disguised, he indicates any cut, thrust, bind or beat and immediately executes a time counter-attack instead of reacting to the opponent's feint of time counter-attack.

In international fencing any movement executed against a counter-attack (action built on tempo) is considered as a counter tempo. This includes both second intention attacks and renewed counter-attacks.

VII. ÉPÉE FENCING

Of the three weapons used in fencing the épée most resembles an actual duelling weapon and follows the methods and concepts of traditional combat with a sword or stabbing weapon. In foil and sabre the scoring of hits is specified by certain conventions and rules which, compared to the unfettered conditions of épée, lends an artificial air to the bout. Although the rules defining the attack, the right of attack, the constitution of a defence, the correct execution of counter-attacks and so on are undisputedly logical, they still leave a sense of something contrived.

Bearing in mind the rules and conventions, translating them into actual practice and including them in the bout all requires additional work and special attention in developing the proper habits and reflexes for foil and sabre. Since no conventions regulate the scoring of hits in épée, the major principle involved is that of hitting first. All the factors which limit the activities of the foil and sabre fencer, which confine the combat within a specific framework and which make learning how to fence a bout even more difficult, do not come into play in épée. Beginners in épée fencing, therefore, are in a favourable position as compared to novice foil and sabre fencers.

The realistic basis and lack of conventions makes épée more popular than foil or sabre in terms of the number of people involved. This popularity is enhanced by the electric scoring system which simplifies matters even further, and by the fact that épée allows more opportunity to the use of natural movements and styles than do the other two weapons. It must be remembered, though, that the most outstanding épée fencers rely on accurate movements and superbly developed technique.

The épée has its origins in the straight sword used extensively in Western Europe quite a while ago. The straight sword was used originally for both thrusting and cutting. As time passed the weapon grew thinner and cuts became ineffective so that today the épée is a thrusting weapon only.

Strange as it may seem, many similarities exist between épée and sabre fencing although the usual comparison made is between épée and foil fencing.

The épée is related to the foil in that:
- both are thrusting weapons,
- both use the same system of positions and movements.

The relationship between épée and sabre is based on a number of factors which reveal a large measure of similarity. They are:
- both include the advanced parts of the body, namely the hand and arm, in the valid target area,
- both rely on the assistance of the forearm and elbow to handle and control the weapon,

- both force the fencer to calculate actions based on two fencing distances which exist simultaneously,
- an apparent similarity in attacks carried out to the arm and hand such as time cuts in sabre and angular thrusts in épée or parrying a time cut followed by a riposte in sabre and parrying a change thrust followed by a riposte in épée.

There are fundamental differences between foil and épée which prevail over the similarities and account for, determine and shape the specific character of épée fencing.

Because the épée is heavier than the foil, more physical strength of wrist and fingers is needed to handle the weapon. Introducing the strength factor into the combat makes épée a more masculine affair. Often the épée fencer needs to have actual physical superiority over the opponent in order to control his weapon in the course of some intense encounters and even body contact which is allowed under the rules of épée.

The larger target area in épée means that defensive actions must be extended to much broader limits.

Hits are scored in épée not according to a conventional priority but temporal priority; that is, whoever hits first.

Two factors in the make-up of the épée are critical to having an effective weapon. They are the point of the blade and the rigidity of the blade.

The point is the means of indicating objectively the materiality of a hit. It also symbolizes that part of the weapon which would inflict a wound or penetrate the opponent's body. Without a sensitive point at the end of the blade, it would be difficult to hit the opponent's wrist, hand or arm because the pointless blade would slip off the target more easily, to which many can attest from experiences in lessons using a pointless weapon.

Many types of point have been tried during the evolution of the épée. The point currently in use is shaped like a disc and is much safer and less damaging to jackets, gloves and other equipment than previous ribbed or spiked designs. Because of this, however, the older designs were more easily and more securely fixed on the target due to their catching on the jacket or other material.

The hand and arm still remain vulnerable to hits but the risk of damage is greatly reduced. The smoother point, however, is more likely to slip off the target and, as a consequence, the fencer runs a greater risk. For this reason, thrusts to the hand and arm are executed less frequently than in previous eras. Coaches promote this but it is no excuse for the neglecting of attacks to the hand and arm or ignoring them to the extent that many épée fencers of the day do.

The fact that fewer thrusts are directed to the hand and arm does not alter the fundamental truth that scoring a clear-cut hit, signalled by a single light, is more likely on the advanced target than on the body.

The second factor, the rigidity of the blade, is important not only because the blade is used to carry the hit but also because it must be able to stop the opponent's thrust from arriving. This requires that the blade be quite rigid.

The need for a rigid blade has also led to a number of technical developments which offer new and different tactical ideas to be put into actual practice.

VII.1. The protective apparel worn in épée fencing

Because the épée is quite a heavy weapon and has a fairly rigid blade, and because the style of fencing calls for and uses more physical strength than either foil or sabre, the possibility of injury is greater. Testimony to this fact exists in the repeated incidence of accidents and injuries caused by the rigid blade in competitions and lessons. It is therefore not enough for the coach or students to know the rules referring to protective apparel of the fencer. The fencer should ensure that jacket, pants and other related items are in good condition before each training session or competition. On occasion the coach should make a routine check of the students' clothing. The possibility always exists that a hit scored on a worn area may cause it to tear and, if the blade gets caught, it could penetrate the jacket and cause injury.

Students may only practise bout fencing while wearing a mask which has no flaws in the mesh or bib. Any dents in the mesh must be hammered out immediately so that the point of an incoming blade cannot get stuck and penetrate during a heavy encounter or forceful action. Wires in the mesh which have spread apart must be moved back together. If the mesh has been repeatedly dented or worn at one place and thus weakened, the mask can no longer be used and must be replaced immediately.

VII.2. Suitability to épée fencing, the time to begin training and the conditions and methods related to training

As mentioned earlier, épée fencing is a masculine sport. It requires a highly developed muscular system and more physical preparation and strength than either foil or sabre.

From the above it follows that the drop in age at which foil and sabre fencing can begin does not apply to épée. A coach may identify future épée fencers from among students in the 10-11-year-old age group based on a prediction of their growing to be quite tall. Specializing in épée, however, should be delayed.

Following an appropriate preparation in foil, students of around 13 of 14 years old may be gradually switched over to épée. This is the optimum age at which to begin training in épée.

To solve the problem of how to prepare future épée fencers, many top coaches

begin training students with the foil. Only when they have acquired the fundamental physical properties needed for épée or have proved themselves capable of
properly conducting a foil bout are the students given the épée.

At this stage the student deemed fit to cope with the increased fencing target
can be taught the special methods of thrusting in épée and other specific movements
characteristic of épée fencing which distinguish it from foil. These specific abilities
and reflexes and sensitivity to the épée should be developed gradually.

The coach must determine the most suitable moment at which to switch the
young foil fencer over to the épée. This should be done before the fencer has
completely internalized the conventions of foil because movements and tactical
concepts which are too ingrained might prevent a successful switch over by a
student otherwise better suited to épée.

If a student of 13 or 14 years old wishes to start fencing, it is still a good idea to
begin his training with the foil because it is easier to handle and control. This
affords an opportunity to limit and polish technical execution and to develop
a refined sensing of the blade. Such a foundation is also indispensable in épée.
Even an experienced épée fencer can benefit from periodic training with the foil
if, for example, he has been forced to miss training for an extended period due to
injury or other such reason.

In days gone by many fencers were equally adept at both foil and épée. Today
this is virtually out of the question because of the number of fencers involved in
the sport and because the standards and intensity of training have increased. Épée
has evolved into a unique sport with its own character and therefore rare is the
fencer who crosses over to the distinct world of foil unless strictly for pleasure and
playful complementary activity.

In selecting épée fencers the coach should give priority to tall students with
a strong physique and long limbs. Only a competitor of superior abilities can
make up for the disadvantages of being short.

From those who start training with the foil, those who carry themselves more
stiffly, who are well-muscled, who have a difficult time loosening up to the degree
necessary for foil and who prove less sensitive to the refined movements needed
in foil, should be switched over to épée.

VII.3. The fundamentals of épée

Épée fencing is founded upon actions and movements used in foil and the material
drawn from this source are adapted in a way that is advantageous to the épée
fencer. The specific characteristics and rules of épée broaden the range of the
chosen actions and often modify the method of execution, giving the épée a more
varied repertory than the foil.

Foil actions adapted in their original form make up the technical basis of épée
fencing. The only difference in execution of these actions is that in épée they

can be carried out against any part of the opponent's body, including the head, arms and legs, hands and feet, and not just the body.

Foil actions which must be modified when adapted to épée fencing form a secondary category in the épée fencer's repertory.

Finally, a third category of actions exist which is made up of actions exclusively belonging to and characteristic of épée fencing. Specific products of épée fencing, they have no counterparts in foil, or counterparts that exist in theory only.

The variety of thrusts in épée is extremely rich. Not only does the épée fencer use the thrust common to foil, but also he must be able to execute angular thrusts and thrusts with opposition. Thus thrusts can be done in three different ways.

The thrust is considered as done in the same way as foil thrust if the blade lies in a straight line at the moment the arm is extended and the movement finished. This line is, in fact, never absolutely straight due partly to the position in which the hand and guard is held and partly to the hand's positioning in the line of the shoulder or even slightly outside the shoulder. Even if the point is directed at a spot on the target lying opposite, the hand never follows the same path as the point. Also, the fact that the blade bends on impact and causes the arm holding the weapon and the épée to rise without a relaxation of the grip or breaking of the wrist excludes the possibility of an absolutely straight line in the final position of the thrust.

Using the thrust common to foil is recommended in situations where the épée fencer has a time advantage over the opponent's anticipated counter-attack. If this time advantage does not exist, the thrust should be executed with opposition by carrying the hand sideways during the thrust, either in the middle of the action or, as is usually the case, in the more critical final stage (see Fig. 158). This move-

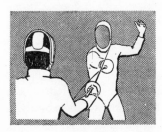

FIG. 158

ment, designed to protect the fencer from being hit, causes the opponent's counter-attack to be driving off-line through the positioning at the right time and to the right extent of the fencer's guard in the line of the opponent's thrust.

Opposition done inward should be more pronounced than opposition done outward since, in the latter, the original hand position of the fencer is already in opposition to some extent. This becomes evident as no substantial difference can be seen between a thrust executed with outward opposition and one done in a manner similar to a foil thrust with little opposition, if any.

The point of the blade, on the other hand, should advance without interruption and maintain its line throughout the thrust.

The angular thrust is designed to place the point in behind the opponent's guard to put it within striking distance. This type of action is almost unknown in foil and used only in exceptional cases by but a few foil fencers. It is used in épée primarily to reach the hand or arm of the opponent whose blade is in line and whose guard protects the advanced target. Its advantage lies in the fact that the angle formed increases the likelihood of scoring a hit while at the same time removing the fencer's arm and hand out of the line threatened by the opponent.

Since the hand and guard move away from the opponent's weapon while executing an angular thrust, the guard and point each travel different paths towards the fencing target. It must be remembered that angular thrusts must come from a closer distance than those executed in a manner similar to foil thrusts.

As in the opposition thrust the blade in the angular thrust can be moved to form the necessary angle at any stage of the thrust. The best time to angulate the blade depends on several factors, including:

● the fencing distance,
● the relative position of the two blades,
● the choice of preparatory movements and other related actions.

If a direct movement with lunge is used, the blade usually takes up its angular position before it is directed to the target. When the fencing distance is long and the fencer intends to use a feint attack which starts to the hand and finishes with an angular thrust, he should conceal his intention as he closes the distance and only execute the final movement at the last possible moment.

It addition, the fencer must be able to execute correct and accurate thrusts in both pronated and supinated hand positions.

The range of defensive movements in épée is broader than in foil, just as it is in terms of offensive movements. Again, this offers a rich variety to the fencer. The character and, in certain instances, even the method of defence in épée also differ from foil fencing.

The first line of defence is provided by the point of the blade held in an appropriate on-guard position and in line. Held in the correct way, without any defensive intention or movement, the weapon offers sufficient coverage to prevent the opponent from executing an attack. The point is activated the moment the opponent begins an action. If the correct on-guard position is taken up, it is impossible for the opponent to execute a direct attack without impaling himself on the fencer's point. The coach should demonstrate this in practice.

The guard also performs an important function in defending the hand and forearm against straight thrusts because it offers protection by hiding the advanced target. Thus no parrying movement is needed.

Counter-attacks are more important and more frequent than parries in épée fencing because of the nature of épée; that is, because there is no convention concerning the priority of hits and because certain parts of the target such as the hand, arm and front leg are at a relatively short distance. Unlike the sabre or foil fencer, the épée fencer does not need to gain conventional advantage in order to execute offensive actions. Counter-attacks, therefore, can be used at any time and against any offensive action of the opponent.

Based on the frequency of execution, two types of defensive counter-attacks can be identified:

- the concise or merged counter-attack, done in one time,
- counter-attacks done in two times, like the parry/riposte timing in foil.

Because the fencing target in épée is much larger than in foil and sabre, any efforts to protect it by parrying would require a major increase in the size of movements which would in turn create many more openings for the opponent to renew his attack or counter-attack on the fencer's riposte. The épée fencer, therefore, should be taught not to use parries against attacks directed below a certain level, but rather use the more effective defensive action of counter-attack. He can also withdraw the leg being threatened or combine this with a counter-attack.

A final defensive option is a special possibility. It involves the withdrawing of the smaller and more mobile target areas such as the hand, arm, leg or foot out of range of an attack. Occasionally this passive method which creates an excellent opportunity for taking over the attack should be combined with blade actions to make it an active defensive approach.

The factors which decide the form of defence chosen by the fencer are several. Besides the fencer's personal preference, the situation or the moment, the actual possibility of executing the preferred movement and the related psychological and objective conditions help to determine whether or not to use an action or substitute it with another.

i. The make-up of the épée and the correct grip

Of the three weapons used today in the sport of fencing the épée most resembles its ancestor, the straight sword used in Western Europe, and has maintained many of its physical characteristics such as the guard which covers the hand and the triangular blade with its channel to allow the blood to drain.

The épée is made up of the blade, the handle, the guard and the locking nut or pommel.

The blade, when viewed in cross-section, is shaped like a triangle with the electric wire running along the channel. The rigidity, or flexibility, of the blade is specified in the rules governing épée fencing.

As in sabre and foil, the blade of the épée can be divided into three sections. This division is based upon practical considerations more in épée than in foil, which relies less on physical strength. The spring-loaded point at the tip of the blade must be able to support a weight of 750 grams as laid down in the international rule book.

The handle is made either of wood or of metal. The French grip can be of either material and is usually covered with rubber, while the pistol grip invariably is made of aluminium (see Fig. 159). The épée equipped with a French grip is held

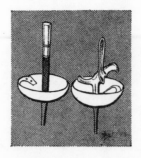

FIG. 159

together by a pommel, while a locking nut is used to hold a pistol grip épée together.

When the épée is assembled, the handle should be bent inward and downward in relation to the line of the blade.

The method of holding an épée equipped with a French handle is the same as that for holding a French foil, except that the thumb and index finger are placed a little farther from the guard, at about 1 centimetre from it. This is done to prevent injury to the fingers in the event of any heavy impacts occurring which, in épée, happens fairly frequently. The holding of the pistol grip and the placement of the fingers on the handle are determined by the actual configuration of the pistol grip.

ii. Vulnerable points of the fencing target

Although the entire body, including the head and limbs, constitutes the target area, certain sections are categorized as vulnerable points because they are more accessible to the attacking blade. Because of this these sections are the ones to which most attacks are directed and on which most hits are scored. Obviously the vulnerable points are those areas of the target lying closest to the opponent and are situated on the arm and flank on the same side as the arm holding the weapon.

The vulnerable points of the target, listed in an order descending the body are, in the case of a right-handed fencer:

- the head,
- the right part of the chest,
- the right shoulder and upper arm, the right elbow,
- the right forearm,
- the right wrist,
- the right flank and hip,
- the right thigh and knee,
- the right leg and foot.

Attacks directed to the head:

- fail into the opponent's central vision, which is less sensitive to perceiving motion and, therefore, results in a delay of defensive reflexes,
- are executed in the highest possible line to which the opponent cannot

easily react by raising his weapon because of the principle of advantage
inherent in the high line.

The vulnerability of the arm, elbow and wrist is primarily attributable to their
proximity to the opponent's point. The fact that these advanced areas are closer
not only means that they are easier to hit but also that the attack arrives more
quickly and less footwork is needed to reach these targets than to reach the body.
The opponent's retreat following an unsuccessful attack is also safer than if he
had closed the distance to reach the body. Also, being constantly aware of the
threat of the rigid blade to the arm and hand, the fencer dares not risk extending
his arm any farther than necessary.

If the fencer fails to land a hit on the advanced target areas he can continue
his attack to the opponent's body rather than search for the target area which
has been missed because this major surface still lies beyond and acts as a secondary
target.

Both the trunk and hips constitute a reliable and secure target because of their
greater size and because they are less mobile than the arms and legs.

Fencers tend to have difficulty in sensing the timing of attacks to the thigh and
foot because these areas lie just at the limits of the fencer's field of vision. Surprise
actions directed to the thigh and foot, therefore, offer a reasonable promise of
success.

VII.4. The on-guard position (Fig. 160)

In the on-guard position for épée the fencer's legs, feet, body and free arm are
positioned in the same way as in the foil on-guard. The distance between the feet
is also the same, although the fencer may close his stance if he thinks this will

FIG. 160

make the leading leg a less vulnerable target. If this is done, the body's weight
should not be transferred to the rear leg, a method formerly adopted, because
such a position inhibits the fencer's ability to make a quick start in any direction
he might wish to move.

The épée fencer must also bend both legs to take up a seated position, but not
in an unnatural fashion. The legs and thighs held at an optimum angle ensure
elasticity in movement and promote the quick execution of the lunge.

The arm holding the weapon is held higher and more extended than in the foil on-guard. An on-guard with the arm completely extended should be avoided except in certain instances which are determined by tactical considerations. Such an extended position causes the muscles to stiffen and leaves little in reserve for a further extension if needed. Even when almost completely extended, there should always be an emergency reserve of one or two inches left for further extension.

On the other hand, the arm is not held with the elbow too bent. This allows the opponent's point to come too close to the target and increases the time and distance required to halt an attack. It also exposes the upper arm and elbow to a greater extent and virtually invites the opponent's hit.

The forearm lies horizontal, with the elbow pulled inward towards the body and the hand held supine. The point of the blade is directed inward and downward, lying slightly below the level of the guard, and towards the opponent's guard.

Holding the hand and blade high:

- offers the optimum starting position for any type of attack or defence the fencer wishes to execute,
- most effectively translates the principle of the high line into practice,
- protects the fencer's arm and hand with the guard almost completely.

The point being directed inward and towards the opponent's wrist:

- facilitates the defence of target areas in front of the body,
- emphasizes the threat which the point represents.

If the hand is held supine:

- the certainty of the thrust is increased because the elbow is prevented from moving laterally in any direction,
- promotes more accurate and limited parries executed with a movement of the forearm.

Only a fully supinated hand position can offer complete coverage to the fencer's forearm and elbow and partial coverage of the arm behind the guard and the point of the weapon.

The prone position of the hand fails to offer an adequate coverage of the target areas lying close to the opponent and fails to ensure the accuracy of the point. The supine position offers the fencer many advantages even if it takes a long time to learn and accommodate, advantages which are worth the effort. If necessary, the coach should teach the student to relax the shoulder in order to hold the hand in the required supine position.

If the on-guard position is adequate:

- the fencer is protected against any direct attack to the advanced parts of the target, namely, the hand, arm, foot and leg,
- the opponent must first deflect the fencer's blade before executing any attack to the body,
- the fencer can more easily avoid the attempted binds of the opponent because of the point's being directed downward,
- attacks in the low line can be countered simply by extending the arm.

Fencers who develop a preference for executing cutovers to the advanced areas of the target and for counter-attacks normally take up an on-guard position different from the one outlined above. They hold the blade more vertically, with the arm bent at the elbow. It is halfway between the on-guard in line and the on-guard customarily used in foil. This position facilitates the execution of cutovers because the first stage of lifting the point has been eliminated. Taking advantage of the inherent peripheral speed, the fencer moves the point towards the target with an accelerating whip-like action.

VII.5. Épée actions

i. Attacks directed to the advanced areas of the target

As already mentioned, the advanced areas of the target are the most vulnerable to attack. For this reason the principles and possibilities of executing attacks to these areas must be examined before looking at other forms of attack.

The limbs are very mobile and present small surface when compared to the rest of the fencing target. To score a hit on these areas which usually are in motion or can be easily moved from one position to another requires a highly developed ability to handle and control the weapon. Practice in handling and controlling the blade requires careful and precise work and constantly taking lessons.

Success of attacks to advanced target areas such as the wrist, forearm, elbow, leg and foot depends on:
- the timing selected in which to execute the action,
- the speed of execution,
- the accuracy of the movement.

In general, simple actions should be used when an attack is directed to the opponent's hand or arm. This is because the opponent is usually set to counter-attack against any offensive movement. The simple actions chosen can be executed with or without a bind and can take the following forms:
- straight thrust, either in opposition or in manner similar to a foil thrust,
- change thrust, similar to the change thrust in foil but with the hand giving opposition during the movement,
- angular thrust.

When the straight thrust or change thrust is used, the hand should maintain its supine position throughout the movement because any change in hand position can cause the point to deviate laterally. A rotation which causes a break in the line of the blade and grip can result in the point being displaced an inch or more. Although this sounds like very little, it can be enough to cause the point to slip off the target, which in the case of advanced target areas is a small surface.

The supine position of the hand maintains the weapon in its position as if it were clamped in a vice and limits possible deviations to a minimum even when a number of thrusts are executed in succession.

If the fencer rotates his weapon, he will find it impossible to hit a specific area because the surface is very small and, proportionate to the magnitude of the rotation, the vulnerable areas recede from his point. For example, as the fencer rotates his weapon while attacking the arm, the deviation in the position of the point causes it to move gradually upward along the arm, pushing the most vulnerable point farther away and thus increasing the risk of a double hit.

During the thrust the hand does not drop below the level of its original position and thus maintains the height of the blade. If the hand drops, the reach of the fencer is shortened, which is an obvious disadvantage and increases the danger of the opponent's counter-attack hitting. When he sees the blade dropping, the opponent can easily seize the high line and its inherent advantage.

The blade may be elevated but only if necessary and only in the final stage of the thrust with an accompanying movement of the arm. The wrist must not be bent nor the grip of the fingers loosened.

In no instance can the fencer lean on the target for support when the thrust hits. It is unnecessary to exert such pressure on the point over and above the specified weight of 750 grams.

Too much pressure on the point:
- is unpleasant for the coach when giving a lesson,
- leads to the fencer leaning on the target for support,
- offers the opponent greater opportunity to execute a counter-attack,
- makes the fencer's return to guard more difficult.

During the thrust the hand must remain in the supine position while the arm is extended. The point and the guard move along separate paths and, as the rear foot pushes the fencer, they approach the target on parallel lines. There should be no additional aiming of the point during the thrust as this might reduce the certainty of the hit finding the target.

The movement of hand and arm must be in complete harmony with that of the feet.

While the lunge is executed the body remains erect and does not fail forward. This is a more important requirement in épée than in foil or sabre. In contrast to foil, the épée fencer returns to the on-guard position from the lunge with the arm holding the weapon remaining extended in order to fend off the threat of a counter-attack by the opponent. Only when the on-guard position has been resumed can the arm be bent. Some fencers develop a bad habit of lowering the blade as they return to the on-guard position. This is a result of carelessness and the more comfortable feeling it affords. It can be eliminated if the coach, during the lesson, executes on occasion counter-attacks after the student has scored a hit and which can be neutralized only if the student returns to the on-guard position with the arm extended.

Executing an attack with a straight thrust is effective only if the opponent leaves his arm unprotected. The arm may be left unprotected either voluntarily or because of movements executed by the fencer. Thrusts done in a manner similar to foil should only be attempted if the fencer has a clear tempo advantage over the opponent and the threat of a counter-attack neutralized with an opposition from the hand.

The thrusts most effective for penetrating a correctly held on-guard position or getting in behind a blade held in line are the angular thrusts. Because the fencer's hand is exposed when he breaks the line of the hand and blade, angular thrusts must be executed quickly and should come as a surprise.

It is recommended to combine angular thrust with a contact of the opponent's blade, usually with a beat. A strong beat done in an unconventional manner can not only delay but sometimes even make a counter-attack impossible to execute.

Angular thrusts of the opponent's hand can come from practically any direction; that is, from above, below, outside or inside. For angular thrusts done from above, outside or inside the hand is held in a supine position; for angular thrusts from below, the hand is held in a prone position.

Provided the fencer considers the appropriate direction in which the point should be set prior to executing an angular thrust, the certainty of the thrust's finding the target is enhanced and, at the same time, the threat of a counter-attack is diminished. An angular thrust from above is used against an opponent's blade which points downward. Angular thrusts from the other directions are determined according to the same analytic process. In the initial stages of teaching angulated thrusts the coach can make things easier for the student by offering a target which is well-exposed and at a favourable angle to be hit. At later stages the target may be kept covered to compel the student to execute angular thrusts in a more realistic context.

Straight thrusts are effective as attacks directed to the knee, leg and foot, although the threat of a counter-attack with stop thrust by the opponent must always be kept in mind. For this reason, thrusts to the foot should be used sparingly and must come as a surprise after proper planning and preparation. They should be introduced with some form of contact with the opponent's blade or when and if the opponent pulls back his arm. Beats are not well suited for introducing attacks to the foot since the opponent's blade returns to its original line immediately following the beat.

Initially the students practise thrusts to the body, shoulder and elbow, later thrusts to the forearm and wrist are included. The process of teaching thrusts is one of a gradual reduction in terms of the target area to be hit.

In the initial stage of teaching thrusts are practised in a manner similar to foil thrusts. Opposition thrusts are included next and finally angular thrusts.

During the fencing lesson any type of thrust can in principle be executed. In practice, however, thrusts to the foot are painful to the coach and those to the head dangerous because of the stiffness of the épée blade. Rarely are these thrusts practised in the lesson. They can easily be executed in the course of bout fencing by a fencer who has the ability to score hits with precision on the hand and arm.

In previous eras the coach wore leg guards for protection when teaching thrusts to the leg, but this is no longer fashionable. To teach thrusts to the head, coaches used to place their hands in front of their faces and the student would hit the elevated target. At the moment the point landed the coach would turn his arm inward to cushion the shock and secure the hit on the target.

Today the coach is advised to wear a protective outer sleeve over his jacket when giving an épée lesson. This reduces the impact of a straight, rigid blade and saves the coach's jacket as well.

When teaching thrusts the coach's presentation and position designed to create the necessary conditions are identical to those described in the chapter on foil fencing. One additional element which is needed when thrusts to the elbow, forearm and wrist are executed is the coach's follow-up movement. This follow-up movement represents an attempt to close or protect the opening or area to which the student has directed his thrust in a manner resembling the actual reaction of an opponent in bout fencing. Imitations of parries and counter-attacks, which constitute follow-up movements, should follow the fixing of the hit by a split second.

The coach, therefore, fulfils a dual function in the teaching of thrusts to the hand and arm. First, he gives an opening in which the student hits and then, following the student's thrust and in harmony with it, attempts to close that opening. The follow-up movement, done immediately after the student's thrust, creates bout-like conditions and also prompts a quicker execution of the student's action.

Even if proper care is taken, the follow-up movement often causes a heavy impact of the student's point on the coach's arm. Because both coach and student are in motion, the relative speed of the two actions is increased and thus raises the force of impact. Thrusts executed by the coach which are quite strong can lead to pains in the joints, which can become chronic. He should, therefore, symbolically represent the conditions of a bout, the intention and not the actual strength of an action, when executing the follow-up movement.

The fencer can adopt a number of different defensive methods against thrusts directed to the advanced areas of the target. These include:

● preventive positions, the most important of which is a correct on-guard,
● counter-attacks with opposition to the opponent's advanced target areas,
● withdrawing the threatened area from the line of attack and counter-attacking with an angular thrust,
● parry and riposte.

Counter-attacks are the simplest and most effective means of defence against angular thrusts. They should be directed to the area of the opponent's target lying closest to the guard and so reduce to a minimum the risk of a double hit. Against angular thrusts from below, the counter-attack is done with downward opposition. Opposition outward is used against angular thrusts from outside, and opposition inward against angular thrusts from inside.

At first, beginners are taught the correct execution of counter-attacks against angular thrusts without any blade contact, later, time counter-attacks introduced with an attack on the blade can be used against angular thrusts.

After executing a counter-attack with a time thrust the fencer steps back and frees his point from the opponent's arm. This allows him to open the distance and defend himself in the event that the opponent continues his attack.

ii. Unwritten rules governing attacks to the body

The farther the area of the target lies from the fencer, the more cautious and thoughtful he must be in executing an attack to it. The fencer should take measure to cover himself when executing an attack to the body, which is the most removed target, from medium distance. Obviously, at close quarters different considerations must be taken into account.

Measures which protect the fencer in the face of a quick and threatening time counter-attack which can come at any moment include:

- a feint, which causes the opponent to move his blade and arm from their original position,
- second intention, which induces a time counter-attack and neutralizes it with a preconceived defensive action,
- a compound attack on the blade, which contains the opponent's attempts to avoid the fencer's actions by executing several changes of transfers in quick succession.

The processes used in providing protection for the impending attack can be different in nature; that is, they can be technical variations or tactical movements. They are designed to allow the fencer to close the fencing distance and score a hit with his thrust while delaying or after parrying the opponent's time counter-attack.

Thrusts to the upper part of the body are never directed at the body, but rather at the shoulder. There are several reasons for this, including the fact that:

- the shoulder is closer to the fencer,
- a hit on the shoulder is more likely to fix.

Attacks to the opponent's body and shoulder are best executed in the fencer's sixth line because it offers the maximum security due to the opposition involved. It is also the position from which it is easiest to renew attacks to the arm and forearm if the initial action fails to find the target.

The épée fencer should refrain from executing first intention attacks to the opponent's body, unless they have been properly prepared and introduced.

iii. Defensive actions

In contrast to foil, there are no conventions in épée specifying the proper and sufficient execution of defensive actions. Since the overriding objective is to hit the opponent before being hit, the most effective defensive action as evidenced many times in practice is an opposition thrust during the opponent's attack which neutralizes the attack while scoring a hit at the same time. This type of action is made up of two elements, one attacking and one defending, which are done simultaneously as in contrast with the two-time defensive rhythm of parry and riposte used in foil.

Time counter-attacks play a much more important role in épée than in either foil or sabre. Because there is no rule of priority to determine when a fencer may execute a time counter-attack, the épéeist must always be aware when he attacks of the possible counter-attack of the opponent which may come at any time.

The time counter-attack can be executed in tempo; that is, hitting before the opponent can hit. It can also be done for other reasons, such as the neutralizing of the opponent's attack or the making of a double hit, keeping in mind the one-twenty-fifth of a second time delay in the signalling of the electric scorer.

Time counter-attacks are best executed against the opponent's hand or arm while taking a short step backward or returning to the on-guard position.

The time degagement thrust, used to avoid the opponent's attack on the blade, often results in a double hit. For this reason this type of time counter-attack is adopted less frequently in épée than in foil.

The derobement, however, which is a release of the blade from the opponent's bind, is preferred much more. This movement, which is characteristic of épée, can be executed effectively only if the fencer waits until the opponent's bind is firm and definite. The later the fencer can release his blade from the bind, the more certain the hit is to find the target before the opponent's hit arrives. This observation is verified when using the electric scoring apparatus. Paradoxically this happens not because the fencer makes the hit but because the opponent's hand or arm moves in a way that causes it to be hit.

The derobement is done with a spiralling movement from the on-guard position while the opponent's blade advances. The fencer releases his blade in line from the opponent's blade but does not extend his arm or execute a thrust. If done in this manner, the opponent's blade in most cases slips off the target because the blade involuntarily pushes past the intended target.

Once the hit has landed, the fencer steps backward, at the same time pushing off the target through a pressure on his point. This type of "taking off" is commonly seen in sabre fencing after the execution of a time cut. If the fencer does not keep proper distance, releasing the blade from the opponent's bind does not result in the fencer scoring a hit.

As well as defensive actions with the point, the usual defensive movements in the form of the parries have an important and specific role to play in épée fencing. Unlike foil parries, however, the parries used in épée offer cover for only a very short time.

The fencer's defensive system should be well camouflaged so that the opponent, who is very familiar with parries, cannot anticipate the fencer's movements. He should also vary the use of the parries since a defensive system based solely on counter-attacks can be neutralized and broken down by the opponent's use of second intention attacks.

The sooner a defensive action is executed, the more a parry followed by a riposte resembles a counter-attack in terms of the duration. The difference between the two is that, in executing a time counter-attack, the fencer does a thrust in order to defend himself while, in executing a parry and riposte, he defends himself in order to carry out a thrust. In épée, the two-time rhythm of parry and riposte, common to foil fencing, is used only when fencing at close quarters.

The characteristic opposition of parries is more pronounced in épée than in foil. Parries are also strong and firm, with an active participation of the forearm. The blade is moved and controlled with the forearm, the wrist being moved only to a minimum.

During the formation of a parry the point of the weapon remains in a central position, close to the opponent's target and line, except in the case of parries done at close quarters. This is necessary in order to facilitate a quick execution of the riposte and is counter-balanced by the firm opposition offered, even in physical terms, by the parry.

Fencers tend to prefer sixth, counter-sixth and second parries. The body, which is the largest part of the fencing target, is most exposed and therefore vulnerable when fourth and circular parries are used. Circular parries, however, are highly effective in defending the hand from attacks directed from above, but should only be used if the opponent's intention has been clearly revealed. The success of the fourth parry, a very effective defensive movement, depends on the speed with which the riposte follows. Third parry can be used to best advantage at close quarters. The on-guard position, the location of the individual parries, and their relationships to each other are shown in Figure 161.

FIG. 161

Most frequently the riposte in épée is executed with contact between the blades being maintained. Usually it is directed to the area of the target lying closest to the point of the weapon about to execute the riposte. For example, after a second parry, the riposte is directed to the lower part of the body or the thigh of the opponent. Often a transfer is used to prevent the opponent from using a renewed thrust.

Parries can occasionally take the form of beat parries. If fencing at close quarters, the only effective riposte is a thrust carried out to the body.

The actions used in épée are based on the same foundations as those in foil, but the system in which they are taught is different. Students practise attacks in parallel with every type of defensive action, including time counter-attacks and defensive movements done with the point. The basic nature of épée offers better opportunities for the fencer to execute the various defensive actions described above than does the other thrusting weapon, the foil.

Fencing – its history and development

Fencing and fighting

Although fencing is probably not as old as fighting, it must be much older than recorded history. Since humans developed weapons, they have constantly studied how to use them more effectively. Their search naturally led them to develop nonlethal practice forms and training methods. Every family, clan, tribe or nation found ways to hone its combat skills, developing fighting traditions which ultimately developed into martial arts. Five-thousand-year-old Egyptian paintings show soldiers training with wooden swords and protective padding. Often enough, a practice session with swords must have turned from a military drill into a friendly contest. At the moment combat preparation turned into play, the *sport* of fencing was born. And at that very moment, I am certain, a fighter from the old school was on hand to lament that the whole spirit of sword-fighting had been ruined.

The Renaissance

The line of development which leads to our modern Olympic sport of fencing begins much later – in Europe, just as the Middle Ages were ending and the features of the modern age were beginning to emerge.

Many forces led to the emergence of what we can call the Renaissance gentleman. The gentleman was subtly different from the knights of preceding generations. He aspired to be a courtier as well as a combatant. Like Chaucer's Squire, he cultivated dancing and the arts as well as jousting. It no longer seemed necessary, practical, or polite for him to carry battlefield weapons on the city streets, let alone indoors. Of course, he still wore his sword – partly for self-defense, but more and more for advertising who and what he was.

The wearing of a sword proclaimed a gentleman's honor and his readiness to defend it. It marked him as a cultivated heir of the knights and heroes of old – the heavily armored mounted fighters who were actually not yet obsolete on the battlefield. As everything in his life was supposed to be, the gentleman's sword was beautiful as well as useful. The sword became an article of costume and an item of fashion.

Fashion is a tyrant. Increasingly, it dictated that swords be lighter and more graceful than battlefield swords, more harmonious with the costumes and manners of the Renaissance. Who would be so uncouth as to walk the streets, or stalk the salons of Paris or Verona, elegantly ruffed and doubleted in the latest fashion, but carrying a two-handed armor-crushing battle sword? Absurd! As well carry an axe or a glaive! Against unarmored (not unarmed!) opponents, the new rapiers were no less deadly. And since the proud gentlemen who carried them were forever ready to draw them in defense of their honor, it was still necessary for every honorable man to learn to use a sword, and use it well.

The rise of technique

Early swordplay was not at all unsophisticated, but it was relatively simple, as really serious hand-to-hand combat must always be. A trained fighter like Prince Hamlet, who aspired to be a hero like his axe-wielding father, will always scoff at the ridiculous excesses of a courtier like Osric. (The so-called "duel" in *Hamlet* actually illustrates some of the conventions of a fencing *exhibition* circa 1600.) The lightness of the new weapons, however, in addition to making practice more pleasurable, led to the development of increasingly complex techniques. These arose because they were spectacular, exciting, and *possible* – for the sheer pleasure of performing them. Like every Renaissance art, the new swordplay was systematized by masters in the leading cultural centers – Spain, Italy, France and Germany – and written down in a succession of classic fencing texts. Regional styles and "secret strokes" were rampant. This is the period of legendary (but historical) swordsmen like D'Artagnan and Cyrano de Bergerac. We see such figures today through the nineteenth-century eyes of Dumas and Rostand and their innumerable successors on stage and screen, and they provide fencing with some of its lasting images.

Fencing was now practiced as an art. Actions developed for use in the *salle d'armes* (fencing room) which would have been too risky to use much on the slippery and uncertain surfaces of the outdoor dueling fields. One such action was the lunge. This one action is so characteristic of the modern sport that it has become almost its trademark. A smooth, lightning-fast elongation of the whole body ("lunge" comes from French *"allonger,"* to lengthen), the lunge replaced the cross-footed "pass" as the means of choice for delivering an attack – as long as you were fencing on a floor rather than grass or gravel. Likewise it became popular to deflect, or parry, an attack (rather than dodge it) with the purpose of launching an immediate reply (the riposte) even without maintaining control of the adversary's blade. Like the lunge, this detached parry-riposte was swifter and more exciting than the moves it supplanted. And like the lunge, it carried a serious risk – of being hit while hitting – a risk that was much more acceptable in the salle d'armes than on the field. Finally, the invention of the mask, around the beginning of the eighteenth century, made it practical to teach and practice even riskier and more elaborate actions – as well as putting an end to a tradition of one-eyed fencing masters. More and more, the martial art of fencing was becoming a sport – a contest with increasingly explicit rules, practiced for the sheer delight of combat play.

The nineteenth century

With the French Revolution and its aftermath, the original context of fencing was largely lost. Gentlemen no longer wore even small-swords on the street; while indoors, court swords were increasingly relegated to a purely ceremonial function. Gentlemen still fought duels, but in post-revolutionary France at least, the duel was a more egalitarian institution. No longer a monopoly of the hereditary aristocrats, honor was available to all who chose to claim it. Since the maintenance of honor rested on one's willingness to defend it with the sword or the dueling pistol, dueling continued. Partially supported by this ethos of symbolic knighthood, fencing as a sport and art continued to grow.

The art of fencing reached one of its undoubted peaks in the nineteenth century. The parry-riposte sequence evolved into an intricate chain of probes and replies, feints and attacks, ripostes, counter-ripostes, and counter-counter-ripostes, delivered with dazzling speed and increasingly elaborate blade work. Fencing actions multiplied, as did the textbooks that expounded them. There were nine distinct parries, which could be executed in four distinct directions. There were at least ten ways of sustaining or breaking contact with the adversary's steel while attacking or defending. These could in turn be combined with the parry positions to produce whole systems of attack and defense which were available to the fencer both for use and for discussion. The luxuriant flowering of fencing actions was quite independent of developments on the dueling field, where the life-and-death nature of the struggle always necessitated more restraint and simplicity.

The supreme weapon of this efflorescence of the sport was the foil, an even lighter and much more flexible descendant of the rapiers and small-swords of previous centuries. The French and Italian names for the foil (*fleuret, fioretto*) mean "little flower" and give an idea of the image of delicacy and grace which the foil projected.

The English word "foil" derives from a word related to "fold," meaning "turned back" like the tip of a blunted weapon. Being "foiled" means being thwarted, as when a fox turns back on its tracks. So the famous cry of "Curses! Foiled again!" has nothing, alas, to do with fencing. The "foils" in *Hamlet* weren't today's fencing foils but blunted, or "bated," rapiers.

The classical foil was invented purely as a training weapon, not a combat arm. In the hands of a master swordsman, of course, it has always been more than that, as the great Jean-Louis proved in a famous fight. Jean Louis, the son of a Haitian woman and a French army officer, was considered the finest (French) swordsman of the Napoleonic era. In a duel against a boastful but capable opponent armed with a sharp smallsword, he used only a blunted foil. Jean-Louis parried all his attacks, touched his adversary (harmlessly, of course) at will, flicked the buttons off his shirt in quick succession, and concluded the encounter by bloodying his opponent's face with a slash from his blunted tip.

The three disciplines

Spurred, perhaps, by the success of foil as recreation, other fencing disciplines arose. Around the middle of the century, the military sabre, a heavy battlefield weapon, was refined and lightened to allow sporting use, beginning its evolution into a fencing weapon. At the same time, a few fencers were decrying what they considered the *excessive* refinement of foil technique. They began training with the epee, a blunted twin of the dueling sword of that period. (Civilians always dueled with this sword – the French *épée de combat* – while military officers might choose the sabre if they preferred.) This developed into the third of the fencing disciplines. With its simpler rules and its closeness to the conditions of a historical duel – if we ignore the element of fear! – epee has always had its devoted adherents.

Epee is the simplest of the weapons to explain. Hits are scored with the point only. They can land anywhere on the body, from the top of the head to the sole of the foot, to the back, to the arms – anywhere. Whoever hits first scores the touch. If both fencers hit at the same time, the touch is scored *against* both of them. The result is that in an epee match, as in a duel, both contestants can lose.

Foil, like epee, scores only with the point. However, the target is limited to the torso of the body, including the whole front of the body from the groin to just below the throat, as well as the back and sides above the top of the hips. (Arms, legs, and mask are not valid.) In other words, the target looks a lot like a short fencing jacket with no sleeves, and in fact, competitors wear a metallic vest so that touches can register. Unlike epee, foil is a *conventional* weapon: if both fencers are hit about the same time, there is a set of rules to decide the touch, not only who hits first. For a fuller explanation, read Appendix C: Priority ("Right of way")

Sabre, like foil, is a conventional weapon with a restricted target area. The sabre target is the entire body above the tops of the legs – torso, arms, and head. Unlike foil or epee, sabre uses both the point and the edge of the weapon, which increases the attacking potential and makes sabre a dashing, aggressive weapon which recalls its cavalry origins.

The growth of fencing

Women as well as men could take up the light and flexible foil, and they did so. Fencing is one of the few combat *sports* in which men and women of all sizes and every degree of physical strength can contend on a more or less equal footing. From the early nineteenth century (if we don't count the eighteenth-century Chevalier d'Eon, a celebrated fencer who lived as a man, but may have been a woman or a hermaphrodite), women were fencing against men and sometimes beating them. A popular series of prints by Rowlandson shows the scandalized fascination this topic held for the public. Sabre and epee, the slightly heavier weapons associated with dueling, held out as masculine preserves well into this century. At present, however, there are world championships and Olympic medals for women's epee, and women's sabre seems to be on the verge of general acceptance.

The rise of fencing as a sport was unaffected by the decline in the frequency and prestige of actual dueling. Fencing epitomizes some of the best values of the culture that produced it: quickness, grace and flexibility of mind and body, accompanied by a soul of honor, courage and courtesy. Since fencing stressed these qualities over brutality and force, it seemed natural for it to become a part of physical education curricula. Not only did it promote confidence, coordination, and trimness – as one nineteenth-century advertisement promised, in terms prophetic of today's leisure industry – it also seemed perfectly designed to build that elusive quality, "character," in the nation's youth. When Sir Richard Burton, the great adventurer, explorer, and translator of *The Arabian Nights* had his portrait painted, he proudly dressed in his fencing master's uniform.

The spread of fencing was part of a transformation of sport itself which had already been going on for some time and has not ended even today. Like fencing, sports in general changed from the private preserve of an elite to a meeting ground for wider and wider groups of people. It became a vehicle for national unity – and somewhat later, for international unity as well.

Fencing was one of the sports at the first Olympic Games in 1896. The rise of international competition led to pressure for standardization of rules among the different fencing nations. In 1913 the International Fencing Federation, or F.I.E. (Fédération Internationale d'Escrime), was born. Nine nations were present at its first meeting. The rules of fencing it issued in the following year are still in use.

In the twentieth century, and especially since the end of the Second World War, fencing has become a genuine world sport. A few of the oldest fencing nations – especially France and Italy, but Spain and Germany as well – dominated international fencing at its inception. Very early on, Hungary joined the ranks of the fencing powers.

Hungary deserves special mention, since this book is devoted to the International School, which developed there. One of its leading pioneers was Italo Santelli, an Italian fencing master. (Giorgio Santelli, the legendary American coach, was Italo's son. Italo started him fencing at the age of six, trained him as a fencing master, and sent him to America to spread the gospel.) Italo was called to Budapest at the beginning of the twentieth century. Hungary itself already boasted a strong national fencing tradition. Here Santelli and others worked to create a practical effective style, avoiding the dogmatism which had crept into some of the older schools.

These great coaches made Hungary a leader in modern fencing. They helped make it possible for a country left tiny and impoverished by the First World War to produce so many champions and teach so much to so many other nations. Even before the Second World War, Hungary's "International" style was strong in all the weapons and dominant in sabre. After the war, the Hungarian approach, with numerous national variations, rapidly became, and remains, the world's dominant school.

The Cold War saw a worldwide transfer of international political rivalries into the world of sport. One result was that Eastern European nations, led by the Soviet Union, crowded into the ranks of the premier fencing powers. Forty years later, the Soviet Union's collapse and the end of the East Bloc did not weaken fencing in these nations. Rather, it produced more national squads to contend for the available medals. Cuba, which reemerged as a fencing power during the Cold War, has also remained very strong. As of the present writing, China and Korea are leading East Asia into the elite group: the World Cup event at Venice in 1997 saw those two nations contend for the team foil title. The Islamic world has also joined the fencing movement. Egypt has a strong fencing tradition, and other Arab countries are investing heavily in fencing squads. Nearly a hundred countries, representing every inhabited continent, have fencing federations and participate in the international fencing movement.

A fencing bout today

What would a swordsman of an earlier day– Hamlet, D'Artagnan, Jean Louis or Sir Richard Burton – think of a bout in today's world sport?

The lighter weapons and increased speed and distance of today's game would dazzle the Renaissance fencers Hamlet and D'Artagnan. They might note with surprise that circling for position is no longer possible: today, a fencing bout takes place in a rectangular area called the strip, or piste, fifteen meters long and up to two meters wide. At the same time, they would immediately understand most of the preliminaries. D'Artagnan would note that much of the ancient courtesy still persists. (Hamlet's manners were much less gallant.)

Sir Richard would be delighted to see that technology had advanced immensely, even since his own innovative century. Electrical scoring, an idea first put forward in the early days of electricity in the nineteenth century, has been in use for most of the twentieth. Fencers' weapons are now attached to an electronic scoring apparatus, and the fencers themselves (in foil and sabre) wear metallic vests that mark the target area.

Modern fencers face each other from their en garde lines, four meters apart, then salute each other, the referee, and the spectators. Both D'Artagnan and Jean Louis would nod approvingly. The nineteenth-century contestant would be completely familiar with the procedure, as the referee calls, "En garde!" and the fencers take their positions. "Ready?" asks the referee, and the fencers respond, "Ready, sir." Then comes the command, "Fence!" and the bout begins. (In international competitions, the commands are all in French, the international language of fencing.)

The old heroes would watch with fascination as fencing began. All of them would be amazed at the athleticism of the athletes and the speed of the weapons. But they would recognize the same essential game.

Once the command to fence is given, play continues until the referee calls "Halt!" for any reason–a hit has been scored, one of the fencers has stepped off the strip, or one of the fencers has broken a rule. Before play resumes, the referee again gives the commands: En garde! Ready! Fence!

Of course, informal bouts – much more familiar to Hamlet or D'Artagnan –, may take place without a referee, without a scoring machine, or for no fixed number of touches. If there is no scoring machine (or no visual judges), the fencers, following the old traditions, are obliged to call any touches that hit them – and to give their opponent the benefit of the doubt!

Current rules have developed to suit the modern nature of fencing as an international competitive sport. In competition, fencing bouts last until one or the other competitor scores a certain number of touches, or until a set time expires. In a "pool," where each fencer fences all of the others, bouts are for five touches. In direct elimination events, bouts may be as long as fifteen touches. If time runs out before one fencer has scored all the necessary touches, the one who is ahead wins.

So far, I think, the old-time swordsmen would understand the modern bout quite well. However, if the two fencers are tied when time runs out, matters can be complicated. In an epee *pool*, both fencers *lose* if the score is tied – reflecting the idea that in a duel, it's possible for both participants to be killed or wounded. In pools in the other weapons, and in direct elimination in all three weapons, the fencers continue for one more minute, "sudden death." Whoever scores first wins.

Now would come the rule that would certainly shock our swordsmen. If no one scores during that minute, so that the score remains tied, the winner is the fencer who *won a coin-toss* just before the sudden-death minute began. Many modern fencers find this incomprehensible, and both Jean Louis and D'Artagnan would be outraged. One can imagine their reaction: A coin-toss to decide a combat? Why not toss a coin in advance and spare yourselves the effort of fighting? (But at least it prevents bouts from going on forever.)

At the end of an *informal* bout, the fencers always shake hands – a gesture, which our courteous heroes would note with grave approval. At the end of a *competition* bout, they don't have to shake hands (tempers may be too hot), but they must still salute.

So how would today's fencing look to the swordsmen of an earlier day?

Fencing today may be scored electronically by externally programmable microprocessors. Today's *salle d'armes* may be a high school gymnasium, a university fencing room, or a church basement as well as a palace chambers or traditional fencing club. Certainly, as our time travelers would have noticed, it is conducted at an unprecedented level of athleticism and practiced by more people, and a broader range of people, than ever in its history. But fencing still shows the features that have always attracted devotees – its heady blend of excitement and vitality with quickness and grace, and its unique combination of mental toughness and alertness with speed and creativity.

Renaissance swordsmen like Hamlet and D'Artagnan, as well as nineteenth-century fencers like Jean Louis and Sir Richard Burton, would surely approve of what they saw.

Safety

1. Safety and responsibility

Quite often, fencing takes place within an institution with clearly defined safety and accountability procedures; for example, a university, school, or formal recreational facility. Just as often, perhaps, a fencing club is a very informal organization in which responsibility is much more vaguely allocated. In the worst case, everyone involved feels that ultimate responsibility lies elsewhere. *Wrong!* Whatever the setting, everyone involved – fencers, spectators, parents, coaches, organizers, and administrators – has a responsibility for safety.

- *The more involved you are, the more you ought to know.*

- *The more responsibility you have, the more you need to know.*

- *The more you know –the more you ought to know and need to know– the more responsibility you have.*

A. Fencing and its risks

- *Fencing is a very safe and relatively painless sport – when practiced safely. Practiced recklessly, it risks serious injury, and worse.*

Frequently, when someone is injured, the injured party sues everyone in sight who can be connected with the accident, whether it's the opponent, the coach, the organizer, the landlord, or the school. Once we are sued, we are already losers – in time, money, and annoyance.

In these highly litigious times, more and more of our behavior seems to be driven by considerations of insurance and the threat of lawsuits. One result is that fearful authorities impose burdensome restrictions on even the most innocuous activities. Everyone suffers. Nevertheless, the main thrust of this section is not how to avoid lawsuits. It is how to reduce unnecessary risks to ourselves and others – how to behave responsibly in a fencing environment.

- *The information offered here is only a shadow of what you need to understand. Flesh it out with instruction, observation, repetition, and practice!*

Most injuries are the familiar sprains and pulls that come from overuse, under-training, or otherwise using the body in a way nature didn't intend it to be used. This means that fencers need to be sure they warm up and stretch properly, and coaches need to impress their fencers with the importance of this phase of practice. Common as they are, these injuries can be minimized by knowledgeable coaching.

However, we have to remember that fencing is not a sport like every other. It is not only a contact sport, but also a combat sport. That is, the fencers – often vigorous athletes in peak condition – are trying as hard as they can to hit each other with metal weapons. Now, when properly maintained, the weapons will not injure a fencer *wearing proper protective gear.* They may very well injure bare or lightly-covered skin; but the only skin a fencer should be showing is the rear (unarmed) hand and the back of the head. (If a fencer turns so as to expose the back of the head, the action must halt.)

- *Whenever one person faces another with weapon in hand, both must be properly supervised, trained, informed, and protected.*

You may think that there's no harm if – without contact – an experienced fencer simply demonstrates an action to another fencer without wearing a mask. But think about it:

- *One of the fencers may stumble or make an unforeseen move, causing an accident;*

- *Someone else fencing in the room may collide with one of the fencers;*

- *The coach (or another safety-minded person) may see the two fencers practicing unprotected out of the corner of an eye and call an emergency halt. This disrupts the entire fencing room and is annoying at best.*

Against these considerations, how much of an inconvenience is it for an experienced fencer to put a mask on?

The good news is that *if fencers are properly outfitted,* the major risks occur only when a weapon breaks. The bad news is that all weapons *will* break sooner or later. When they do, the remnant may be a sharp spike. Even then, the gear now in use will almost always protect the fencer against serious injury – *but only if the fencer is wearing it!*

Other dangers in a fencing room are to the people who are not actually fencing – people who may be going around unprotected and unwary. They are not wearing masks, so a carelessly carried point can strike them in the face. They may not be watching the action, so that fencers can collide with them. They can be oblivious to the electrical equipment and trip over a cord. They are less likely than the fencers to be aware of the risks. Unattended children may toddle into harm's way.

In summary, the risks of serious injury in fencing are real. *But –*

- *They can be minimized so effectively that fencing can be a very safe sport indeed.*

- *Safety demands alertness, foresight, and restraint on the part of everyone in volved – fencers, non-fencers such as spectators and parents, and organizers such as coaches and supervisors.*

B. Three Rules for Fencers

By *fencers* I mean everyone in the fencing room who is carrying a weapon – or was just carrying a weapon–or ever *intends* to carry one.

For fencers, safety comes down to three common-sense rules:

- *The first is concern for others*: **keep your point down!** *(when you are not fencing)*

- *The second is alertness:* **keep your eyes open!** *(all the time)*

- *The third is foresight:* **use proper equipment!** *(when you are fencing)*

Almost every serious accident I have ever heard of in fencing involves neglect of one or more of these rules. The others seem unavoidable, a coach's nightmare. The only comfort is that it is much more likely that you will be involved in a *traffic* accident on your way to the fencing room than that you will see one of these freak *fencing* accidents in your entire fencing career.

1. Keep your point down

Keep your point down means that when you aren't fencing, you are responsible for seeing that your weapon can't do anyone any harm. The safest thing is to put it away, but this isn't always practical or necessary. If you don't put it away, keep it where no one can trip over it or run into it. If you need to keep it in your hand, keep the point down. In any other position, someone can run into it and get hurt – or *you* can turn suddenly and run it into someone else.

When you're not fencing, you have to stay out of the way of people who are. Until you learn to do these things, you are a constant nuisance and potential hazard to everyone around you.

2. Keep your eyes open

Keep your eyes open means maintaining a constant alertness with *all* the senses – not just the heightened alertness of bouting, but a larger awareness of the whole room.

You have to *see*

- *that you are fencing where another pair of fencers can back into you*

- *that a non-fencer has wandered across the fencing strip behind your opponent, just as you launch your attack*

- *(if you are the non-fencer, you have to avoid doing that!)*

- *that your opponent's mask has slipped (faulty equipment) or that he has turned his back to you, exposing the back of his neck (an illegal move)* – and you must stop in time.

- *that your opponent is about to back into a wall, into another fencer, or over a cliff!* – and you must immediately stop fencing and correct the situation.

- **that an unsafe action is taking place anywhere in the fencing room** – and you must take immediate and appropriate action.

You have to *hear*

- *someone calling a halt to your bout*

- *someone pointing out a dangerous condition* – and you must stop immediately and take appropriate action.

You have to *feel*

- *that you are about to hit too hard*

- *that your blade has broken* – and you must release the weapon immediately.

Keeping your eyes open also means that if you see something unsafe going on, you yourself must take immediate and appropriate action.

3.   Use Proper Equipment

Always use proper equipment means using regulation equipment that you have checked for safety.

- **a regulation weapon** *that's properly assembled and maintained, without weakening kinks or bends (with experience, it's often possible to tell when a blade is ready to break).*

- **a mask** – *of course* – *and one that's not weakened by rust or dents.*

- **a jacket** – *of course* – *and one without holes which a point could find.*

    Masks and jackets should generally not be yard-sale specials or attic heirlooms. Show these to the coach before you use them.

- **a glove** *with a cuff long enough to cover the opening of your `sleeve. Fencing regulations specific half the length of the forearm).*

- **leg covering**: *it doesn't matter what the others are doing or how hot it is. You may not mind bruises on your thigh, but punctures are another matter.*

- **breast protection** *for women* – *required by the rules of fencing*

- **groin protection** *for men* – *not required by the rules of fencing, but by some national federations, many clubs and schools, and ordinary common sense.*

- *an **underarm protector.***

The underarm protector or plastron needs a bit of explanation because its importance may be less obvious. It is crucial. Much of the body is reasonably well protected by bone or muscle or both. The exception is the armpit, where only a layer of skin stands between your opponent's point and your lungs or heart. Of course, a regulation fencing jacket is reinforced at that point. Unfortunately, there remains the chance that a point will enter the cuff or penetrate the sleeve and travel up the arm, *under the jacket,* to the armpit. The underarm protector defends very effectively against this possibility. *Always* wear one when you fence.

Here I should say something about the FIE requirements for fencing equipment. The FIE has set very high strength standards for masks and jackets, and rightly so. The very high level of athleticism at international competitions generates immense forces. But does *everyone* need equipment that meets FIE standards (the jargon is "FIE-homologated")? Is FIE-homologated equipment worth the considerable extra cost?

Some national federations, and even some private fencing clubs, require their members to wear FIE-homologated equipment. In my opinion, this is an insurance-driven decision. Accidents involving the penetration of well-maintained conventional equipment have always been very rare. In addition, not even FIE-homologated equipment can resist every puncture. Consequently, if given a choice, every decision-maker must attempt to balance – responsibly – cost, convenience, and safety.

C. For non-fencers, especially parents

By non-fencers, I mean parents, friends, and spectators – the people who are in the fencing room whose purpose isn't to fence, coach, or officiate. The rule for you is to keep your eyes open!

In addition, parents of very young fencers have a special role: to look out for them. Young children can't be expected to remember all the safety rules all the time – though they can be told to – and other people aren't as likely to watch them as closely. Coaches should have eyes in the backs of their heads; but parents will still have that extra sixth sense that tells them when their offspring are going to do something unpredictable.

D. For coaches and organizers

I have just outlined some areas that are the responsibility of the *individuals* in the fencing room. All of these are *also* the responsibility of the coach. The coach is responsible for the safety of the entire group. A coach has to see *everything* that's going on and not allow *anything* that he or she isn't willing to take responsibility for.

When I say "responsible," I mean both morally and legally.

Why morally responsible? Someone might object that the adult members of the group are responsible for themselves. Yes, they are – partly. They are also relying on your judgment and leadership as the trained expert. You may be letting so-and-so fence epee in shorts because you tell yourself, "She's an experienced adult who knows the risks," while she may be saying, "It can't be too dangerous because Coach is letting me do it." Of course, as an adult, she's *partly* responsible, morally, for any consequences of her recklessness. But so are you, for condoning it. If you're not ready for this, you might want to rethink why you want to coach.

Second the coach may well have a legal responsibility in the event of a lawsuit. This flows from the fact that coaches are presumed to be experts. Even if they don't have a signed contract, a fencer or a parent may rely on them to teach, coach and supervise their children.

What this means is that insofar as the coach is the person in charge, the coach takes – *must* take – responsibility for the fencing room and its occupants.

None of this means that the coach must do everything by himself. A good coach delegates. A good coach finds and encourages people who want to take responsibility. That's the only way to get the job done *and* stay sane. *But* –

- *In the end, the coach **has** – and therefore must **take** – responsibility.*

2. A safety checklist for coaches and organizers.

A. In any emergency...

☐ What steps are to be taken in the event of an emergency? Who has what responsibility? Does everyone know his or her task in advance?

☐ Where is the nearest telephone? Where is the nearest hospital? Where is the nearest first aid kit?

☐ How is an ambulance to be directed?

☐ Which responsible adult in the room knows first aid? Is currently certified?

☐ Who else needs to be notified? Is there a phone list?

☐ Will your system work even if you aren't there to supervise it? (If not, what are you going to do about it?)

B. The fencing room

☐ Are the exits and exit routes clearly visible and understood by all?

☐ Is the surface suitable for fencing?

☐ Has the surface been checked *today?* – floor swept, strips fastened down securely, etc.?

☐ Is the fencing area laid out safely? Are obstructions close to the fencing area padded?

☐ Is there sufficient run-off space behind each end of the strip? Beside each strip?

☐ Is there enough extra space for referees and scorers?

☐ Are there any obstructions in the fencing area that need to be removed?

☐ Is there a safe place for spectators and nonparticipants?

☐ Is the electrical equipment safe to use?

☐ Are the strips laid out so that they don't interfere with each other? Do fencers understand that they should fence parallel to each other?

☐ Is the room planned so that necessary traffic doesn't interfere with fencing?

☐ Have signs been placed or people assigned to warn of unavoidable hazards?

C. The equipment

☐ Is equipment regulation? If not, what are your reasons for allowing its use? Is there a stated policy?

☐ Is the footgear adequate for conditions?

☐ Is the protective equipment in good condition?

☐ Masks: are there dents, rust spots, weak areas, loose straps?

☐ Gloves, jackets, etc.: are there holes, worn spots, or dangling strips of loose fabric?

☐ Do fencers know when wearing full equipment is mandatory and when it is optional? Do you have a clear policy? How do you make it known?

☐ Are fencers wearing equipment correctly?

☐ Does it fit right?

☐ Are fencers using equipment safely and with discipline?

D. The fencers

☐ Have fencers signed consent/waiver/release forms? They are probably worthless as legal protection, but they are one step in a process of education for both coaches and fencers.

☐ What steps have you taken to educate your fencers about safety?

☐ Are fencers physically and mentally prepared to fence – in general and today?

☐ Have the fencers or their parents made any risk factors – medical or otherwise – known to the coach?

☐ Are fencers properly warmed up/stretched out?

☐ Is anyone excessively fatigued, overheated, emotionally stressed, etc.?

☐ Is everyone alert and attentive? (How can you tell?)

☐ Is everyone aware of proper form and safe technique? (Why are you sure?)

☐ Disciplined and responsible in behavior? (What steps have you taken to ensure this?)

E. Non-fencers in the fencing room

☐ Is there a safe place for them?

☐ Have fencers been alerted to their presence?

☐ Have you made them familiar with any restrictions on their movement, hazardous conditions, etc.?

F. The coaches

☐ Do you have a plan for the training and development of the fencing group as a whole?

☐ Do you have a plan for each fencer?

☐ Are your plans adapted to individual differences?

☐ Do you understand your varying obligations
  — to beginning fencers?
  — to young fencers?
  — to adult fencers

☐ Who can conduct training in your absence? Are they clear about safety procedures and individual differences?

☐ What steps are you taking to improve your skills
  — As a coach?
  — As a trainer?
  — As a helper in an emergency?

G. Insurance

Now for the *least* important question on this list – that is, if you have taken care of the rest, for only then will you have protected your fencers be able to face any contingency with confidence:

☐ Do you and your club have liability insurance?
  (Circumstances vary from country to country; the US Fencing Association (USFA) offers insurance to member clubs.)

Priority ("right of way")

Foil and sabre are called "conventional" weapons. Of course, "conventional" doesn't mean "mundane", but rather that these weapons are governed by certain conventions – rules for deciding what happens if both fencers are hit at about the same time. (In epee, if this happens, both fencers are counted as hit) The convention is also called priority or, more colloquially, right of way.

Priority originated as part of serious training for smallsword fighting, as a way of forcing fencers to think prudently instead of reacting automatically. It developed into one of the outstanding features of fencing as a sport. What it does is to reduce the role of blind instinct and replace it with logical thought. (It is fitting that priority began to develop during the period known as the Enlightenment!)

When we are attacked, one of the most natural and instinctive reactions is to counterattack. It's the "fight" part of the fight-or-flight response. It frequently works in boxing, where you can take a punch to give a punch. In a sword fight with sharp weapons, the risks are much more serious. The likely outcome is what the French called *le coup á deux veuves* – the two-widow stroke. Since a dead duelist was unlikely to come back for more fencing lessons, fencing masters had to teach their students to practice in a way that encouraged prudence, but not timidity. The idea behind priority, therefore, is not to *eliminate* the counterattack – which is, after all, *sometimes* the best move – but to move it from the realm of blind instinct into the realm of reason.

To understand priority at its most basic, consider these cases:

1. You and your opponent face each other, on guard. At the command to fence, you straighten your arm and lower your weapon so that your point threatens her target area. She ignores this and attacks. She runs on to your point, but she hits you. Who scores the touch?

You do. In a real fight, you both would have been seriously wounded, but it would have been your opponent's fault. She saw your threat but did nothing to protect herself. You were behaving rationally; she wasn't.

2. At the command to fence, you step forward. Your opponent begins to straighten her arm for an attack. You react by lunging into her. Both of you are hit. Who scores the touch?

She does. You failed to avoid her threat. The double hit is "your fault."

3. Your opponent steps forward and lunges at you. You deflect his attack and answer with an immediate thrust (the riposte). Meanwhile, he "replaces" his point and hits you, so that you are both hit at the same time. Who scores the touch?

You do. Once his attack was deflected (parried), your opponent should have anticipated your riposte.

The general principle should be clear. A threat to the target, made while the arm is extending, has priority over a hit that is made in reaction to the threat – unless the threatening point has been deflected from its course or, in sabre, the threatening blade has been blocked (the parry). After the parry, the defender's immediate riposte has priority over the attacker's continuation, unless the riposte in turn is parried, and so on.

In practice, there are many difficult, borderline cases, which have led to some slight complications in the rules.

First, the "threat" of an attack doesn't exist if the attack begins too far away to hit. The rule limits the attacking distance to the length of one advance and lunge. With a running attack, the initial threat only lasts until the rear foot lands.

Second, attempting and failing to deflect the opponent's blade – on offense or defense – loses the priority.

Third, simply coming forward, no matter how aggressively, does not constitute a threat. An attacking threat only exists when the arm is extending and the weapon is threatening the target. Think about these instances:

1. I step forward without extending, then lunge and hit you. *Before my arm has begun to extend*, you extend and hit me. It's your touch. You attacked while I was still preparing to attack.

2. I step forward, still without extending, lunge, and hit you. This time, you react by attempting to parry my attack, *but you miss my blade*. You immediately reach forward and hit me. It's my touch. You were reacting to my late-developing attack.

The extended, threatening arm (point in line) has the priority only as long as it is "maintained." It can be maintained while retreating, or standing still, but not while moving forward. Imagine that I attack by stepping forward and lunging with extended arm. My attack falls short without you parrying it. Now –

1. I hold my position, or retreat with extended arm, and you attack "onto it," with the result that we're both hit. *It's my touch*: I maintained the line.

2. I continue my forward movement with extended arm as you begin your counteraction. *It's your touch*: I lost the line when I started forward after my attack.

Does this all sound confusing? Are you asking yourself how anyone can keep these rules in mind and fence at the same time? Don't worry. Right of way is part of the special satisfaction of foil and sabre. If you can't stand it, there's always epee. But you can *learn* it! And even if you fence epee, which doesn't use the convention, you need to understand it. Right of way trained duelists to anticipate their opponents' reflexive counterattacks. In the same way, epee fencers can plan to avoid counterattacks – or take advantage of them, if that is in their interest.

If you have followed this condensed explanation, you already have a basic understanding. To develop a real *feeling* for right of way – to make right of way second nature – requires time, attention, and patience.

APPENDIX D

Fencing Resources

1. Bibliography and suggestions for further reading

a. Books cited by Lukovich (mostly in Hungarian)

Bay, Béla-Rerrich, Béla-Tilli, Endre: Tór-és párbajtörvívás. Budapest, 1953.
Beke, Zoltán-Polgár, József: The Methodology of Sabre Fencing. Budapest, 1963.
Czirják, József: Testneveléselmélet 1. Budapest, 1962.
Duronelly, László: Vívás. Budapest, 1951.
Gerentsér, László: A modern magyar kardvívás. Budapest, 1944.
Lukovich, István: Vívás. Budapest, 1968. (In Hungarian)
Lukovich, István: Felkészülés és taktika a vívásban. Budapest, 1969.
Lukovich, István-Mecseki, Attila: A vívás oktatásának általános módszertana és mechanikuja. Budapest, 1967.
Nádori, László: Edzéselmélet. Budapest, 1968.
Ozoray (Schenker), Zoltán: A modern magyor kardvívás. Budapest, 1958.
Ozoray (Schenker), Zoltán: Säbelfechten. Corvina, Budapest, 1961.
Rerrich, Béla-Tilli, Endre: A magyar vívás kézikönyve. Budapest, 1954.
Szabó, László: Fencing and the Master. SKA Swordplay, 1997.
Tilli, Endre-Rerrich, Béla: A kardvívás. Budapest, 1954.
Tornanóczy, Gusztáv-Gellér, Alfréd: A vívás kézikönyve. Budapest, 1942.
Vass, Imre: Epee Fencing. SKA Swordplay, 1997.

b. In print, in English, and useful

Evangelista: Encyclopedia of the Sword (Greenwood, 1995)
_____: The Art and Science of Fencing (Masters, 1996)
FIE: Rules of Competition (AFA, CFF, USFA, etc., every year)
Garret, Kaidanov, and Pezza: Foil, Sabre, and Epee Fencing (Penn State, 1994)
Gaugler: A Dictionary of Universally Used Fencing Terminology (Laureate, 1997)
_____: History of Fencing (Laureate, 1997)
_____: The Science of Fencing (Laureate, 1997)
Lukovich: Electric Foil Fencing (SKA Swordplay, 1997)
Pitman: Fencing, Techniques of Foil, Epee, and Sabre (Crowood, 1988)
De Silva: Fencing: The Skills of the Game (Crowood, 1992)
Szabó: Fencing and the Master (SKA Swordplay, 1997)
Vass: Epee Fencing (SKA Swordplay, 1997)
Westbrook: Harnessing Anger: the Way of an American Fencer (Seven Stories, 1997)

c. Older, but still valuable

Angelo: The School of Fencing (Land's End Press, 1971)

Barbasetti: The Art of the Foil (E. P. Dutton, 1932)

_____: The Art of the Sabre and the Epee

de Beaumont: Fencing: Ancient Art and Modern Sport (Barnes, 1978)

Campos: The Art of Fencing (Vantage Press, 1988)

Castello: The Theory and Practice of Fencing (Charles Scribner, 1933)

Castle: The Schools and Masters of Fence (Arms & Armour Press, 1969)

Deladrier: Modern Fencing (U.S. Naval Institute, 1948, reprint 1954)

Hutton: The Sword and the Centuries (Charles E. Tuttle, 1980)

Morton: Martini A-Z of Fencing (Queen Anne, 1988)

Nadi: The Living Sword: A Fencer's Autobiography (Laureate Press, 1994)

____: On Fencing (G. P. Putnam, 1943) (Laureate Press, 1994)

Palffy-Alpar: Sword and Masque (Davis, 1967)

2. Fencing on the Internet

There's more fencing on the Web than you can shake a foil at! To get an idea, just ask one of the better search engines – Alta Vista is my favorite right now – for fencing (you'll have to disregard references to cattle fencing, the fencing of stolen goods, and the like!), for *escrime,* and for *esgrima.* This section is just a starting point.

a. Newsgroup (UseNet): rec.sport.fencing

Rec.sport.fencing, also known as r.s.f., is by far the largest fencing forum on the Internet. You will find open discussion on all fencing-related topics – questions, answers, arguments, complaints, proposals, humor,. The FAQ (see below) is posted monthly. Tournaments are announced and results are posted. If you will be visiting Oshkosh, Almaty, or Adelaide and want to fence there, you can get on line to ask where. (You can also check the list of national fencing organizations later in this resource section.

Rec. sport.fencing: subscribe through whichever Internet Service Provider (ISP) you use.**Rec.sport.fencing digest:** If you don't get newsgroups or don't want to read through a lot of separate messages, you can get the digest – which is actually all of the day's messages – at the end of the day.

Send to majordomo@cs.wisc.edu with text "subscribe rsf

b. FAQ (Frequently Asked Questions):

A treasury of fencing information, frequently updated (and gratefully acknowledged here). Posted monthly to the newsgroup and available for download via FTP at

Region	FTP Address	Directory
North America:	*ftp.uu.net*	*/usenet/news.answers*
	rtfm.mit.edu	*various directories*
Europe:	*ftp.uni-paderborn.de*	*/pub/FAQ*
	ftp.Germany.EU.net	*/pub/newsarchive/news.answers*
	grasp1.univ-lyon1.fr	*/pub/faq*
	ftp.win.tue.nl	*/pub/usenet/news.answers*
Asia:	*nctuccca.edu.tw*	*/USENET/FAQ*

c. Websites

The Web is volatile. The list below makes no pretense of completeness; rather, it offers some excellent places to start. Also check the supplier listings for some great supplier sites.

1. National and international organizations

Check these out for official information, rankings, club links, how to become a member, championship result, rankings, announcements, and key phone numbers. Most of the sites have more than this, and I try to mention some of it in the notes below.

F.I.E.: http://www.calvacom.fr/fie/
The International Fencing Federation on-line. In French. Fencing rules, international schedule, world rankings, much more.
British Fencing (the AFA): *http://www.netlink.co.uk/users/afa/index.htm*
The Sword magazine, links to British clubs, more.
Canadian Fencing Federation: http://www.fencing.ca
Belgian Fencing: http://www.synec-doc.be/escrime/maison/
An excellent fencing dictionary, numerous club links
Danish Fencing: http://meyer.fys.ku.dk/~sthansen/
An unofficial page with club listings and many links.
Italian Fencing: http://www.bull.it/coni/federa/e-fis.html
Professional Fencing League: http://www.profence.com/
United States Fencing Association: http://www.usfa.org
Fencing rules in English, results, club links, much more.
US Fencing Coaches Association: http://www.netheaven.com/~kos/usfca/

2. Fencing Links:

These reference pages will lead you to more clubs, organizations, and on-line resources around the Web

Fencing all over the world: http://www.ii.uib.no/~arild/fencing/patch2/www_pages.html

Fencing Links: http://www.m2c.com/links/fencing.htm

Fencing on the Internet: http://hcs.harvard.edu/~fencing/internet/net.html

3. Where to get it: Manufacturers, suppliers, & outfitters

Notes:

1. Super **websites** are listed in **boldface**

Websites (URL's) are <u>underlined.</u> On many browsers, prefixes and suffixes (like http:// or .htm) are unnecessary.

2. Country code follows each country's heading. International dialing protocols may differ from domestic (Do you or don't you dial an initial "1" or "0?" Be patient.

AUSTRALIA (61)
Aladdin Sports (Leon Paul Dealer)
55 Jessie Street, West Preston VIC 3072
TEL: 3 9483-3077 FAX: 3 9816-3357
EMAIL: pears@cs.latrobe.edu.au
http://www.cs.latrobe.edu.au/~pears/aladdin/Master.html
Fencing International Equipment
Angelo Santangelo, Maestro of Arms
47 Dalrymple Avenue, Chatswood, NSW 2067
TEL: 2-419-8968
Fentec Sports
48 Clara St, Camp Hill QLD 4158
TEL: (07) 395 3852
Jeff Gray Fencing
93 Sherwood Street, Revesby NSW. 2212
TEL: 2-9773 4515 FAX: 29 792 4083 Email:
jeffgray@acay.com.au

AUSTRIA (43)
Fechtsport Michael Martin
Dr. Gohren-Gasse 22, A-2340 Mydling
TEL: (43) 2236 471370 FAX: (43) 2236 471378

BELGIUM (32)
Bambust (France-Lames, Uhlmann)
625 Brusselse steenweg
1900 Overijse – Jesus-Eik
TEL: (0)2 657 42 89 or (0)2 687 65 71
http://www.synec-doc.be/escrime/materiel/bambust.htm
Frank Delhem Sport (Uhlmann dealer)
Gijsbrecht van Deurnelaan 31
 Bus 6, B-2100 Deurne
TEL: (32) 3 6442676 FAX: (32) 3 6442707
http://www.synec-doc.be/escrime/materiel/delhem.htm

BRITAIN (44)
Blades
35 Edinburgh Drive,
Staines, Middlesex TW18 1PJ
TEL: 01784 255-522 FAX: 01784 245-942
Duellist Enterprises
1 Barrowgate Road, Chiswick, London W4
TEL: 0181 747 9629
Forest City Park Road ,Timperley,
Altricham, *Cheshire* WA14 5QX
TEL:161 969 0441 FAX 161 272 0255

Gladiators
101 High Street,
Evesham, Worcestershire WR11 4DN
TEL:0386 421296 FAX 0386 421298
Merlin Enterprises
24 Prices Lane, York YO2 1AL
TEL/FAX 01904 611537
Leon Paul (Manufacturer, distributor, supplier)
Units 1 & 2, Cedar Way, Camley St., London NW1 0JQ
TEL: (0171) 388-8132 FAX: (0171) 388-8134
http://www.netlink.co.uk/users/afa/leonpaul/lp1.htm#cat
Rome Fencing Equipment
29 Grange Way, Broadstairs, Kent CT10 2YP
TEL/FAX: (01843) 866588
White Knights
Freepost DL780, Spennymoor, Co. Durham DL16 6BR
TEL: 0941 159598 or 01388 811352 FAX: 01388 811352
EMAIL: Knights@joust.demon.co.uk

CANADA (1)
Fencing Equipment of Canada
2407 Bayview Place, Calgary, Alberta T2V 0L6
TEL: (403) 281-1384 FAX: (403) 281-0043
Allstar (Herb Obst Agency)
CP 788 Succursdale NDG,
Montreal, Quebec H4A 3S2
TEL:(514) 482-2140 FAX: (514) 485-9283
Agents: Halifax: Barbara Daniel (902) 457-9228
            Winnipeg: Milton Himsl (204) 284-4138
            Ottawa: Ron Millette (613) 235-2226
            Saskatoon: Dennis Duncan
            (306) 664-8527
            Vancouver: Zbig Pietrusinski
            (604) 984-2157
Prieur-PBT
Vijay Prasad
383 Tamarack Dr., Waterloo, Ontario N2L 4G7
TEL: (519) 885-6496 FAX: (519) 888-6197

DENMARK (45)
Allstar-Danmark
Skoldhoj Alle 6F, DK-2920 Charlottenlund
TEL: 39638463 FAX: 39623760

FRANCE (33)
BLAISE FRERES SARL (Blade makers)
Z.I. de Trablaine,
42500 LE CHAMBON-FEUGEROLLES
TEL: 16-77538624 FAX: 16-77567482
Cero-Soudet
18 rue Nemours, 75011 Paris
TEL: 48 06 48 48 FAX: 47 00 05141
Escrime Technologies/Fencing Technologies
(Manufacturer of scoring machines)
1 rue Danton Besancon 25000 FRANCE
TEL:3 81-61-16-05 FAX: (33) 3 81-61-13-67
EMAIL: EscrimeTec@aol.com or richard-marciano@uiowa.edu.
or marciano@sdsc.edu
France Lames (Blade makers)
B.P. 60 Z.I. La Borie,
43120 MONISTROL SUR LOIRE
TEL: 16-71660507 FAX: 16-71665204

Glisca Escrime
1073 Chemin de Teyssières, 84380 MAZAN
TEL: 16-90698515 FAX: 16-90698150
Prieur (Manufacturer, distributor, supplier)
31 Boulevard Voltaire, 75011 Paris
TEL: 43 57 89 90 FAX: 43 57 80 11
Soudet (see Cero-Soudet)
Uhlmann/Allstar (of Lyon)
7, rue Leonard de Vinci,
69120 Vaulx-en-Velin, Lyon
TEL: 78 79 28 96 FAX: 78 80 11 33
Uhlmann/Allstar (of Paris)
138 rue de Chevilly,
94240 L'Hay-les-Roses, Paris
TEL: 46 87 26 70 FAX: 46 87 24 68

GERMANY (49)
Artos (Manufacturer)
Riemengasse 46, 88486 KIRCHBERG/ILLER
TEL: 73 54 8913 FAX: 49-73 54 1482
Allstar Fecht-Center
(Manufactuer, distributor, supplier)
Carl-Zeiss Strasse 61, 72700 Reutlingen
TEL: 7121 9500-0 (central line)
(English, French, Spanish)
7121 9500-22 or -25
7121 9500-15 (Italian)
FAX: 7121 9500-99
EMAIL: allstar@t-online.de (Management), or allstar1@t-online.de (Export Dept.)
http://home.t-online.de/home/allstar/homepage.htm
Uhlmann Fecht-Sport (Manufacturer, distributor, supplier)
Uhlandstrasse 12, 88471 Laupheim
TEL: 7392 6018
http://home.t-online.de/home/uhlmann-fechtsport/
Fecht-Sport H. Lieffertz
Eibenweg 3, D-50767 Köln
TEL/FAX: +49 221 795254 FAX: (49) 7392 2373
EMAIL: Sjoerd@change.gun.de
http://www.trv.de/fecht-sport-lieffertz.htm (could not confirm)

ITALY (39)
Allstar-Italia di Mazzini Lucia
Via Nostra Signora di Lourdes 72,
I-00167 Roma
TEL/FAX: 6 6638830
Dueci Escrime
Via di Mezzo Nord, 256,
56023 NAVACCHIO (PISA)
TEL: 50-777654 FAX: 50-775249
Negrini Fencing Line (Manufacturers)
Vicolo Scala Santa, 24,
37129 VERONA
TEL: 45-80011984 FAX: 45-8002755
Novascherma
Via Trieste 12, 31055 QUINTO DI TREVISO
TEL: 39-422-378477 FAX: 39-422-378477

JAPAN (81)
Dalt Co., Ltd.
1-630 Meguro Meguro-ku, Tokyo153
TEL: 3-34901460 FAX: 81-3-34952457
TOKYO FENCING Co. Ltd.
171 1 F Chateau Mejiro Building
23-18-2 Takada Toshima-Ku, Tokyo
TEL:/FAX: 3-53962813

MEXICO (52)
Blade Mexico
Christina & Louis Arredondo
TEL: 5 2 359 0430 FAX 5 358 5797

NETHERLANDS: (31)
Stichting Topschermen Den Haag
Van Galenstraat 14M, NL-2518 EP Den Haag
TEL/FAX: 70 3640624

NEW ZEALAND (64)
Barry Moore Academy of Fencing
1/4A MacMurry Rd., Remuera Auckland
TEL/FAX 9524 8456
Email: bj-pj@ihug.co.nz
PORTUGAL (35)
Joao Firmino Paulino Cabral
Av. Curry Cabral 9 1Esq.,
Venda-Nova, P-2700 Amadora
TEL:1 4744040 FAX:1 3978376

RUSSIA (7)
LAMMET
9/23 2-d Baumanskaya str., 107005 MOSCOW
TEL: 095-2618018 FAX: 095-2618018
MEGASTAR
Loukinskaia 7 appt. 405, 119634 MOSCOW
TEL: 095-3185477 FAX: 0953185477
VNITI
Maly pr. P.S. 87, 197022 St. Petersburg
TEL: 812-2321040 FAX: 8122331854

SPAIN: (34)
Es.Fid SA
Av. Madrid 171-177, Esc. Isda 3070, E-08028 Barcelona
TEL: 3 2112933 FAX: 3 4186844

SWITZERLAND: (41)
APRILIA SPORT
Birmensdorferstrasse 99, 8003 ZURICH
TEL:1-4614030
FAX: 1-4614031
Fechtsport Rdber & Co.
Blattliring 7, CH-6403 K|ssnacht am Rigi
TEL: (41) 41 816759

USA (1)
American Fencers Supply
1180 Folsom St., San Francisco, CA 94103
TEL: (415) 863-7911 FAX: (415) 431-4931
Belle and Blade
124 Pennsylvania Ave, Dover, NJ 07801
TEL: (201) 328-8488
Blade Fencing Equipment, Inc.
212 West 15th St., NY, NY 10011
TEL: (212) 620-0114 FAX: (212) 620-0116
http://www.blade-fencing.com
Blue Gauntlet
246 Ross Ave., Hackensack, NJ 07601
TEL: (201) 343-3362 FAX: (201) 343-4175
Colonial Distributing Fencing Equipment
PO Box 636, 330 N. Fayette Drive, Cedarburg, Wisconsin 53012
TEL: (414) 377-9166 FAX: (414) 377-9166
Commodore Systems *(Scoring machines)*
(Saber 3-weapon box)
P.O. Box 22992. Nashville, TN 37202
TEL: 1-800-627-4903 TEL:(615) 329-9398
FAX: (615) 329-0640 EMAIL: howardef@macpost.vanderbilt.edu
Cheris Fencing Supply
5818 East Colfax Avenue, Denver, CO 80220
TEL: (303) 321-8657 TEL:1-800-433-6232 FAX: (303) 321-8696
Le Touché of Class
TEL: 562-428-8585 FAX: 562-428-8385
EMAIL: letouchecl@aol.com
URL:http://members.aol.com/terykins/Fencing/Fencing.html
M.A.S. Weapons
5600 E. 36th St. N. #7, Tulsa, OK 74115-2101
TEL: (918) 835-0467 FAX: (918) 835-6663
contact: Kevin Mayfield
Physical Chess (main store)
2933 Vauxhall Rd, Vauxhall, NJ 07088
TEL: (908) 964-1211 or 1-800-FENCING
FAX: (908) 964-3092 EMAIL: physchess@aol.com
Physical Chess (New York City)
2067 Broadway, New York, NY 10023
TEL:(212) 595-3636

The Fencing Post
1004 Bird Avenue, San Jose, CA 95125
TEL: (408) 297-4448 FAX: (408) 297-8960
http://www.thefencingpost.com.htm
EMAIL: saul@thefencingpost.com
Alexandre Ryjik Fencing Equipment
4094 Majestic Lane Suite 163, Fairfax, VA 22033
TEL: (703) 818-3106
George Santelli, Inc.
465 South Dean St., Englewood, NJ 07631
TEL: (201) 871-3105 FAX: (201) 871-8718
http://www.santelli.com
Southern California Fencers Equipment
16131 Valerio Street, Van Nuys, CA 91406
TEL: (818) 997-4538 FAX: (818) 998-8385
Triplette Competiton Arms
162 W. Pine St, Mt Airy, NC 27030
TEL: (910) 786-5294
Uhlmann International
Wolf Finck, Pres. USA Headquarters
Fayetteville, GA 30214
TEL: (770) 461-3809
Vintage Sporting Equipment
P.O. Box 364, Sheboygan, WI 53082
TEL: (800) 690-4867 FAX: (414) 459-9666
Zivkovic Modern Fencing EquipmenT
77 Arnold Road. Wellesley Hills, MA 02181
TEL: (617) 235-3324 FAX: (617) 239-1224
http://www.fas.harvard.edu/~zivkovic.htm

---

4. Fencing organizations around the world

Abbreviations: A=Association; Am= Amateur; Esgrima = Esg
Fencing = Fg; Federation = Fed, Fédération = Féd; Federacion
= Fedc;.
When **mailing**, the name of the country as listed must be
   included as the last element of the address, except
   when the mailing address is in a different country .
   (Example: Armenia, below).In this case, the country to
   mail to, in CAPITAL LETTERS is the last element of the
   address.
To **telephone or fax**, dial your code for international access,
   followed by the complete listed number

INTERNATIONAL FENCING FEDERATION
(FIE) Fédération Internationale d'Escrime
32, Rue La Boetie 75008 Paris, FRANCE
TEL:33 145.61.14.72 FAX 33 1 45.63.46.85
http://www.calvacom.fr/fie

ARABIA (see Saudi Arabia)
AUSTRALIA Australian Fg Fed
P.O. Box 7517, Melbourne, VIC 3004
TEL:(61) 3 9510 8399 FAX: (61) 3 9510 2722
ANTILLES (Netherlands Antilles)
NederlandsAntilliaanseaSchermbond
Marsweg 20, Curaçao FAX: 599-9 616825
ARGENTINA Fedc Argentina de Esg,
Calle Bolivar 358 3°, dep. 6,
P.O.B.1066 Buenos Aires
TEL: 54-1 3427717, FAX: : 54-21 270622
ARMENIA Armenian Fg Fed,
64 route deTroinex, 1256 Troinex Geneva,SWITZERLAND
ARUBA Aruba Fg Fed S.A.B.A.,
P.O.B. 319 St. Nicolaas
TEL: 297-8 47216 FAX: 297-8 37133
AUSTRIA Oesterreichischer Fechtverband,
Blattgasse 4 1030 Vienna
TEL: 43-1-714 14 47 FAX: 43-1-714 14 46
AZERBAIJAN Azerbaijan Fg Fed,
98A, Leningradski Prospekt, Baku
TEL: 7-8922 648145

BAHREIN Bahrein Fg Fed
Bahrain Defence Force Military Sports Union, P.O.B. 245
BELARUS Belarus Fg Fed,
Av. F. Skaryna 49 ap. 307, 220005 Minsk
TEL: 7-0172 277964 FAX: 7-0172 331839
BELGIUM Royal Belgian Fg Fed,
12, rue Général Thys Boîte 3, 1050 Brussels TEL: 32-2
6440033, FAX: 32-2 6440397
BULGARIA Bulgarian Fg Fed, 18 Bd Tolboukhin, Sofia
TEL: 359-2 865320 FAX: 359-2 879670
BOLIVIA Fedc Boliviana de Esg
Casilla 447, Santa Cruz
FAX: 591-42 50939
BRAZIL Confed. Brasileira de Esg
Av. Brasil 2540, CEP 20930, S. Cristoras,
Rio de Janeiro 23
TEL: 55-21 5893006 FAX: 55-21 5893006
BRITAIN British Fg (AmFgA)
1 Barons Gate 33-35 Rothschild Road,
London W4 5HT
TEL: 0181 742-3032 URL http://www.netlink.co.uk/users/afa/
CANADA Canadian Fg Fed
1600 Prom. James Naismith Drive,
Gloucester, ON K1B 5N4
TEL: 1(613) 748-5633 FAX: 1(613) 748-5742
  http://www.fencing.ca
CHILE Fedc Chilena de Esg, Tarapaca 739, Santiago de Chile
TEL: 56-2 6395089 FAX: 56-2 6395089
CROATIA Croat Fg Fed, Tig Sportiva 11, 41000 Zagreb
TEL: 38-41 339333, fax 38-41 325864
CHINA Fg Ass'n of the People's Republic of China
9 Tiyukuan Street, Beijing
TEL: 86-1 753110 FAX: 86-10-7123110
COLOMBIA Fedc Colombiana de Esg
Calle 28, n° 25 – 18 Santa Fe de Bogota
TEL: (57) 1 2327589 or (57) 1 2455457 FAX: (57) 1 2859396
COSTA RICA. Fedc Costaricense dE Esg
ACE 1702-2050, San Pedro FAX: 506-257801
CUBA Am Fg Fed, Calle 13, n° 601,
Zona Postal 4, Habana de Cuba
TEL: 537 408416, FAX: 53 7 409037
CYPRUS Cyprus Fg Fed,
P.O. Box 4212 Limassol Cyprus
TEL: 357-5 324033 FAX: 357-5 325838
CZECH REPUBLIC Czech Fg Fed,
Mezi Stadiony, Post Schranka 40,
6017 Prague 6 FAX: 42-2 353007
DENMARK Dansk Faegte Forbund,
Idraettens Hus,
Brondby Stadion 20, 2605 Brondby
TEL: 45-43 26 20 97, FAX: 45-43 26 26 27
ECUADOR Comite de Esg de Pichincha,
Palacio de los Deportes Queseras Medio (La Vicentina),
P.O.B. 381 – Quito
FAX: 59-32-479236
EGYPT Egyptian Fg Fed,
Jardin de l'Ezbekieh, Cairo
TEL: 20-3 912513, FAX: 20-2 5912513
EL SALVADOR Fedc Salvadorena de Esg
Sala Esg, Palacio de los Deportes.
Centro de Gobierno, San Salvador
TEL: 503-713486 FAX: 503-231923
ESTONIA Estonian Fg Fed,
Regati 1 Talinn EE 0103
TEL: 372-2- 238343 FAX: 372-2-238387
FINLAND Suomen Miekailulitto,
Radiokatu 12, 00240 Helsinki
TEL: 358-01582410 FAX: 358-0 145237
FRANCE Féd Francaise d'Esc,
No.43 - 14 rue Moncey 75009 Paris'
TEL: 33-1 44532750 FAX: 33-1 40239618
GERMANY Deutscher Fechter Bund
Am Neuen Lindenhof 2 53117 Bonn
TEL: 49-228-989050 FAX: 49-228-679430
GEORGIA Georgian Fg Fed
Pr. I. Tchavtchavadze 49/b, 380062 Tblisi
TEL: 7-8832 292875 FAX: 7-8832 292876

GREECE Hellenic Fg Fed,
59 Skoufa St. 10672 Athens
TEL: 30-1 3607507 FAX: 30-1 3614197
GUATEMALA Fedc Nacional de Esg
12 Avenida y 25 calle,
Zona 5, Edificio N° 12 Guatemala
TEL: 502-2-312680, FAX: 502-2-324469
HONDURAS Fedc de Esg de Honduras
Apartado Postal 688, Tegucigalpa D.C.
TEL: 504-322420 FAX: 504-380559
HUNGARY Magyar Viviszovetseg
Dozsa Gyorgy ut 1-3 1142 Budapest
TEL: 36-1 2522149 FAX: 36-1 2522149\
ICELAND Skylminganefnd ISI,P.O. Box 3343, IS-123 Reykjavik
INDIA Fg Association of India
48, Gulmohar Enclave, New Delhi
FAX: 91-11-4636953
INDONESIA Ikatan Anggar Seluru Indonesia,
Stadion Utama Seneyan (Kanselarij)
Jakarta Pusat 10270
TEL: 62-21 5200897 FAX: 62-21 513151
IRAN National Olympic Committee of Iran
N° 44 12th Avenue, Gandhi Street, Teheran
FAX: 98-21 8882857
IRELAND Irish Am Fg Fed
24 Flemingstown Park, Churchtown, Dublin 14
TEL: 353-1 6670400 FAX: 353-1 6670240
ISRAEL Israeli Committee of Fg
c/o Sports Fed, 4 Marmorek St. TEL: Aviv
TEL: 972-4 386480 FAX: 972-3 6856270
ITALY Federazione Italiana Scherma
Viale Tiziano 74 00196 Roma
TEL: 39-6 36858304 FAX: 39-6 36858139
JAPAN Japanese Fg Fed,
1-1-1 Jinnan, Shibuya-Ku Tokyo
FAX: 81 33 48 12 379
JORDAN Jordan Fg Fed
POB 925150, Amman
TEL: 962-6-606825 FAX: 962-6-604717
KAZAKHSTAN Kazakhstan Fg Fed,
1 Abay 48 480072 Almaty
TEL: 7-3272 541295 FAX: 7-327 2 675088
KIRGHYZTAN 17 Togholok Moldo Street, 720033 Bishkek
TEL: 7-3312 210685
KUWAIT AmFgA, POB 23665, Safat 13097
TEL: 965-2554785 FAX: 65-2550546
LATVIA Latvian Fg Fed,
Kirova Street 49, Riga 226050
TEL: 371-2-288613 FAX: 371-2-284412
LITHUANIA Lithuanian Fg Fed,
Graiciuno, 2028 Vilnius
TEL: 7-0122 641331 FAX: 7-0122 641331
LUXEMBOURG Féd Luxembougeoise, B.P. 2017 Luxembourg
TEL/FAX: 352-496523
MACEDONIA Fg Association of the former Yugoslavian
Republic of Macedonia,
Kosarkarska sala/grad.park Skopje
MALAYSIA Malaysian Fg Fed, P.O.Box 1275
Jalan Pantai Bharu 59800 Kuala Lumpur
TEL: 60-3 7572433 FAX: 60-3 7358138
MEXICO Fedc Mexicana de Esg
Av. del Conscripto y Anillo Periferico 11200 Mexico, D.F. Mexico
TEL: (52) 5 6045053
MOLDOVA Moldovan Fg Fed,
73 Stefan cel Mare Street
277064 Kishinev, TEL: 7-0422 224133
MONACO Féd Monegasque d'Esc,
Stade Louis, II 7 Avenue des Castellans, MC 98000
TEL: 33-93 250707 FAX: 33-93 305054
NETHERLANDS
Koninklijke Nederlandse Algemene Schermbond
PO Box 18690, 2502 ER The Hague
TEL/FAX: 31 70 3211 705
NEW ZEALAND. New Zealand AmFgA,
P.O. Box 2380, Christchurch
TEL: 64-3 3665580 FAX: 64-3 3668381

NICARAGUA Fedc National de Esg
Mongolia una cuadra al Sur,
Barrio Altagracia, Managua
TEL: 505-2-71341 FAX: 505-2-663704
NORTH KOREA People's Democratic Republic of North Korea
Fg Association Dongsin 2 Dongdaewon District Pyongyang
NORWAY Norges Fekteforbund
Hauger skolevei 1,13351 Rud
TEL: 47 22 87 46 00 FAX: 47-67 132989
PANAMA Comision Nacional de Esg de Panama,
B.P. 1834, Panama 1
TEL: 57-2639979 FAX: 57-2637908
PERU Fedc Peruana de Esg
Estadio Nacional, Puerta 19, 2° piso, Lima
PHILIPPINES Philippine AFA, c/o Mr. Celso L. Dayrit, President
38 San Agustin Street, Pasig TEL: 632-597294 FAX: 632-6715019
POLAND Polski Zwiazek Szermierczy,
ul. Zlota 9 m 4b 00-019 Warsaw
TEL: 48-2 2272825 FAX: 48-2 2272825
PORTUGAL Federacao Portuguesa de Esg, Rua do Quelhas
32-44, 1200 Lisboa.
TEL: 351-1 3978713 FAX: 351-1 3978376
PUERTO RICO Fedc Am de Esg,
Apartado 4507, Comité Olimpico,
San Juan P.R. 00924 FAX: 809-7216805
ROMANIA Fedc Romania de Esg,
Strada Vasile Conta 16, 70139 Bucarest,
TEL: 40-1 2115572 FAX: 40-1 2100161
RUSSIA Russian Fg Fed,
Loujnetskaia Naberejnaia, 8, Moscow
TEL: 7-095 2011329 FAX: 7-095 2011325
SAUDI ARABIA Saudi Fg Fed,
P.O. 58938 Riyadh 11515
TEL: 966-1 4821022 FAX: 966-1 4822026
SINGAPORE AmFgA of Singapore 815,
Upper Serangoon Rd, Singapore 1953,
TEL: 65-2835566 FAX: 65-2859276
SLOVAKIA Slovak Fg Fed,
Junacka 6 832 80 Bratislava
FAX: 42-7 2790551
SLOVENIA Slovene Fg Fed,
Hubadova 6, 61000 Ljubljana
TEL: 38-61 342092 FAX: 38-61 273460
SOUTH AFRICA South African Am Fg Fed
POB 19085, Wynberg 7824
TEL: 27-21-7614967 FAX: 27-21-7614968
SOUTH KOREA Korea AmFgA,
Rm. 107, Olympic Gym. n° 2, Oryung-Dong, Songpa-gu, Seoul
TEL: 82-2 4204289 FAX: 82-2 4204235
SPAIN Real Fedc Espanola de Esg
Ferraz 16, 28008 Madrid
TEL: 34-1 5597400 FAX: 34-1 5476835
SWEDEN Svenska Faktfforbundet,
Idrottens Hus, 123 87
TEL: 46 8-605 60 00 FAX: 46 8-604 33 99
SWITZERLAND Féd Suisse d'Esc, Secrétariat central,
Hauptstrasse 5043 Holziken
TEL: 41-64 810281 FAX: 41-64 810283
TAIWAN Chinese Taipei Fg Association
5th Fl., N° 20, Chu Lun Street Taipei,
TEL: 886-2-7758718 FAX: 886-2-7781663
THAILAND AmFgA of Thailand
Multidisciplinary Lab, Faculty of Science, Mahidol University,
Rama 6 Rd , Bangkok 10400
FAX: 66-2 2461358
TUNISIA Tunisian Fg Fed,
Cité des Jeunes, Av. Mohamed V, 1002
Tunis Belvedere
TEL: 216-1766950 FAX: 216-1795567
TURKEY Turkish Fg Fed,
Sanayi Cad. 28 Nushet Atav is Hani Ulus Ankara
TEL: 90-4 3106692 FAX: 90-4 3117247
TURKMENISTAN Turkmenistan Fg Fed
34 rue Khoudajberdiev 744000 Achkhabad
TEL: 7-363 253844 FAX: 7-3632 510484

UKRAINE Ukraine Fg Fed,
42 Kujbisheva Street Kiev
TEL: 7-044 2200200 FAX: 7-044 2201294
URUGUAY Fedc Uruguay de Esg,
Canelones 982, Montevideo
TEL: 598-2 920877 FAX: 598-2 925107
UZBEKISTAN Uzbekistan Fg Fed,
83, Tashkent Street 70029 Tashkent
TEL: 7-3712 559647
UNITED STATES United States Fg Association
One Olympic Plaza
Colorado Springs, CO 80909-5774
TEL: 1(719) 578-4511 FAX: 1(719) 632-5737
http://www.usfa.org EMAIL usfencing@aol.com
VENEZUELA Fedc Venezolana de Esg
Apartado Postal 535, Barquisimeto
TEL: 58-2 5456227 FAX: 58-51 735286
VIRGIN ISLANDS Virgin Islands Fg Association
470 Mountain Oaks Parkway,
Stone Mountain GA 30087 U.S.A.
TEL: 1-404-4132523 FAX: 1-809 7750267
YUGOSLAVIA Yugoslav Fg Fed,
Strahinjica Bana 73a, 11000 Beograd
TEL: 381-11 631 272 FAX: 381-11 68